The 150
Healthiest
Slow Cooker Recipes
on Earth

FAIR WINDS
PRESS
BEVERLY, MASSACHUSETTS

The 150 Healthiest Slow Cooker Recipes on Earth

The Surprising, Unbiased Truth about
How to Make Nutritious and Delicious Meals
that Are Ready When You Are

Jonny Bowden, Ph.D., C.N.S., and Jeannette Bessinger, C.H.H.C.
Authors of *The Healthiest Meals on Earth*

First published in the USA in 2012 by
Fair Winds Press, a member of
Quayside Publishing Group
100 Cummings Center
Suite 406-L
Beverly, MA 01915-6101
www.fairwindspress.com

16 15 14 13 12   1 2 3 4 5

ISBN: 978-1-59233-494-0

Digital edition published in 2012
eISBN: 978-1-61058-184-4

Library of Congress Cataloging-in-Publication Data is available.

Photography by Bill Bettencourt

Printed and bound in Singapore

The information in this book is for educational purposes only. It is not intended to replace
the advice of a physician or medical practitioner. Please see your health care provider before
beginning any new health program.

FROM JONNY

. . . to my beautiful Michelle . . .

. . . the ultimate "slow cooker" . . .

it took us a long time . . .

. . . but it was so worth it.

FROM JEANNETTE

I dedicate this book to my husband Jay,

my daughter Jesse, and my son Julian.

You are the light of my life

and make everything possible.

Clockwise from top left:
Pungent, Light, and Clear Thai Seafood
Stew; Mega Omega Piquant Artichoke,
Olive, and Anchovy Sauce; Antioxidant-
Burst Raspberry Peach Cobbler; and
Low-Carb Sesame Turkey Meatballs

CONTENTS

2 | STOCKS, SAUCES, PURÉES, AND INFUSIONS

3 | SIDE DISHES

4 | APPETIZERS AND SNACKS

5 | DRINKS, DESSERTS, AND BREAKFASTS

Introduction

When I was in my twenties I backpacked through Europe with my brother and a college friend. One of the places we went to was Rome, and one of the places we visited there was the Spanish Steps in the world-famous Piazza di Spagna. The area is gorgeous, typically Italian, and simply bursting with history, authenticity, and tradition.

And no one loved the area more than Italian writer Carlo Petrini.

So you can imagine how he felt when, in 1986, McDonald's announced it was building a restaurant there.

To protest the opening, Petrini organized a demonstration, which evolved into the Slow Food Movement, and in 1989, delegates from fifteen countries assembled in Paris to sign its founding manifesto. Today the Slow Food Movement has more than 100,000 members with chapters in 132 countries.

Which brings us to the slow cooker.

Fast-food restaurants have changed the way we eat, but more important, they have changed the way we *think*. Not just about food, but about everything. The fast-food mentality has permeated our lives, assisted by dozens of technological innovations that make things easier but also faster and in many ways more superficial. We want what we want and we want it *now*. This minute. That kind of thinking has affected everything from the way we conduct our relationships (Internet dating, speed dating, Facebook "friends") to the way we handle money (buy now, pay later, or not at all).

The Slow Food Movement was, and is, important—and not just because it strives to preserve regional and traditional cooking and sustainable agriculture. It's also important because of what it says about our lives. It gives people a chance to say, "Hey! Slow down! Let's smell the roses and enjoy the scenery."

So at its heart, the Slow Food Movement is about being present. It's about mindfulness. It's about being in the moment.

For many people, cooking has always been an act of love. Fresh ingredients, carefully and conscientiously selected, prepared at the height of their flavor and nutritional power, served lovingly and proudly at a sit-down, leisurely meal for family and friends. And in some small way, that is the tradition and spirit whose essence is captured by slow cooking.

The slow cooker is actually the perfect compromise between the modern need for food that's convenient and fast, and the wistful nostalgia for beautiful, flavorful meals that simply can't be gotten at the drive-through takeout.

Something good, or *potentially* good, came out of the financial crisis of the late 2000s. Restaurant outings fell, same-store sales at restaurants fell from the previous year, and people began eating at home more. In the previous recession, families cut back by eating fewer meals out, but they wound up buying frozen meals at the supermarket. Not this time. According to food industry consultant Liz Sloan, Ph.D., in 2009, "We have the highest level of in-home cooking in the United States since 1992."

Enter the slow cooker.

What if you could shop for fabulous ingredients, assemble and prepare them in a relatively easy way, go to work, and come home with a scrumptious, flavorful, utterly nutritious meal? That's the promise of the slow cooker, and it never fails to deliver.

No more "slaving over a hot stove," but also no more need to depend on fast food. This is the perfect compromise, delivering nutritionally dense, fresh-cooked meals yet not requiring you to spend hours chopping, dicing, sautéing, blending, heating, and pot watching. For virtually every recipe in this book you merely buy the stuff, do a little prep, throw it in the slow cooker, and leave it alone. Hours later when you're ready to eat, there it is. Nutritious and delicious.

Those of you who are computer savvy know the term GIGO. It's shorthand for "garbage in, garbage out," meaning that the output of the computer is only as good as the stuff you put in it. It can calculate the answer to a ridiculously complex math question faster than you can blink, but if you feed it the wrong information, the answer will still be wrong. And it's kind of the same thing with food.

The best recipe in the world will only turn out to taste as good as the ingredients you use to make it. And the slow cooker, perfectly suited to bringing out complex flavors, really shines when you use the best ingredients, which we've tried to do. So let's talk about some basics when it comes to choosing ingredients.

CHOOSE THE RIGHT KIND OF MEAT

With all the talk about how "bad" meat is for you, you might be forgiven for wondering why we use so much of it in this book (and, frankly, in all our other cookbooks as well). Is meat really the health hazard that mainstream health professionals seem to think it is?

Actually, no. But God is in the details, so let's clear up a few things about meat.

First, some background. Cows are *ruminants*, which means that their natural diet is pasture. "You are what you eat" applies equally to animals, and to a cow, pasture- or grass-fed is the equivalent of "whole foods." Cows are *not* meant to eat grain. It causes them to become acidic and also creates meat that is high in inflammatory omega-6 fats and low in beneficial anti-inflammatory omega-3s.

In addition, cows raised on grain are typically factory farmed, meaning they live short, brutish lives in confined quarters. Cows from factory farms, also known as confined animal feedlot operations, or CAFOs, are fed substantial amounts of antibiotics, plus growth hormones and steroids to fatten them up before slaughter. The result is meat that is heavily laced with drugs you don't want in your diet.

Grass-fed beef, however, is, forgive the pun, a whole different animal. Because grass is so rich in nutrients, the fat of grass-fed beef is richer in anti-inflammatory, heart-healthy omega-3s and *lower* in pro-inflammatory omega-6s. In addition, grass-fed beef contains measurable amounts of conjugated linoleic acid, or CLA, a particularly healthful fat that has been found to reduce tumors in animals by a significant amount. Several studies suggest that grass-fed beef has greater levels of vitamins A and E as well as antioxidants like glutathione and superoxide dismutase (SOD) that help fight cancer.

Grass-fed beef is also healthier because of what it does *not* have. According to a report in *Time*, the U.S. Department of Agriculture (USDA) has determined that grass-fed ground beef is 65 percent lower in saturated fat, while grass-fed New York strips are 35 percent lower. (Full disclosure: I strongly believe that we have wrongfully demonized saturated fat and blamed it for many things that it does not actually do, a subject I've written about extensively in columns and books. But I realize that many people don't share that opinion, so for those of you who are worried about saturated fat, it's worth mentioning that grass-fed meat has less of it.)

But here's something that's not controversial at all: antibiotics in your food are not good. And you're way less likely to be consuming said antibiotics when you eat grass-fed meat. Why? Because when cows are raised in crowded pens, they get sick a lot and are routinely fed antibiotics as a precautionary measure. When they're raised on pasture they are *not* routinely fed antibiotics, nor are they "fattened up" on steroids or hormones. The result is beef that is far better for you than ordinary supermarket meat.

There's a lot of confusion about the labels "organic" and "grass-fed," which sometimes overlap. Organic beef simply means the cow was fed *organic grain*.

Well, this is *marginally* better because the grain fed to the cows is free of pesticides, but the important thing to remember is that beef shouldn't be raised on a grain diet in the first place. Though most grass-fed meat is also organic, given a choice between the two, grass-fed trumps organic every time.

All meat labeled "grass-fed," however, is not necessarily the same. Many grass-fed ranches send their cattle to feedlots for the final weeks of life, where they are fattened up on corn and sometimes given growth hormones. "You should look for *100 percent grass-fed*," advises Lowell Novy, whose own ranch (www.novyranches.com) produces only 100 percent grass-fed meat. Up to 2002, the USDA allowed the label "grass-fed" to be used when 80 percent or more of the animal's diet was pasture. This regulation was recently updated—USDA-certified grass-fed meat is now 100 percent grass-fed. Without the USDA-certified label, however, you can't be completely sure.

By 2006, more than 1,000 U.S. ranchers had switched to an all-grass diet for their cattle. Pasture-raised beef still constitutes only 1 percent of the nation's meat supply, but sales reached approximately $120 million in 2005 and are expected to grow at least 20 percent per year over the coming decade.

Obviously, raising a 100 percent grass-fed animal is far more expensive and time-consuming than raising one in a feedlot farm, and the price of the meat reflects that. Dry-aging—a process by which the meat is left to "age" for 21 days before being sent to market and one that is not done by every grass-fed ranch—drives the cost up even more (warehousing costs money!). And though the end product is undeniably healthier, many consumers want to know whether the taste is worth the extra cost.

The answer is an unequivocal yes. In our "unofficial" taste tests, we cooked up some sample rib-eyes, burgers, and T-bones donated by Novy Ranches as well as some from U.S. Wellness Meats and served them in a blind taste test to a panel that included two families and one seven-year-old. The verdict was unanimous: each person (except the seven-year-old) said the beef was otherworldly—succulent, juicy, tender, and delicious.

The seven-year-old simply asked whether she could have some more.

U.S. Wellness Meats delivers all over the country. Find them at www.grasslandbeef.com.

FISH TOXIN FEAR PUT IN PERSPECTIVE

The main concern most people have with fish is mercury, which is understandable because it's one of the most potent toxins on the planet. But you probably don't have to fear it as much as you think.

First, let's be honest: nearly all fish and shellfish contain slight traces of mercury. But for most people the risk from that trace amount is not a health concern. In fact, a large study of more than 173,000 men and women found that mercury exposure from eating fish doesn't increase heart-related problems. In the study, researchers found that people who reported eating the most fish showed somewhat higher levels of mercury but they didn't have any increase whatsoever in heart disease or stroke. In fact, those with the highest concentration of mercury actually had a 15 percent *lower* risk of heart disease compared to those with the lowest concentrations.

The reason for that surprising finding has to do with cost-benefit analysis. Those in the study with the higher levels of mercury were *also* those who ate the most fish, and those who ate the most fish were *also* consuming the most omega-3 fats (found primarily in cold water fish like salmon). Apparently, the enormous benefit of increased consumption of omega-3 fats outweighs the risk involved in ingesting a slight amount of mercury from fish.

"I think this really shuts the door on the worry about heart risk or toxicity to the heart at these exposure levels," said the lead author of the study, Dariush Mozaffarian, M.D., a heart expert at the Harvard School of Public Health. "And that's an important message, because there may be a lot of adults who are at risk of heart disease who may be confused or concerned about eating fish, or are shying away from fish because of their concerns about mercury. Our study suggests they don't need to worry about heart risks."

Now I'm no mercury apologist. We should avoid it like the plague. But avoiding fish because of the possibility of ingesting a small amount of mercury has some pretty steep costs. Nutrients such as omega-3 fatty acids, iodine, iron, and choline, present in fish such as wild salmon, shrimp, pollock, cod, canned light tuna, and even catfish, are vital to brain development. Researchers found that these nutrients may even lessen the effects of dyslexia, autism, hyperactivity, and attention deficit disorder.

Scientific findings presented at a conference sponsored by the governments of the United States, Norway, Canada, and Iceland and assisted by the United Nations' Food and Agricultural Organization supported the notion that all Americans, *especially* pregnant and nursing women and children, should eat seafood twice a week despite the current concerns about pollution contamination. The American Heart Association recommends at least two fish meals a week. This recommendation is included in the USDA's dietary guidelines as well. The nutrients found in seafood help reduce the risk of death by heart attack and prevent a host of chronic health problems.

And while we're on the subject of fish, let's talk specifically about salmon, one of our favorite fish and one that figures prominently in several of the recipes in this book.

Salmon, as you may know, is one of the best sources in the world for omega-3 fatty acids. These fats, called "wellness molecules" by Andrew Storr, M.D., of Harvard Medical School, are helpful for heart and brain health. They lower triglycerides and blood pressure and even improve mood.

So we love salmon.

But the problem is that salmon has become so darn popular that it's now a commodity. Salmon are now routinely raised on what are called "salmon farms," where thousands of them are crowded into small areas called "net pens," with serious consequences for both the fish and the surrounding waters. Salmon farms pack the salmon in like sardines, which obviously makes the spreading of disease a virtual certainty. So the salmon farmers do exactly what the factory farmers do with their cattle—they feed them massive amounts of antibiotics.

They also feed them grain. Now salmon in the wild are natural carnivores, dining happily on such fare as sardines, krill, mackerel, and other fish. They don't thrive on grain any more than factory-farmed cows do. And because of their heavy grain diet, their fat has a higher proportion of pro-inflammatory fats like omega-6s. What's more, according to independent lab tests by the nonprofit Environmental Working Group, seven out of ten farmed salmon purchased at grocery stores were contaminated with PCBs (polychlorinated biphenyls) at levels that raise serious concerns.

Wild salmon, on the other hand, are a whole different story. They get their natural red color not from artificial colorings (the way farmed salmon often do) but from a fantastic antioxidant called *astaxanthin*, which is naturally found in the krill they like to eat. They aren't pumped full of antibiotics and they have low levels of omega-6 fats. All in all, wild salmon are the way to go and it's the reason we feel so strongly that you should try to get wild whenever possible. We get all our salmon directly from Alaska from Vital Choice, a superb company of third-generation Alaskan fisherman who are committed to sustainable fishing and to selling a pristine, clean product free of as many contaminants and metals as possible.

Find Vital Choice at www.vitalchoice.com. They even have a terrific Dr. Jonny "starter pack" featuring all of my favorite Vital Choice products!

CHICKEN WITH GOOD KARMA

From time to time, you'll hear us refer to "pastured chicken" in glowing terms. And you might wonder, "What the heck is that?"

TIPS FOR SLOW COOKING HEALTHY MEALS

You can leave your slow cooker totally unattended, but be careful when handling because their bases become hot to the touch. Consider these other tips when using your slow cooker.

Temperature Safety: Because the slow cooker raises the temperature of a dish gradually and, on the low setting, can remain at a low temperature, avoid removing the lid except by recipe direction or toward the end of cooking time, especially on the low setting. Food-borne bacteria cannot remain alive at a temperature of 165°F (73.8°C), so you need to keep meats and dairy in particular at that temperature or higher.

Liquids: There is little to no moisture loss in a slow cooker, so you generally need less liquid than in stove-top cooking. The foods themselves will also release juices and fats with little evaporation, so plan accordingly.

Meats: In general, the fattier the cut of meat, the longer cooking time it requires. So the leanest cuts, such as skinless chicken breast, take about two-thirds of the time of chicken thighs, which take about half the time of marbled stew beef. Also, you may wish to brown cuts of beef for a richer flavor before slow cooking. This extra step is not necessary for cooking the meat to doneness, but is more for aesthetic reasons. The exception to this is ground meat, which should generally be fully browned on the stove and drained before adding to the slow cooker. Add fish and other seafood at the end of cooking time, or prepare "packet style" and cook over a shorter period, as with our Zested and Light Lemon-Garlic Tilapia with Roasted Shiitakes.

Vegetables: The vegetables best suited to the slow cooker are the harder root vegetables because they can hold their shape and texture over longer cooking times. You can also prepare leafy greens, though they are best in sauces or liquids, and hardier greens and other colored vegetables, such as green beans and yellow squash, but they generally require far less cooking time. When cooking root veggies, cut them into small, bite-size cubes, chunks, or slices and place them on the bottom of the cooker. The smaller the cut size, the quicker the cooking time, which is important to note when pairing with meats, which may require more time. Add the lighter vegetables in the last hour of cooking time, and the most delicate, such as peas, in the last 10 to 15 minutes of cooking time.

Beans: The simplest method to cook beans in the slow cooker is to soak them in water to cover overnight, drain the soak water, and cook them in fresh water or sodium-free broth (salt can toughen beans and increase their cooking time, so do not add any, even in broth, until the last 30 minutes or so). Lentils and split peas are the exceptions, because they do not need to be presoaked and generally require less cooking time than other legumes. Some tender beans, such as navy, can soak and go right into the slow cooker. But other, hardier beans, such as chickpeas, need to be brought to a boil on the stove top for about 15 minutes after soaking and before being put into the cooker. Rinse and add a 2-inch (5 cm) square of soaked kombu to the cook water to increase beans' digestibility. You can remove or dice and include at the end of cooking time.

Dairy: Yogurts, cow's milk, and creams can separate over an extended cooking time, so plan to add them toward the end of cooking time when using unless specifically directed otherwise in a recipe.

Grains: The long-cooking whole grains do very well in the slow cooker: pearl barley or barley groats and whole oat groats, for example. The quicker-cooking grains, such as brown rice or quinoa, should be added closer to the end of cooking time, In general, grains require a very liquid base for cooking, such as a brothy stew or soup.

One grain-based ingredient that does *not* do well in the slow cooker, however, is pasta, including couscous. If you are making a pasta-based dish, cook it on your stove top according to package directions and add it to the finished slow cooker recipe.

Glad you asked.

Chickens were first domesticated in Asia about 8,000 years ago, and came to the United States by way of Europe in the fifteenth century. The average American eats about 80 pounds (36 kg) of chicken per year, which makes it by far the main source of animal protein in the American diet.

The high demand for chickens has created bottom line–driven factory farms where chickens live and die in terrible conditions. They're kept alive pumped full of antibiotics and nasty chemicals, and genetically engineered to grow artificially quickly—and the people who work in such factories also suffer terrible injuries in the attempt to keep up with speeded-up assembly lines. (Full disclosure: the same is probably true for beef slaughterhouses as well.)

Grass-fed, pastured, organic chickens, grown the old-fashioned way, are still available throughout the United States from family farms that care about their animals and provide them with good, healthy diets and lifestyles. Their meat is much healthier and tastier than industrial chicken, and they come free of bad karma!

DAIRY AND EGGS—THE CHOLESTEROL MYTH

I love eggs and eat them almost every day. And I'm talking the whole egg, folks, complete with yolk. (The last time I ate an "egg-white omelet" was around 1985!) Which probably makes some of you wonder, "What about cholesterol?"

Well, that's a subject for a whole other book, but let's just get the basics out of the way. You have nothing to fear from the cholesterol in eggs. Dietary cholesterol, the kind found in egg yolks, for example, has minimal impact on your blood cholesterol. Minimal. Seriously. That's been known for quite a while, and the only exception is the approximately 1 to 2 percent of the population with a condition called *familial hypercholesterolemia*. The other 98 to 99 percent of folks needn't worry.

Not only that, but the effect of eggs on heart disease cannot be predicted by looking at their cholesterol content. Eggs contain incredible nutrients—protein, folic acid, B vitamins, lutein, and zeaxanthin for the eyes, choline for the brain—and, as Larry King used to say, "I'm just gettin' started!" As Walter Willett, M.D., chairman of the department of nutrition at the Harvard School of Public Health and a professor of medicine at Harvard Medical School, has said, "No research has ever shown that people who eat more eggs have more heart attacks than people who eat few eggs."

I recommend that you get eggs from pastured or free-range chickens. These eggs have a higher omega-3 content, which makes them even better for you.

So I'm a huge fan of eggs, but I do have reservations about dairy, which is not a great thing for everyone. It's one of the seven top allergens; about 75 percent of the people on the planet are lactose-intolerant, and dairy, particularly milk, causes digestive upset and mucus production in a certain percentage of people. That doesn't mean you shouldn't eat it, just that you should be aware that, despite massive propaganda from the dairy industry, it's not for everyone.

So in a lot of recipes that call for milk, we've included alternatives if you're one of the many who doesn't do well with cow's milk. Try almond milk or rice milk, which have wonderful flavors and work just as well in a lot of recipes. And, if you can get it, try raw milk, one of nature's great health foods. Because it hasn't been heated to high temperatures, it contains the enzymes that are destroyed by pasteurization. (The politics of raw milk and the dairy industry are far too arcane to go into in this book, but let's just say that the "dangers" of raw milk are greatly exaggerated.)

WHY YOU SHOULDN'T AVOID FAT

While we're on the subject of dairy, let's talk for a minute about the issue of fat. Most of us have been brainwashed into believing that the less fat we eat the better, and have been trained to gravitate toward skim milk, or nonfat yogurt and cheese. Not so fast.

A 2010 study reviewed sixteen years of data on more than 1,500 adults to investigate the relationship between dairy consumption and mortality. Disappointingly, there was no consistent association between *total* dairy intake and mortality. But when investigators compared those in the study who had the highest intake of *full-fat dairy* with the participants who had the lowest, those with the *highest* intake (about 339 grams or 12 ounces per day) had a 69 percent reduction in their risk for death from cardiovascular disease.

The reason for that reduction in risk seems to be a particular fatty acid called *trans-palmitoleic acid*, which is only found in dairy fat. A 2010 study published in the *Annals of Internal Medicine* found that those with the highest circulating levels of this fat had a whopping 60 percent lower incidence of diabetes. Those with the highest levels also had lower body mass index (BMI, a measure of overweight); smaller waist circumference; higher levels of HDL, or "good" cholesterol; lower triglycerides; less insulin resistance; and lower levels of C-reactive protein, a marker for general inflammation.

"We found that blood levels of this fatty acid, which is exclusively found in dairy fat, are associated with a strikingly lower risk of diabetes as well as markers of metabolic risk like insulin resistance," lead researcher Mozaffarian, of Harvard University, told me.

I haven't recommended no-fat dairy for more than a decade. When manu-facturers make no-fat versions of foods that naturally contain fat, the no-fat versions invariably contain more sugar and carbs and are generally way worse for you than the foods they replace. Ironically, calcium, which is why a lot of people turn to dairy in the first place, is much better absorbed in the presence of some fat. For all these reasons, we recommend that when you do use dairy you avoid the no-fat kind and go for either full-fat, or—if you're trying to re-duce calories—the low-fat kind. (Remember, our Paleolithic ancestors didn't eat "low-fat caribou." The fat is in the food for a reason, and avoiding it at any cost is turning out to be a bad idea!)

WHAT ABOUT ORGANIC?

Despite the best efforts of the food industry to make us think our food just magically somehow appears in the supermarket aisle, our food actually *comes* from somewhere. And where it comes from—where and how it grows in the case of plants, and what it eats and how it is raised in the case of animals—has a lot to do with its quality. So let's start with a basic premise, one that we've al-ready seen quite clearly when it comes to beef, chicken, and fish: the quality of the food we eat comes from the quality of the food *our food* eats.

This maxim applies even when we're talking about fruits and vegetables. Studies have shown that carrots grown in one section of the country do not have the same nutrient composition as carrots grown in another part of the country. (The practice of studying this sort of thing was abandoned because it pissed people off. Grapefruit growers in one part of the country did not want data out there showing that grapefruits grown in *another* part of the country had more vitamin C. Agribusiness is dedicated to selling us the concept that "carrots are carrots, beef is beef.")

But agribusiness interests aside, *where* a food comes from can make a big dif-ference in its nutritional composition, and *how* it was produced makes a big dif-ference in its chemical composition. A fruit or vegetable grown in soil depleted of minerals is going to be less nutritious than one that's grown in soil rich in nutrients. If an apple is sprayed with a ton of chemicals, pesticides, or fumigates, and then artificially treated to make it bigger, rounder, redder, more uniform, pol-ished, and more appealing to the eye, it stands to reason that a chemical analysis of that apple is going to look a lot different than an analysis of an apple growing wild on a farm somewhere. Now whether or not those measurable differences have any real impact on our health is a matter of huge debate.

Agribusiness would like you to think that they don't.

I suspect that they do.

Which brings us to organic foods. The whole idea of the organic food movement—the "spirit" of the movement, if you will—was a desire to return to basics, just as the Slow Food Movement was a desire to return to the basics of a different (but related) sort. It was fueled by a fervent wish to consume the healthy products of the small, sustainable farm where fruits and vegetables and cows and pigs and chickens and horses lived in an interdependent atmosphere of pastoral tranquility, where food, whether animal or vegetable, was grown (or raised) the old-fashioned way. The organic movement valued a time and place where animals were not fed growth hormones and steroids and antibiotics and where crops were left to fend off the elements with their own protective antioxidants and anthocyanins rather than with chemical pesticides and carcinogenic fumigates, and where "Roundup Ready," genetically modified plants (GMOs) were unknown.

People who wanted organic food were voting both *for* their health and *against* a marketplace that was increasingly providing them with "food products" bearing less and less resemblance to anything that could once be considered real or whole food—stuff that grew out of the ground, fell from a tree, or was harvested from healthy animals grazing on pasture or wild fish swimming in uncontaminated waters. Buying organic represented a return to natural, and presumably healthier, foods.

At least that was the hope.

It was a noble ambition. But fulfilling it presented problems, the most significant of which was how to provide this kind of "nonindustrialized" boutique food to huge numbers of people over vast distances in a largely urban society. The solution? What Michael Pollan, in his brilliant book, *The Omnivore's Dilemma*, calls "Big Organic." Successfully delivering organic food to vast numbers of people in an industrialized society requires the same scale of operation as delivering processed, packaged foods to supermarkets. A small family farm just can't compete. The economics of survival in the competitive food business required that the organic producers mimic the large, factory farms and production facilities of their nonorganic brethren. The ideal of the organic movement—the small, sustainable, pastoral farm—simply didn't fit into a business model in which hundreds of thousands of pounds of "product" are moved vast distances on a daily basis. Hence, as Michael Pollan writes,

I discovered organic beef being raised in "organic feedlots" and organic high-fructose corn syrup—more words I never expected to see combined. I learned about the making of . . . organic TV dinner, a microwaveable bowl of "rice, vegetables, and grilled chicken breast with a savory herb sauce." Country Herb, as the entrée is called, turns out to be a highly industrialized organic product, involving a choreography of thirty-one ingredients assembled from far-flung farms, laboratories, and processing plants scattered over a half-dozen states and two countries, and containing such mysteries of modern food technology as high-oleic safflower oil, guar and xanthan gum, soy lecithin, carrageenan, and "natural grill flavor." Several of these ingredients are synthetic additives permitted under federal organic rules. So much for "whole" foods.

So much for whole foods, indeed.

So is the organic food we buy in large chains like Whole Foods and Wild Oats any better than the stuff we buy in the A&P or Costco? It's a difficult question. Certainly, the term *organic* has been co-opted. (When you routinely see products like "organic soda" and "organic sugar" and "organic chocolate cereal" you have to ask some serious questions.)

But as far as fruits and vegetables go, organic can assure us that we're ingesting fewer toxic chemicals. Buying organic food can therefore remove at least *one* source of potential carcinogens from our daily diet, which, particularly in the case of foods that are highly contaminated when conventionally grown (like coffee and strawberries), makes it worth the price.

At least for me.

But does "organic" guarantee us a more nutritious product? Maybe. As Pollan writes, "[O]rganic blackberries . . . having been grown in a complexly fertile soil and forced to fight their own fights against pests and disease, are in some quantifiable way more nutritious than conventional blackberries." He's supported by at least one scientific source (*Journal of Agriculture and Food Chemistry*, vol. 51, no. 5, 2003). And more recent studies have tested the effects of different growing methods on antioxidant levels and revealed that several organic growing methods can increase the broad antioxidant content of produce. "On average, antioxidant levels increased by about 30 percent in carefully designed comparative trials," said Donald Davis, Ph.D., a biochemist at the University of Texas. "Organically grown produce offers significantly enhanced health-promoting qualities, contributing to the achievement of important national public health goals."

So, yes, I buy organic, whenever possible. I just don't kid myself any more that the label refers to something that came from a farm like the ones on which I collected eggs from the barnyard as a kid.

If you want that kind of real food, it's going to take more than just looking for the organic label on your supermarket food. You might need to join a food collective. Go to a farmers' market. Grow your own food. Or, if you can, go to a local farm and buy your food there. See where it comes from. Say hello to the people who grow it. If you're lucky enough to be able to do that, you'd be giving yourself a real gift.

So all things considered, organic food has the edge over nonorganic. However, we have to take price into account. Organic fruits and vegetables are, let's face it, more expensive.

What to do, what to do?

Here's what I do: I check with the Environmental Working Group. For years now, this terrific nonprofit group dedicated to consumer interests has tested fruits and vegetables for pesticide contamination and published a list of 100 foods ranked according to their level of contamination. The twelve "dirtiest" crops are known colloquially as "the Dirty Dozen," and those are the ones I always buy organic. (The least contaminated crops are known as the "Clean Fifteen.") From time to time, the group updates the list based on recent samples. As of this writing, the Dirty Dozen are:

1. Apples
2. Celery
3. Strawberries
4. Peaches
5. Spinach
6. Nectarines (imported)
7. Grapes (imported)
8. Bell peppers
9. Potatoes
10. Blueberries (domestic)
11. Lettuce
12. Kale/collard greens

Download a wallet-size guide to the Dirty Dozen and the Clean Fifteen at www.foodnews.org/walletguide.php.

In addition, I'd recommend getting organic meat, milk, and coffee. Although, as mentioned, grass-fed trumps organic if you have to choose, organic meat still offers a layer of protection against pesticides that nonorganic meat doesn't. Same with milk. And coffee is one of the most sprayed crops on the planet, so whenever possible, I'd go with organic coffee as well.

WHAT THE LABEL DOESN'T TELL YOU

A word about the nutrition data at the end of every recipe.

We're so accustomed to reading nutrition labels and looking for the fat content and calories that we often miss the bigger picture. Some of these recipes have more fat than you may be used to. (Remember that the percentage of fat in your diet has absolutely *no* relationship to any major health outcome, a fact confirmed by Willett, of Harvard University, and a fact I've written about many times before.) Also keep in mind that the nutrition facts at the end of the recipe (or on the label of any food) don't tell the whole story.

There are thousands of plant chemicals—polyphenols, flavanols, flavonoids, antioxidants, carotenoids—that have significant health properties, and they're not listed anywhere on an ingredients label or a nutrition facts panel. These terrific compounds are what make whole foods healthy, but they often fly beneath the radar. While it's interesting to know the amount of protein, fat, and carbohydrates in any given recipe, remember that the ingredients you'll use in these recipes offer far more health benefits than you can glean from simply knowing their calorie or fat count.

What Chef Jeannette and I have tried to do in this cookbook, as well as the four others we've written together so far, is to make it easy, fun, and affordable to bring healthy meals to your family's table, meals everyone will enjoy, meals that won't break the bank, and meals that will nourish your body and nurture your soul. Meals and recipes simply can't be evaluated solely on the basis of how many calories or how many grams of fat (or protein or carbs, for that matter) they contain.

You also have to factor in such things as joy.

Because if food isn't, after all, a joy, then we might as well take a pill for our nutrition and call it a day.

The slow cooker is a great tool for discovering or *re*discovering the joys that good food (and good health) can bring to your life.

We hope these recipes help you do just that.

Enjoy the journey.

—Dr. Jonny

How to Cook the Healthiest Slow Cooker Recipes on Earth

Slow cookers have come a long way in the past twenty years. There is a wide variety of possible sizes and features to choose from, and they all have subtle differences. But ultimately, all varieties of slow cookers have one main function: to gradually cook your food at a controlled, steady temperature over time. Because nearly all of your prep work takes place at the beginning of cooking time and then you can walk away (or go to work!) and leave it unsupervised, the slow cooker is also a huge kitchen convenience tool.

The slow cooker allows for the slow development of rich flavors, as in pungent infusions such as our Fresh Thai Oil Infusion. It also allows for the nearly effortless preparation of dried beans (try our Enzyme-Rich Pineapple Pepper Chili) and whole grains, such as our Whole-Grain Asian Shiitake Barley. In short, it's tailor-made for preparing the most nutritious foods in some of the most delicious ways.

Although it has been around for years, the slow cooker is currently enjoying a renaissance among busy, working families. In our expanding efforts to prepare healthy, whole foods in the shrinking amounts of time we have available to us, the slow cooker is emerging as a cornerstone of what we call the "new cooking technology" of our age. So pull yours out of the closet and dust it off. Or better yet, invest in a new model that does everything but clean the kitchen. Either way, you'll want to test it out and start making easy, tasty, nutrition-packed dishes for yourself and your family. You may well find yourself a slow cooker convert.

SLOW COOKER INFORMATION

Unless otherwise indicated, the recipes in this book will all cook up in a 4- or 4½-quart (3.8 or 4.2 L) slow cooker (typically allows for 4 to 6 entrée servings). In general, most of them will do just as well in a 6-quart (5.7 L) cooker (6 or 7 entrée servings). We do occasionally call for a smaller 1- or 2-quart (1 or 1.9 L) model (1 to 3 entrée servings) or a larger 6- or 7-quart (5.7 or 6.6 L) model (6 to 9 entrée servings) for a few of the recipes, but for the most part these recipes are very forgiving.

Every make and model of slow cooker has its own characteristics. This makes it nearly impossible to standardize recipe directions, especially cooking time, for all types of slow cookers. As a result, you need to get to know your own cooker(s) well so that you can adjust the recipes as needed. I had a cooker for years (my first one) that seemed to dry out my meats no matter what I tried. I thought that's what slow cookers did: dry out meats. I learned to add stew beef and cuts of chicken toward the end of cooking time and didn't find it as convenient as the cookbook promised. Then I bought a newer model with adjustable temperatures and suddenly found my meats cooking to juicy perfection along with everything else.

If you're in the market, my advice is to invest in a good one. I'm a believer in quality appliances because they generally offer consistent performance and last for years, even decades, with no problems. I will make mention of two of my favorite high-end models here because they are that good. I have utterly fallen in love with the All-Clad 7-quart (6.6 L) anodized aluminum slow cooker. Not only is it big enough to fit two whole chickens (very convenient for making soup stocks), but it also has a programmable timer and dual heat settings that automatically switch to warm at the end of cooking time. The best feature, however, is a safe, nonstick insert that can move between the stove top and the slow cooker. Although there are some stove top–safe stoneware models, as far as I know, this is the only nonstick model that allows you to brown vegetables and meat, or melt fats or cheeses, and then drop it right into the cooker. It has revolutionized slow cooking for me.

My second plug is for the VitaClay dual slow cooker/rice cooker. This cooker has a natural clay pot insert that allows you to cook perfect grains every time. It doubles as a rice cooker and does something unique and wonderful to stew beef. It cooks a little hotter than a true slow cooker, but the healthy clay pot and grains option makes it a high-quality, high-value two-fer.

If you are working on a tight budget, however, and planning to slow cook only occasionally, there are multiple models of excellent slow cookers on the market that are very economical. Look for a well-reviewed model that has the features you like the most.

FAVORITE FEATURES

Following are some additional handy features to look out for in different models.

Attached lid: Slow cookers keep the liquid/moisture content of a dish intact, and consequently the lid is often covered with condensation. One handy feature that removes the hassle of the wet lid is an attached, hinged lid that allows you to simply flip it open without needing to put the lid into the sink.

Clamps for travel: Some units have a handy clasp feature for the lid, which allows you to seal and fix the lid in place for easy transport. These units will often also include an insulated carrying case—great for parties or potlucks.

Timer: Many units have a programmable timer, some with advance settings so you can set them to start at a future time.

Heat settings: Some units have more than one heat setting. Most have high and low, but some also have high/low, which alternates heats, allowing you to temporarily bring things to a boil and then reduce the heat. Another handy feature is autowarm, a default setting so that when a dish is complete, it automatically switches to warm and keeps your dish from burning or growing cold.

—Chef Jeannette

The Mains

The slow cooker really shines when it comes to making healthy and hearty main dishes. Once you've experienced the convenience and freedom, you'll wonder why you ever cooked any other way. And those extra hours in the pot do wonders for bringing out rich flavors you never even knew were there. Enjoy—you're in for many a treat!

MEAT

Tangy Tomato Grass-Fed Pot Roast

High-Protein Two-Bean 'n Sirloin Tip Chili

Real Deal Beef Stew with Orange and Clove

New England Corned Beef and Cabbage

Clean Loaded Sloppy Joe with a Kick

Vegetable-Loaded Beef and Barley Stew

Grass-Fed Beef with Butternut Squash and Cherries

Simplest High-Fiber Beefy Tacos

CLA-Rich Beef Biryani

Leaner, Savory Slow-Cooked Meatloaf

Iron-Rich Ground Sirloin Borscht

Moroccan Braised Lamb Shanks in Fresh Tomatoes and Red Wine

Beanie Slow-Cooked Shepherd's Pie

Taste of India Lamb

High-Fiber Curried Mulligatawny Lamb Stew

Luscious, Leanest Lamb Chops

POULTRY

Versatile, Lean, and Easy Chicken Base

Lower-Sugar BBQ Pulled Chicken Thighs

Chunky German Digest-Ease Sausage and Sauerkraut Stew

Easiest Lean Artichoke Chicken

Clean Peanutty Thai Chicken

Lean Dried Apricot Chicken and Wild Rice Soup

Easy Asian Sweet Chili Chicken

Veggie-Rich Asian Chicken Stew

Low-Cal Fiesta Mexi-Chicken

Flavorful, Fiber-Full Moroccan Chicken

Lean Lemon-Apricot Chicken

In-a-Pinch Protein Pesto Chicken and Mushrooms

Free-Radical-Fighting Kalamata Chicken

Spinach, Basil, and Feta–Stuffed Chicken Rolls with Pignolis

Sweet and Saucy Free-Range Chicken Thighs

Satisfying, Spicy Lemon Chicken

Indian Super-Spice-Rubbed Chicken

Quick Sesame Teriyaki

Low-Carb Lettuce Wraps

Savory Slow Cooker Tender Turkey Drumsticks

Flavanol-Rich Cocoa Chicken Mole

Jamaican Jerked Turkey Legs

Low-Cal Tropical Turkey Breast

Turkey and Fruit-Sweetened Cranberry Sauce Supper

Lean and Green Stuffed Peppers

Lean and Easy Taco Salad

MEATLESS

Loaded Split Pea Sweet Potato Soup

Sweet Tooth–Buster Sweet Potato Apple Soup

Enzyme-Rich Pineapple Pepper Chili

Mighty Minestrone

Lean Green Curried Tofu

Low-Cal Caribbean Black Bean Soup

Seeded and Stuffed Carnival Squash

Liver-Lovin' Root and Cabbage Stew

Vitamin C–Rich, Three-Pepper 'n Bean Chili

High-Fiber Italian White Bean Soup

No-Cream of Leek and Potato Soup

Rich and Creamy High-Fiber Sweet Potato Peanut Bisque

Flavorful, High-Fiber Curried Spinach and Lentils

SEAFOOD

Gifts from the Sea Chowder

Pungent, Light, and Clear Thai Seafood Stew

Choline-Rich Shellfish Jambalaya

Sea Scallops Mediterranean

Light Louisiana Creole Shrimp Soup

Piquant Hot Tuna and Cannellini Stew

Tangy Tomato-Soused Salmon Patties with Pineapple and Miso

Zested and Light Lemon-Garlic Tilapia with Roasted Shiitakes

Omega-Rich Dilled Salmon Dijon

TANGY TOMATO GRASS-FED POT ROAST

INGREDIENTS

1 large sweet onion, quartered

4 medium-size carrots, peeled, halved, and quartered lengthwise

1 large sweet potato, peeled and coarsely chopped

2 cups (300 g) peeled, seeded, and cubed butternut squash

1 can (14.5 ounces, or 406 g) tomato sauce

3 tablespoons (48 g) tomato paste

¼ cup (60 ml) apple cider vinegar

1 tablespoon (11 g) Dijon mustard

4 cloves garlic, minced

2 teaspoons minced fresh ginger

1 tablespoon (15 g) xylitol (or 2 teaspoons [10 g] Sucanat)

½ teaspoon each salt and cracked black pepper

½ teaspoon ground cumin

½ teaspoon ground turmeric

¼ teaspoon cayenne pepper

⅛ teaspoon ground cloves

2 to 2 ½ pounds (910 to 1,135 g) boneless chuck roast

FROM DR. JONNY: Those of you who have been kind enough (or bored enough) to read all of my introductory notes to what's now about four cookbooks' worth of recipes are probably familiar with my culinarily deprived childhood. Family dinners in the Bowden household in Jackson Heights, Queens, were a nice way to bond, but the food . . . well, not so much. One dish we had all the time, which I really liked, was pot roast. Now the thing about pot roast in the slow cooker is this: when you use chuck roast, the extra fat slowly tenderizes the meat, making it literally "fall apart" tender. But when you use conventional chuck roast, you're getting factory-farmed meat with all the toxins (like antibiotics, steroids, and hormones) that get stored in that fat. The solution? Use grass-fed meat. The fat is perfectly healthy, the animals aren't fed all kinds of chemicals, and you still get that amazingly tender texture and an even richer taste. This version of pot roast—unlike my mother's, bless her kitchen-challenged soul—uses a tangy, flavorful tomato sauce to jazz up the meat. (The acid in the tomatoes and vinegar is a great tenderizer!) And the flavors permeate the orange veggies, so rich in compounds like carotenoids, which act as powerful antioxidants. The veggies make that sauce so succulent you'll want to sop up every juicy bite.

Combine the onion, carrots, sweet potato, and butternut squash cubes in a slow cooker.

In a medium-size bowl, whisk together the tomato sauce, tomato paste, vinegar, mustard, garlic, ginger, xylitol, salt, pepper, cumin, turmeric, cayenne pepper, and cloves until well combined.

Place the roast over the vegetables and carefully pour the tomato sauce over all.

Cook on high for 4 hours, or on low for 6 to 8 hours, until the meat is tender and cooked through.

YIELD: 6 to 7 servings

PER SERVING: Calories 473.8; Calories From Fat 286.9; Total Fat 31.8 g; Cholesterol 90.7 mg; Sodium 686.3 mg; Potassium 1,052.1 mg; Total Carbohydrates 21.4 g; Fiber 4.4 g; Sugar 9.2 g; Protein 25.7 g

HIGH-PROTEIN TWO-BEAN 'N SIRLOIN TIP CHILI

FROM DR. JONNY: The word *protein* comes from the Greek, meaning "of prime importance," an excellent description of why we need it. Protein provides the raw materials for practically every important structure and chemical in the human body. This dish offers a double-barreled dose of protein from both animal and plant sources: beef, one of the most bioavailable and usable sources of protein on the planet, and beans, an excellent vegetarian source of protein (about 12 grams per cup). But finding a high-protein dish that's also high in fiber is the Holy Grail for healthy eating. Look no further. In addition to protein and a host of vitamins and minerals, beans also provide between 11 to 17 grams of fiber per cup, making them one of the greatest high-fiber foods of all time. (One study assessed the antioxidant power of 100 fruits, vegetables, and other foods and beans were a clear winner. Their ORAC score—a measure of total antioxidant power—was higher than even blueberries!) Strongly recommended: grass-fed beef. It's higher in omega-3 fatty acids, lower in "pro-inflammatory" omega-6s, and noticeably absent of any steroids, hormones, or antibiotics. This flavorful chili is a party favorite among Jeannette's family.

INGREDIENTS

2 pounds (908 g) leanest sirloin tip

1 teaspoon salt, divided

½ teaspoon cracked black pepper

2 ½ tablespoons (38 ml) olive oil, divided

2 large Vidalia onions, chopped

1 large red bell pepper, seeded and chopped

1 jalapeño pepper, seeded and finely chopped

6 cloves garlic, minced

3 tablespoons (23 g) chili powder

¾ teaspoon ancho chile pepper
   (or use cayenne pepper)

1 ½ teaspoons ground cumin

1 teaspoon dried oregano

2 cups (470 ml) beef broth

1 ½ cups (353 ml) Corona beer (or other
   lager-style beer)

1 can (14.5 ounces, or 406 g) tomato purée

1 can (14.5 ounces, or 406 g) fire-roasted
   tomatoes, undrained

⅓ cup (90 g) tomato paste

⅓ cup (47 g) dried polenta (coarse ground
   cornmeal)

1 can (15 ounces, or 420 g) white kidney beans,
   drained and rinsed

1 can (15 ounces, or 420 g) red kidney beans,
   drained and rinsed

1 teaspoon Sucanat

½ cup (50 g) chopped scallion

½ cup (8 g) chopped fresh cilantro

Trim any visible fat from the meat and cut into bite-size pieces. Season the meat with ½ teaspoon of the salt and the cracked pepper. Heat 1 tablespoon (15 ml) of the oil in a large skillet over medium-high heat and brown the meat on all sides. Transfer the meat to the slow cooker.

Reduce the heat to medium, add the remaining 1½ tablespoons (23 ml) oil, the onions, bell pepper, and jalapeño pepper to the pan and cook for 5 to 7 minutes, until the onions are soft and translucent. Add the garlic, chili powder, chile pepper, cumin, and oregano and cook, stirring constantly, for 1 minute.

Transfer the pan contents to the slow cooker. Add the broth, beer, tomato purée, fire-roasted tomatoes, tomato paste, and polenta to the mixture and stir gently to mix well.

Stir in the beans, Sucanat, and remaining ½ teaspoon salt and mix well. Cook on high for 5 hours, or on low for 8 to 9 hours, until the meat is tender and the sauce is thick. Stir in the scallion and cilantro just before serving.

YIELD: 12 servings

PER SERVING: Calories 349.8; Calories From Fat 88.2; Total Fat 12 g; Cholesterol 63.5 mg; Sodium 923.1 mg; Potassium 847.5 mg; Total Carbohydrates 31.5 g; Fiber 8.2 g; Sugar 6 g; Protein 26.4 g

FROM CHEF JEANNETTE

This chili is great served with baked corn chips and grated Jack cheese. You can also make a flavorful high-protein, low-cal garnish by combining 12 ounces (340 g) plain Greek yogurt (or low-fat sour cream) with the juice and zest of ½ lime, 2 cloves minced garlic, ⅓ cup (16 g) chopped chives, and sprinkles of salt and cracked pepper. Serve each bowl with a dollop of garnish.

REAL DEAL BEEF STEW WITH ORANGE AND CLOVE

INGREDIENTS

1 red onion, left whole, peeled

8 whole cloves

1 pound (454 g) baby carrots

3 large parsnips, peeled and sliced

1 sweet onion, chopped

1 ½ pounds (680 g) leanest chuck (shoulder roast), cut into 1 ½ to 2-inch (4 to 5 cm) cubes

¾ teaspoon salt

½ teaspoon cracked black pepper

1 can (14 ounces, or 392 g) sliced stewed tomatoes, drained

1 cup (235 ml) beef broth (or 1 cup [235 ml] water with 2 teaspoons [10 g] organic beef Better Than Bouillon)

2 tablespoons (40 g) blackstrap molasses

1 ½ tablespoons (23 ml) apple cider vinegar

3 cloves garlic, crushed and chopped

2 teaspoons orange zest

1 teaspoon ground coriander

¼ teaspoon ground cinnamon

⅓ cup (50 g) raisins

FROM DR. JONNY: You haven't lived till you've tasted real beef stew made in a slow cooker. We always recommend grass-fed meat because it is free of hormones, steroids, and antibiotics, and the fat is much higher in omega-3s (and much lower in inflammatory omega-6s), resulting in a far healthier meat. If you can't get grass-fed, at least go for organic, and if neither is available, choose the shoulder roast because it has the least fat of the chuck. Chuck is actually a fattier meat, but you'll need that extra fat because it really helps the meat hold up better to the long cooking time. Beef remains the best source of iron as well as vitamin B_{12}, which is critical for the metabolism of every single cell in your body! This rich and aromatic stew has a tender bite, enhanced by the delicious taste and texture of the iron-rich molasses, and will gratify your taste buds with its subtle hints of orange and clove. Fun fact: Onions are one of the best sources of a terrific anti-inflammatory, anticancer plant compound called *quercetin*.

Stud the red onion evenly with the cloves and place it in the cooker. Add the carrots, parsnips, and sweet onion.

Season the beef cubes with the salt and pepper and place on top of the veggies. Pour the tomatoes over the beef. In a medium-size bowl, whisk together the broth, molasses, vinegar, garlic, zest, coriander, and cinnamon and pour over all.

Cook on high for 3 to 4 hours, or on low 5 to 6 hours, until the vegetables and beef are tender. Add the raisins during the last 30 minutes of cooking time. Remove the studded red onion before serving.

YIELD: 6 servings

PER SERVING: Calories 698.2; Calories From Fat 358.4; Total Fat 39.8 g; Cholesterol 116.8 mg; Sodium 747.6 mg; Potassium 1,441 mg; Total Carbohydrates 53.7 g; Fiber 11.3 g; Sugar 20.9 g; Protein 33.3 g

NEW ENGLAND CORNED BEEF AND CABBAGE

INGREDIENTS

4 baby turnips, unpeeled and quartered

4 carrots, peeled and thickly sliced on the diagonal

1 yellow onion, quartered

2 cups (470 ml) vegetable broth (or water)

1 to 2 cups (235 to 470 ml) pure apple cider

One 3-pound (1,362 g) corned beef brisket, fat trimmed

2 tablespoons (22 g) hot mustard

½ teaspoon cracked black pepper

1 small head green cabbage, cored and cut into 8 equal wedges

FROM DR. JONNY: Corned beef is actually just salt-cured beef, and the dish itself has nothing to do with corn. The word *corn* comes from Old English and is used to describe hard particles or grains—in this case, the coarse grains of salt used for curing. The common practice of salting beef as a way of preserving it figures prominently in many cultures, from Jewish to Caribbean to Irish. And corned beef does beautifully slow cooked. We paired it with cabbage, one of the great health foods of all time because of its generous helping of cancer-fighting chemicals called *indoles*. Cabbage is also loaded with powerful antioxidants like sulforaphane, which can disarm damaging free radicals and help fight carcinogens. We replaced the traditional white potatoes in this dish with turnips, which are actually in the same vegetable family as cabbages (the Brassica family, also known as Vegetable Royalty!). Turnips are a "highfoluve" food, which means it fills you up without costing you a lot of calories. They provide 3 grams of fiber, more than 250 mg of potassium, 18 mg of vitamin C, and 51 mg of calcium, all for a miserly 35 calories per cup! If a recipe could be a poster child for "a healthy dish," this one would be it!

Combine the turnips, carrots, and onion in the bottom of a 6- or 7-quart (5.7 or 6.6 L) slow cooker. Pour the vegetable broth and cider over all (use 1 cup [235 ml] of cider for 6-quart [5.7 L] and 2 cups [470 ml] for 7-quart [6.6 L]). Lay the brisket on top and coat with a layer of mustard. Sprinkle on the black pepper. Lay the cabbage wedges on top of the brisket, cover, and cook on low for 8 to 9 hours, until the meat is cooked through and tender.

YIELD: 6 servings

PER SERVING: Calories 570.6; Calories From Fat 315.8; Total Fat 35 g; Cholesterol 123.3 mg; Sodium 3,177.5 mg; Potassium 1,277.2 mg; Total Carbohydrates 26.5 g; Fiber 6.4 g; Sugar 9.4 g; Protein 37.2 g

CLEAN LOADED SLOPPY JOE WITH A KICK

INGREDIENTS

1 pound (454 g) leanest ground beef

1 yellow onion, finely chopped

6 cloves garlic, crushed and chopped

1 red bell pepper, cored, seeded, and finely chopped

1 jalapeño pepper, seeded and minced

1 chipotle pepper in adobo sauce, minced

1 can (14 ounces, or 392 g) black beans, drained and rinsed

1 can (14 ounces, or 392 g) fire-roasted diced tomatoes, drained

1 can (14 ounces, or 392 g) tomato sauce

1 ½ tablespoons (30 g) blackstrap molasses

1 ½ tablespoons (23 ml) apple cider vinegar

1 teaspoon ground cumin

1 teaspoon dried oregano

1 teaspoon chili powder (use ancho chile powder, if you have it)

1 teaspoon salt

½ teaspoon ground allspice

FROM CHEF JEANNETTE

Use gloves when working with hot chile peppers and be careful not to touch your eyes!

Serving Suggestions: My favorite healthy and delicious way to serve sloppy Joes is to ditch the bun and stuff the mix into crisp, raw or blanched red bell peppers or hollowed-out heirloom tomatoes (use a melon baller to empty them quickly). It's also great served over a bed of crisp, fresh hardy green lettuce such as chopped romaine hearts garnished with raw red onion. This Joe mix has a kick, so the extra raw veggies also help cool the bite.

FROM DR. JONNY: First time I ever tasted a sloppy Joe, or even heard the term, was at Camp Awosting for Boys in Connecticut, and they served this big plate of greasy mystery meat in some kind of gooey sweet brown sauce on a white hamburger bun. Of course, at the time, I thought it was great. But really, now, canned sloppy Joes? With unidentifiable meat, high-fructose corn syrup, and enough sodium to choke an artery? You can do better! And we did—using grass-fed beef, beans for fiber and antioxidants, tomatoes for lycopene, three different kinds of peppers, a fabulous mix of spices that evokes the Southwest, and one of the healthiest sweeteners on earth, blackstrap molasses. Take that, Camp Awosting! This is a unique and healthy slow-cooked Joe mix that will knock your socks off!

In a large skillet over medium-high heat, combine the beef and onion and cook until the meat is completely browned, no pink remaining, about 6 minutes. Add the garlic and cook, stirring frequently, for about 1 minute. Drain any excess oils and transfer the contents to a slow cooker.

Add all the remaining ingredients and stir well to combine. Cover and cook on high for 3 to 4 hours, or on low for 5 to 6 hours, or until the vegetables are tender.

YIELD: 6 servings

PER SERVING: Calories 260.8; Calories From Fat 40.2; Total Fat 4.5 g; Cholesterol 46.9 mg; Sodium 924.8 mg; Potassium 1,236.2 mg; Total Carbohydrates 31.4 g; Fiber 9.2 g; Sugar 8.4 g; Protein 23 g

VEGETABLE-LOADED BEEF AND BARLEY STEW

INGREDIENTS

1 large sweet onion, chopped

1 green bell pepper, seeded and chopped

2 carrots, peeled and sliced

2 parsnips, peeled and sliced

2 ribs celery, sliced

1 ½ pounds (680 g) stew beef, cubed

4 cups (940 ml) beef stock (try Bone-Strengthening Beef Stock and add ½ teaspoon salt)

1 can (14.5 ounces, or 406 g) diced tomatoes, undrained

¼ cup (60 ml) Burgundy wine

1 teaspoon sweet paprika

1 teaspoon dried oregano

1 teaspoon dried basil

¾ teaspoon each salt and cracked black pepper

12 ounces (335 g) fresh green beans, sliced into 1 ½-inch (4 cm) pieces

¾ cup (150 g) pearl barley

FROM DR. JONNY: Barley is an excellent food choice for those concerned about type 2 diabetes or pre-diabetes because the grain contains essential vitamins and minerals and is an excellent source of dietary fiber, particularly beta-glucan soluble fiber. It's also an extremely low-glycemic grain, scoring a mere 20 on the glycemic index and (even better) 8 on the glycemic load (anything under 10 is low, low, low!). Research shows that barley beta-glucan soluble fiber promotes healthy blood sugar by slowing the entrance of glucose (sugar) into the bloodstream. So barley gets a thumbs-up from us, and when you combine it with grass-fed beef and a bunch of nutrient-dense vegetables you have something pretty close to a nutritionally perfect meal. Note: No white potatoes were harmed in the making of this recipe, because there are none! Fun fact: Ancient Romans used to wear celery around the neck to ward off a hangover after a particularly demanding night of Roman-style orgies! More recently, studies have shown that substances in celery called *phthalides* relax muscle tissue in the artery walls and increase blood flow!

Combine the onion, bell pepper, carrots, parsnips, celery, and stew beef in the slow cooker.

Pour the stock and tomatoes over all and add the wine, paprika, oregano, basil, salt, and pepper, cover, and cook on low for about 4 hours. Add the green beans and barley and cook for 2 more hours, or until the beef and barley are cooked through and tender.

YIELD: 8 servings

PER SERVING: Calories 296.5; Calories From Fat 41.4; Total Fat 4.7 g; Cholesterol 0 mg; Sodium 670.5 mg; Potassium 1,223.3 mg; Total Carbohydrates 39.9 g; Fiber 10 g; Sugar 8.9 g; Protein 25.4 g

GRASS-FED BEEF WITH BUTTER-NUT SQUASH AND CHERRIES

FROM DR. JONNY: During a presentation at the Tucson Festival of Books, Chef Jeannette and I spoke about the joys and benefits of grass-fed meat but were surprised to hear how many people in the audience didn't know what that was. Moreover, those who did told us it was next to impossible to find. So here's the scoop: everything you ever heard about meat being bad for you came from studies where people ate processed meat (like bologna, salami, hot dogs, and other deli specialties) and regular factory-farmed meat (loaded with antibiotics, steroids, and hormones). Grass-fed beef is raised on its normal diet of pasture, has a completely different fat makeup, has no hormones, steroids, or antibiotics, and tastes 100 percent better (at least to my taste buds). As far as availability, you can usually find it at farmers' markets, although more and more health-conscious grocery stores (at least in big cities) are now carrying it as well. You can also order online from companies like U.S. Wellness Meats at www.grasslandbeef.com. Both Chef Jeannette and I always recommend grass-fed, with its higher concentration of omega-3 fats, its CLA content (conjugated linolenic acid—a fat that has anticancer activity), and its lack of all the stuff that makes conventional meat unhealthy. Fun fact: A 2008 study compared two groups of rats, one of which had their diet supplemented with whole tart cherry powder. The rats that received the tart cherry supplement didn't gain as much weight, didn't build up as much body fat, and showed much lower levels of inflammation, which has been linked to heart disease and diabetes.

INGREDIENTS

12 ounces (336 g) frozen dark cherries

1 medium butternut squash, peeled, seeded, quartered, and sliced

1 large sweet onion, sliced

1/2 cup (60 g) dried, juice-sweetened tart cherries

1 1/4 pounds (568 g) cubed stew beef

1 can (14 ounces, or 392 g) diced tomatoes, undrained

2 tablespoons (30 g) quick-cooking tapioca

2 teaspoons tart cherry or apple butter, unsweetened (optional; we like Eden Organics)

3/4 teaspoon salt

1/2 teaspoon black pepper

1/4 teaspoon ground cinnamon

FROM CHEF JEANNETTE

Serving Suggestion: Try this dish served over hot jasmine rice.

Place the frozen cherries, squash, onion, and dried cherries on the bottom of the slow cooker. Top with the beef cubes.

In a medium-size bowl, combine the tomatoes, tapioca, cherry butter, if using, salt, pepper, and cinnamon and mix well to thoroughly combine. Pour the tomato mixture over all and cook on high for 4 to 5 hours, or on low for 5 to 6 hours, until the beef is cooked through but still moist and the squash is tender.

YIELD: 6 servings

PER SERVING: Calories 253.2; Calories From Fat 43.3; Total Fat 4.8 g; Cholesterol 0 mg; Sodium 518.3 mg; Potassium 776.9 mg; Total Carbohydrates 32.7 g; Fiber 3.9 g; Sugar 11.9 g; Protein 22.8 g

SIMPLEST HIGH-FIBER BEEFY TACOS

INGREDIENTS

1 pound (454 g) leanest ground beef

1 yellow onion, finely chopped

4 cloves garlic, minced

2 serrano chiles, seeded and finely chopped

1 can (16 ounces, or 454 g) highest-quality
vegetarian refried beans

1 cup (115 g) shredded sharp Cheddar cheese

1 jar (16 ounces, or 454 g) high-quality salsa

12 small sprouted corn tortillas

2 heirloom tomatoes, chopped

2 cups (110 g) shredded lettuce

1/3 cup (77 g) low-fat sour cream (or use plain
Greek yogurt with a squirt of lime juice for
fewer calories)

1/3 cup (5 g) chopped fresh cilantro

FROM DR. JONNY: Up until I moved to beautiful Southern California, where I now live happily with Emily and Lucy Bowden (that's the pit bull and the Argentine Dogo, respectively), I couldn't have told you the difference between a taco, a burrito, and a tamale. I know, I know. But Mexican food really wasn't my thing. You'd go into the restaurant and they'd bring out a bunch of fried chips, the dishes would be swimming in rice and sauce, the portions would be enormous, and everything seemed to be stuffed into some kind of high-carb wrap that was made with corn or flour. Now I've come to love Mexican food, especially in the versions that Chef Jeannette prepares. This taco—I now know what they are!—is way higher in fiber than the standard fare, largely from the refried beans, but it's also a whole lot cleaner. We use only grass-fed beef (which you won't find in Mexican fast food!), and we add a ton of fresh veggies. This is how real, healthy Mexican food was meant to taste!

In a large skillet over medium-high heat, combine the beef and onion and cook until no pink remains, about 6 minutes. Add the garlic and cook, stirring frequently, for 1 minute. Drain any excess oils and transfer the contents to a slow cooker.

Stir in the chiles, refried beans, cheese, and salsa. Cover and cook on high for 3 to 4 hours, or on low for 5 to 6 hours, until the mixture is cooked through and bubbling. Stir and serve over the warmed tortillas with the tomato, lettuce, and a dollop of sour cream, and garnished generously with the cilantro.

YIELD: 6 servings

PER SERVING: Calories 378.5; Calories From Fat 119.6; Total Fat 13.5 g; Cholesterol 71.9 mg; Sodium 1,070 mg; Potassium 823.8 mg; Total Carbohydrates 36.6 g; Fiber 8.7 g; Sugar 6.7 g; Protein 29.3 g

CLA-RICH BEEF BIRYANI

INGREDIENTS

1 large yellow onion, quartered

4 cloves garlic, crushed

1-inch (2.5 cm) cube fresh ginger, peeled

2 teaspoons ghee (or olive oil)

³/₄ teaspoon ground cumin

³/₄ teaspoon ground coriander

¹/₂ teaspoon ground cardamom

¹/₂ teaspoon ground cloves

¹/₂ teaspoon ground cinnamon

¹/₂ teaspoon each salt and pepper

1 pound (454 g) top round beef, cut into 2 by
    ¹/₂-inch (5 by 1.3 cm) pieces

1 cup (130 g) frozen peas

²/₃ cup (150 g) plain low-fat Greek yogurt

¹/₃ cup (50 g) toasted cashews (optional)

FROM CHEF JEANNETTE

Time-Saver Tip: Omit the ghee and spice-sautéing step and add the spices directly to the onion mixture.

FROM DR. JONNY: I never get tired of making the case for grass-fed beef, so if you've heard my rant before, please forgive me, and if you haven't, here it is: Grass-fed meat is a whole different animal—forgive the pun—from its factory-farmed brethren. The typical supermarket meat we buy is unfortunately the stuff that gives meat such a bad reputation. Of course it's a killer—it's loaded with hormones, steroids, and antibiotics and is high in inflammatory omega-6 fats and low in omega-3s. But grass-fed meat has none of those problems. Cattle fed on pasture don't get sick as much, so they don't need preemptive doses of antibiotics. Nearly all grass-fed ranches are organic and don't use hormones or steroids. And grass-fed meat is rich in a particular kind of cancer-fighting fat called CLA (conjugated linolenic acid), which is not found in the meat, milk, or butter from factory-farmed animals. You'll love the rich taste it imparts to Indian biryani—already filled with savory spices to begin with. Slow cooking lets the meat infuse with those multilayered flavors, and cool yogurt is the perfect accompaniment.

Combine the onion, garlic, and ginger in a food processor and process into a purée. Set aside.

Melt the ghee in a small sauté pan over medium heat and stir in the cumin, coriander, cardamom, cloves, cinnamon, salt, and pepper. Heat, stirring constantly, for 1 to 2 minutes, or until the spices are very fragrant, then add to the onion mixture. Pulse briefly to combine.

Combine the onion-spice mixture and beef in a slow cooker and stir to coat.

Cover and cook on low for 4 to 5 hours, until the beef is cooked through but still tender.

Stir in the peas and yogurt for last 15 minutes of cooking time. Garnish with the cashews, if using, and serve.

YIELD: 4 servings

PER SERVING: Calories 314; Calories From Fat 117.8; Total Fat 13.5 g; Cholesterol 81 mg; Sodium 459.2 mg; Potassium 631.1 mg; Total Carbohydrates 16.3 g; Fiber 3.1 g; Sugar 3.8 g; Protein 32.2 g

LEANER, SAVORY SLOW-COOKED MEATLOAF

INGREDIENTS

1 pound (454 g) baby carrots

1 egg

1 ½ tablespoons (23 ml) Worcestershire sauce (use organic to avoid high-fructose corn syrup)

¾ cup (180 g) low-sugar ketchup or barbecue sauce, divided

½ cup (40 g) whole rolled oats

½ sweet onion, finely chopped

½ medium green or red bell pepper, seeded and finely chopped

1 pound (454 g) leanest ground beef

1 pound (454 g) leanest ground turkey

1 teaspoon salt

½ teaspoon cracked black pepper

FROM CHEF JEANNETTE

Time-Saver Tip: If using a larger slow cooker, form two longer, thinner loaves and cook them on high for 1 ½ hours and then on low for 1 ½ to 2 more hours, or until cooked through.

Variation: For a flavorful alternative to the more classic meatloaf, substitute a fruit chutney for the ketchup or barbecue sauce. Try our recipe for Lower-Sugar Curried Mango Nectarine Chutney or even a high-quality jarred version, such as pineapple pepper.

FROM DR. JONNY: When I was a kid, meatloaf was the homemade version of Hamburger Helper. Basically, you took low-quality beef, mixed it up with lots of white bread crumbs and other fillers, baked it in the oven for a bit, and voilà: ordinary meatloaf. Not bad, but nothing special. We made it better. Using half ground turkey cuts the calories of this normally high-cal dish, and cooking in the slow cooker is not only incredibly *easy*, but it also gives you a deliciously *tender* meatloaf. (In case you haven't heard me say it before, please only use grass-fed beef. Not only does it taste better, but it's also much better for you!) We swapped out those nutritionally empty bread crumbs for oats, adding fiber and important nutrients (like beta-glucan, which is great for prostate health and may help lower cholesterol). The leftovers freeze exceptionally well—keep some handy for a quick, protein-rich snack.

Place the carrots in one layer in the center of a slow cooker.

In a large bowl, beat the egg lightly. Add the Worcestershire, ½ cup (120 g) of the ketchup, oats, onion, and bell pepper and mix well to combine. Break up the meats and add to the bowl. Evenly sprinkle the salt and pepper over all. Using your hands, gently but thoroughly mix to combine well. Do not overwork the meat or your meatloaf will be tough. Shape into a round loaf to fit your slow cooker. (Note: I like to use my 7-quart [6.6 L] cooker for this because it is easier to remove the loaf at the end.) Place the loaf on top of the carrots (this will prevent a soggy bottom and allow any excess fats to drain into the carrots and flavor them deliciously).

Cover and cook on low for 4 to 6 hours, until the meatloaf is cooked though. At the end of the cooking time, turn up the heat to high, brush the top of the loaf with the remaining ¼ cup (60 g) ketchup, cover, and cook for 15 to 30 minutes longer, until the sauce is set.

YIELD: 6 to 8 servings

PER SERVING: Calories 226.5; Calories From Fat 74.8; Total Fat 8.6 g; Cholesterol 106.4 mg; Sodium 691.8 mg; Potassium 513.3 mg; Total Carbohydrates 43.1 g; Fiber 2.5 g; Sugar 5.6 g; Protein 24.2 g

IRON-RICH GROUND SIRLOIN BORSCHT

INGREDIENTS

1 pound (454 g) leanest ground sirloin

1 large yellow onion, chopped

2 cloves garlic, minced

4 large beets, peeled and chopped

4 large carrots, peeled and chopped

2 ribs celery, chopped

2 medium Yukon gold potatoes, unpeeled and chopped

1 cup (90 g) thinly sliced green cabbage

6 cups (1,410 ml) beef broth

1/4 cup (65 g) tomato paste

2 teaspoons organic beef Better Than Bouillon

1 teaspoon caraway seeds

1/2 teaspoon each salt and freshly ground pepper

3 tablespoons (45 ml) red wine vinegar

1/2 cup (115 g) low-fat plain Greek yogurt

1/4 cup (16 g) chopped fresh dill

FROM DR. JONNY: For reasons I'll never understand, whenever I enthusiastically recommend beets, people scrunch up their noses. Did I miss the memo that says you're not supposed to like them? Maybe my fondness for beets goes back to my Jewish grandmother, who made the best borscht in Brooklyn. Later, while working on the original Off-Broadway production of *Little Shop of Horrors*, which was located in the heart of the heavily Jewish Lower East Side (later gentrified and renamed the "East Village") of New York, I used to go the Jewish luncheonette across the street, which had the distinction of offering either hot borscht (unusual!) or the traditional cold kind. Anyway. Beets are a legendary food for the liver, helping it perform its duties as detoxification central. They're a perfect accompaniment to ground sirloin—not a typical borscht ingredient, but who said we had to be typical? Original, yes. Boring, no. You'll love this rich, beefy soup!

In a large saucepan over medium-high heat, combine the sirloin, onion, and garlic. Cook for 5 to 6 minutes, or until cooked through, with no pink remaining. Remove from the heat, drain any excess fat, and transfer to the slow cooker. Add the beets, carrots, celery, potatoes, cabbage, broth, tomato paste, bouillon, caraway seeds, salt, and pepper.

Stir to mix well, cover, and cook on low for 6 to 7 hours, or until all veggies are tender. Stir in the vinegar during the last 10 minutes of cooking time.

In a small bowl, combine the yogurt and dill and store in the fridge while the soup is cooking. Serve in individual bowls with a generous dollop of the dilled yogurt.

YIELD: 6 servings

PER SERVING: Calories 243; Calories From Fat 45.2; Total Fat 5 g; Cholesterol 48 mg; Sodium 1,261.7 mg; Potassium 1,249.1 mg; Total Carbohydrates 27.2 g; Fiber 5.7 g; Sugar 10.2 g; Protein 24.1 g

MOROCCAN BRAISED LAMB SHANKS IN FRESH TOMATOES AND RED WINE

INGREDIENTS

1 1/2 tablespoons (23 ml) olive oil

6 lamb shanks

1 large sweet onion, chopped

1/2 cup (55 g) shredded carrot

1 rib celery, finely diced

1 clove garlic, minced

2 cups (470 ml) dry red wine

3 or 4 medium ripe heirloom tomatoes, chopped (about 3 cups [540 g])

1 cinnamon stick

1/2 teaspoon ground cloves

1/2 teaspoon ground allspice

1 tablespoon (20 g) honey

1/2 teaspoon each salt and freshly ground black pepper, or to taste

FROM DR. JONNY: Lamb is the meat from young sheep that are less than one year old. That immediately tells you that this animal is much less likely to have accumulated a ton of toxins and other chemicals in its meat and fat than, say, a factory-farmed dairy cow that's been fed antibiotics, steroids, and the wrong kind of food (grain) for the four or so years until it's sent to the market for beef. In addition, lamb is a terrific source of protein and iron, providing 20 percent of the recommended daily intake of iron for men and 12 percent for women. And remember, iron from meat—called *heme iron*—is the most absorbable form of iron there is. Lamb also contains almost half the daily requirement for zinc (so important for immunity) and more than 100 percent of the daily requirement for vitamin B$_{12}$! Braising is a great technique for the slow cooker because of the low controlled temperature. This recipe makes fall-apart-tender lamb—utterly delicious!

Heat the oil in a large skillet over medium-high heat. Add the lamb shanks and cook until lightly browned on all sides, 7 to 9 minutes. Transfer to the slow cooker. Add the onion, carrot, and celery to the skillet and cook, stirring frequently, for 7 to 8 minutes, or until just beginning to brown. Add the garlic and cook for 30 seconds. Add the wine, tomatoes, cinnamon stick, cloves, and allspice and bring to a simmer, stirring well to incorporate all the browned bits in the pan. Stir in the honey, salt, and pepper and pour the mixture carefully over the lamb shanks in the slow cooker. Cook on high for about 4 hours, or on low for about 7 hours, until the lamb is tender and easily comes off the bone. Remove the cinnamon stick before serving.

YIELD: 6 servings

PER SERVING: Calories 606.1; Calories From Fat 308.5; Total Fat 34.3 g; Cholesterol 152 mg; Sodium 347.8 mg; Potassium 976.1 mg; Total Carbohydrates 15.2 g; Fiber 3.1 g; Sugar 8.5 g; Protein 43.5 g

BEANIE SLOW-COOKED SHEPHERD'S PIE

INGREDIENTS

1 pound (454 g) leanest ground lamb

1 large white onion, diced

6 cloves garlic, minced

1 can (15 ounces, or 420 g) small white beans,
    drained and rinsed

1 1/2 tablespoons (16 g) Dijon mustard

1 tablespoon (1.7 g) minced fresh rosemary
    (or 1 teaspoon dried, chopped)

1 1/4 teaspoons salt, divided

1 teaspoon freshly ground black pepper, divided

1/3 cup (27 g) shredded Parmesan cheese

3 cups (675 g) cooked mashed potatoes

1/2 cup (24 g) chopped chives

2 teaspoons garlic powder

FROM DR. JONNY: Shepherd's pie is actually a variation on an old traditional dish called "cottage pie," which was basically a meat pie made with beef topped with a mashed potato crust. These days, shepherd's pie tends to mean a meat dish where the meat is actually mutton or lamb (the thinking being that shepherds deal with sheep, not beef!). Regardless, it's a delicious dish and the slow cooker is an ingenious way to do it. We used lean ground lamb, and we lowered the starch (and the carbohydrate load) by swapping out the traditional corn for white beans. The white beans not only add a nice amount of fiber and extra protein, but they also create a really creamy dish. This dish is absolutely terrific for leftovers and even works for a nontraditional (but very filling and energizing) breakfast! Seriously! Fun fact: The term *shepherd's pie* first appeared in the 1870s. The "Cumberland pie" is a version of shepherd's pie with a layer of bread crumbs on top.

In a large skillet over medium-high heat, cook the lamb and onion until no pink remains, about 7 minutes. Drain the oils, stir in the garlic, and cook for 1 minute, stirring frequently. Transfer the contents to a slow cooker and add the beans, mustard, and rosemary, 3/4 teaspoon of the salt, and 1/2 teaspoon of the pepper, stirring well to combine. Sprinkle evenly with the cheese.

In a medium-size bowl, combine the mashed potatoes, chives, garlic powder, the remaining 1/2 teaspoon salt, and the remaining 1/2 teaspoon pepper and mix well. Spread the potatoes evenly over the lamb and smooth out.

Cover and cook on high for 3 to 4 hours, or on low for 4 to 6 hours, until heated through. Remove the lid for the final 20 to 30 minutes of cooking time to allow for the evaporation of any excess moisture before serving.

YIELD: 6 servings

PER SERVING: Calories 415.4; Calories From Fat 133.8; Total Fat 20.2 g; Cholesterol 62.2 mg; Sodium 1,169.4 mg; Potassium 562.8 mg; Total Carbohydrates 35.5 g; Fiber 5.9 g; Sugar 2.8 g; Protein 21.1 g

INGREDIENTS

1 red onion, quartered

6 cloves garlic, crushed

1 chunk peeled, fresh ginger, about 1 inch
      (2.5 cm) square

¼ cup (60 ml) red wine vinegar

1 tablespoon (6.8 g) ground turmeric

1 tablespoon (6 g) ground coriander

2 teaspoons ground cumin

¾ teaspoon salt

½ teaspoon black pepper

½ teaspoon red pepper flakes

2 ½ pounds (1,135 g) lamb stew meat
      (2-inch [5 cm] cubes)

1 can (14.5 ounces, or 406 g) crushed tomatoes

TASTE OF INDIA LAMB

FROM DR. JONNY: Lamb is a wonderful source of protein, not to mention B vitamins, iron, and zinc. For this recipe, look for precut stew meat or slice up some boneless shoulder. (The shoulder cut is way less expensive than the loin cuts.) If you use the shoulder, be aware that it's a tiny bit fattier, so trim away any visible fat if you want a less oily dish—and fewer calories! The flavorful Indian marinade is similar to a classic vindaloo—a popular Indian curry dish in which spices are plentiful. We prepare ours in the slow cooker using a tomato base. The marinade is heavy on the turmeric, a super-spice known for its profound anti-inflammatory and anticancer activity. Fun fact: The name "vindaloo" originates from the Portuguese "Carne de Vinha d'Alhos," a dish of pork, wine, and garlic.

Place the onion, garlic, and ginger into a food processor and process until puréed, scraping down the sides as necessary. Add the vinegar, turmeric, coriander, cumin, salt, pepper, and red pepper flakes and process until well incorporated. Transfer the contents to a glass storage container and add the lamb cubes, tossing well to coat. Cover and refrigerate overnight. Transfer the contents to a slow cooker and stir in the crushed tomatoes. Cover and cook on low for 5 to 7 hours, until the lamb is cooked through and tender.

YIELD: 6 servings

PER SERVING: Calories 431.7; Calories From Fat 242.1; Total Fat 25.7 g; Cholesterol 133.3 mg; Sodium 527.1 mg; Potassium 297.2 mg; Total Carbohydrates 10 g; Fiber 2.6 g; Sugar 0.1 g; Protein 37 g

HIGH-FIBER CURRIED MULLIGATAWNY LAMB STEW

FROM DR. JONNY: Lamb is a wonderful source of protein that also happens to contain a fair amount of minerals such as calcium, magnesium, phosphorus, and potassium. And it makes a fabulous stew. This one, a classically "Irish" stew, has an Indian flair, largely because of the addition of curry. I especially love the inclusion of the apple, a flavor treat that adds just a touch of unexpected sweetness (and crunchiness) to this hearty dish. The low-calorie vegetables add to the volume without packing on many calories, making this a nutritionally dense dish that offers a heck of a lot of nutrition without breaking the caloric budget. The puréed chickpeas add not only a nice helping of fiber (12.5 grams per cup) and protein (14.5 grams) but also give this delicious stew a much-appreciated additional heartiness. Rich and filling, but low in calories.

INGREDIENTS

1 tablespoon (15 ml) olive oil

1 sweet or yellow onion, chopped

2 ribs celery, chopped

2 medium carrots, peeled and sliced

1 medium green bell pepper, cored, seeded, and chopped

1 medium green apple, peeled, cored, and chopped

3 cloves garlic, minced

6 cups (1,410 ml) chicken stock

⅓ cup (90 g) tomato paste

2 teaspoons curry powder

¼ teaspoon cayenne pepper

¾ teaspoon salt

½ teaspoon cracked black

1 medium Yukon gold potato, unpeeled and chopped

1 pound (454 g) cubed lamb stew meat

1 can (15 ounces, or 420 g) chickpeas, drained and rinsed

In a large skillet or sauté pan, heat the oil over medium heat. Add the onion, celery, carrot, bell pepper, and apple. Cook for 6 minutes, stirring often. Add the garlic and cook for 1 minute.

While the veggies are softening, in a large bowl whisk together the chicken stock, tomato paste, curry powder, cayenne pepper, salt, and black pepper and set aside. Add the sautéed veggies to the slow cooker. Top with the potatoes and lamb and pour the broth over all. Cook on high for 4 to 5 hours, or on low for 6 to 7 hours, or until the veggies and lamb are tender.

Add the chickpeas to a food processor or blender and process until nearly smooth, adding 1 tablespoon (15 ml) water, if necessary. Add to the stew and stir in well to incorporate. Cook for 20 minutes longer.

YIELD: 6 to 8 servings
PER SERVING: Calories 312; Calories From Fat 113.3; Total Fat 12.24 g; Cholesterol 45.4 mg; Sodium 785.3 mg; Potassium 662.6 mg; Total Carbohydrates 31.4 g; Fiber 5.1 g; Sugar 8.6 g; Protein 19.4 g

INGREDIENTS

1 large yellow onion, sliced and separated into
 rings
2 tablespoons (30 ml) balsamic vinegar
2 tablespoons (30 ml) chicken broth or water
1 tablespoon (14 g) unsalted butter, melted
1 tablespoon (11 g) Dijon mustard
2 cloves garlic, minced
1 tablespoon (1.7 g) minced fresh rosemary
 (or 1 teaspoon dried)
1 tablespoon (2.4 g) minced fresh thyme
 (or 1 teaspoon dried)
½ teaspoon dried oregano
½ teaspoon each salt and freshly ground
 pepper
8 loin lamb chops
Fresh mint leaves, for garnish (optional)

FROM CHEF JEANNETTE

If desired, you can transfer the onions
and juices to a large skillet and cook over
medium-high heat for a few minutes until
the sauce is slightly reduced and thickened
before serving.

LUSCIOUS, LEANEST LAMB CHOPS

FROM DR. JONNY: Lamb is not only an excellent source of high-quality protein, but it's also a good source of iron and B vitamins. And lamb provides about 45 percent of the daily requirement for zinc, essential for growth, healing, and a healthy immune system. (Plus the zinc and iron found in lamb are easily absorbed by the body.) Half the fat in lamb is unsaturated, and most of that is monounsaturated—the same kind found in olive oil and so prominent in the Mediterranean diet. The loin chop is the leanest, and in this recipe, the slow cooker blends the flavors of the onion and fresh herbs beautifully with the rich taste of the meat. This dish also has a lovely finishing kick of balsamic vinegar.

Layer the onion rings in the bottom of the slow cooker. Pour the vinegar, broth, and butter over all. In a small bowl, combine the mustard, garlic, rosemary, thyme, oregano, salt, and pepper and stir to combine. Rub the mixture evenly over the lamb chops and lay the chops over the onions. Cover and cook on low for 4 to 6 hours, until the lamb is cooked to the desired doneness. Remove the chops and stir the onions and juices before serving. Garnish with the mint, if using.

YIELD: 4 servings
PER SERVING: Calories 673.2; Calories From Fat 414.5; Total Fat 46 g; Cholesterol 204.3 mg; Sodium 541.7 mg; Potassium 1,002.7 mg; Total Carbohydrates 5.5 g; Fiber 0.9 g; Sugar 2.5 g; Protein 55.6 g

VERSATILE, LEAN, AND EASY CHICKEN BASE

FROM DR. JONNY: You've undoubtedly heard me rant and rave about the huge difference between store-bought, factory-farmed meat from Concentrated Animal Feeding Operations, or CAFOs, and grass-fed meat, which is a real health food. The same distinction applies to chicken. Raised (if you can call it that) in confinement in battery cages, these poor birds have a wretched life and produce inferior meat tinged with all the junk they have been fed (such as antibiotics, steroids, and the like). Free-range chickens get to roam around pecking at their natural diet of worms and grass—their meat is much higher in omega-3s and generally healthier to eat. This recipe is an excellent and easy way to use the slow cooker to best advantage and provides the bonus benefit of having a cooked protein on hand all the time!

INGREDIENTS

½ cup (120 ml) chicken broth or water
4 shallots, peeled and crushed
1 bay leaf
½ teaspoon black peppercorns
1 or 2 chickens (3 to 4 pounds, or 1,362 to 1,816 g each)
1 teaspoon salt

Combine the broth, shallots, bay leaf, and peppercorns in the bottom of a 6- or 7-quart (5.7 or 6.6 L) slow cooker. Use 1 or 2 chickens depending on how much cooked chicken you would like and the size of your slow cooker. Lightly salt the chickens all over and arrange in the slow cooker. Cover and cook on low for 7 to 9 hours, until the chicken is cooked through.

Remove the chickens and allow to cool enough to handle. Remove the meat from the carcasses and discard all skin, cartilage, and bone. Dice or shred the chicken or cut away in whole pieces. Use, refrigerate, or freeze cooked chicken in small portions to have a quick protein on hand anytime.

YIELD: 3 to 4 cups (1,120 to 1,400 g) per chicken
FOR ENTIRE RECIPE: Calories 587.1; Calories From Fat 340; Total Fat 37.6 g; Cholesterol 204.8 mg; Sodium 2,881.5 mg; Potassium 851.5 mg; Total Carbohydrates 14.9 g; Fiber 0.3 g; Sugar 0.4 g; Protein 45.3 g

FROM CHEF JEANNETTE

Use cooked chicken to quickly make enchiladas, tostadas, tacos, wraps, hot barbecue chicken salads, cold mayo or tahini salads, quick chilis, etc. It's great with our Immune-Boostin', Gut-Bustin' Fiery BBQ Sauce.

LOWER-SUGAR BBQ PULLED CHICKEN THIGHS

INGREDIENTS

⅓ cup (80 g) lower-sugar ketchup

¼ cup (65 g) tomato paste

¼ cup (60 ml) apple cider vinegar

1 tablespoon (11 g) hot or Dijon mustard

1 tablespoon (15 ml) Worcestershire sauce (use organic to avoid high-fructose corn syrup)

2 tablespoons (30 g) Sucanat or xylitol

4 cloves garlic, minced

1 teaspoon sweet paprika

½ teaspoon each salt and freshly cracked black pepper

¼ to ½ teaspoon ground chipotle chile, to taste

1 small sweet onion, finely chopped

2 pounds (980 g) boneless, skinless chicken thighs

FROM CHEF JEANNETTE

Serving Suggestions: Try serving this rolled up into large, tender lettuce leaves, stuffed into hollowed-out bell peppers (precook cored peppers for 5 minutes in boiling water , and drain well before stuffing), or over a bed of sautéed greens such as collards or kale.

FROM DR. JONNY: So here's the place where I get to rant about why Chef Jeannette and I don't use pork. There's nothing inherently unhealthy about pork, which is a perfectly fine meat. Problem is, the treatment of factory-farmed pigs is so horrendous that I simply can't justify eating it under any circumstances. Pigs are smart and social—some say as much so as dogs—and without going into the gruesome details, we both feel we simply can't contribute to increasing the demand for factory-farmed pigs. If you can find humanely raised pigs that haven't been routinely brutalized, by all means go for it. (At the present time, only Niman Ranch [www.nimanranch.com] has come close to raising pigs in a way that could be reasonably called "humane.") I'm hoping that the equivalent of "grass-fed" pork will become more common in the next decade so that we can all enjoy this meat without guilt. The point here is that chicken thighs are a great alternative to pork and work beautifully in this recipe. Sure, the thighs have a bit more fat than white meat, but that actually helps keep them from drying out in the slow cooker. (We do remove the skins, though, just so the dish doesn't have a greasy feel. No worries. It doesn't.) Bonus points: your taste buds will never notice that the tangy, full-flavored barbecue sauce was made with way less sugar than the store-bought kind!

In a medium-size bowl, whisk together the ketchup, tomato paste, cider vinegar, mustard, Worcestershire sauce, Sucanat, garlic, paprika, salt, pepper, and ground chile until well combined.

Make a layer of onion on the bottom of the slow cooker. Lay the chicken thighs over the onion and pour the sauce evenly over all. Cover and cook on high for 2 to 3 hours, or on low for 4 to 5 hours, or until the chicken is cooked through but still juicy. Using two large forks, pull apart and finely shred the tender thigh meat and stir well to mix with the sauce. The mixture will thicken slightly as it cools.

YIELD: 6 to 8 servings

PER SERVING: Calories 175.6; Calories From Fat 41.6; Total Fat 4.6 g; Cholesterol 94.1 mg; Sodium 448.3 mg; Potassium 414.3 mg; Total Carbohydrates 9.2 g; Fiber 0.9 g; Sugar 6.8 g; Protein 23.2 g

CHUNKY GERMAN SAUSAGE AND SAUERKRAUT STEW

INGREDIENTS

4 links (4 ounces, or 112 g each) smoked (or spicy) chicken sausage, sliced into thick half-moons

1 small yellow onion, chopped

4 to 6 baby new potatoes, quartered

8 ounces (225 g) cremini mushrooms, sliced

2 ribs celery, thinly sliced

2 small carrots, sliced into thin half-moons

1 can (15 ounces, or 420 g) small white beans, drained and rinsed

24 ounces (680 g) sauerkraut, drained and rinsed

4 cups (940 ml) chicken or vegetable broth

1 $^1/_2$ tablespoons (23 ml) white wine vinegar

$^1/_2$ teaspoon each salt and freshly ground pepper

$^3/_4$ teaspoon caraway seeds (optional)

1 bay leaf

FROM DR. JONNY: If all you know about sauerkraut is from ballpark hot dogs, be prepared for a shock. Sauerkraut is actually a naturally fermented food, and that alone earns it a place among the healthiest menu items on the planet. Naturally fermented foods include yogurt, real olives (the kind that sit out in brine in the olive bars, not the kind that are chemically processed in the little jars), tempeh, miso, authentic soy sauce, and the Korean dish kimchi. When foods are naturally fermented, they are rich in enzymes and the "good bacteria" known as probiotics, which stimulate the immune system and help with digestion and assimilation of nutrients. Chef Jeannette used lower-calorie chicken sausage for the meat, which blends perfectly with the new potatoes and mushrooms. The nice dose of fiber from the beans adds even more nutrition to this already scrumptious stew.

In a 6-quart (5.7 L) slow cooker, combine all the ingredients and stir gently to combine. Cover and cook on high for 4 to 6 hours, until the vegetables are tender.

YIELD: 10 servings

PER SERVING: Calories 154.3; Calories From Fat 17.1; Total Fat 2.7 g; Cholesterol 7.5 mg; Sodium 1,086.5 mg; Potassium 555.7 mg; Total Carbohydrates 23.7 g; Fiber 5.8 g; Sugar 2.4 g; Protein 9.3 g

EASIEST LEAN ARTICHOKE CHICKEN

FROM DR. JONNY: Artichokes are like the lobster of the veggie community—you have to really dig to get at the good parts, but in the end it's worth it. Artichokes have a number of active chemicals with health benefits for a wide range of conditions. These include *silymarin* (the active ingredient in the herb milk thistle), which has a long and distinguished resume as a plant compound that helps protect and nourish the liver. And artichokes are known for their effects on gastrointestinal upset—one study showed that 85 percent of patients with GI upset who were given extract of artichokes experienced significant relief from nausea, stomach pain, and vomiting. Chef Jeannette created this spicy artichoke sauce to perfectly complement the breast meat of chicken, a wonderful source of protein and slightly lower in calories than the dark meat. But the best thing about this recipe is how simple it is to make. (Okay, maybe tied for best—that tangy artichoke sauce is a definite plus!)

INGREDIENTS

12 ounces (336 g) mini baby carrots

4 small boneless, skinless chicken breasts

1 can (14 ounces, or 392 g) artichoke hearts, drained and halved

1 jar (6 ounces, or 168 g) high-quality artichoke hearts marinated in olive oil, undrained

¼ cup (60 ml) dry white wine

Juice and zest of ½ lemon

½ teaspoon each salt and freshly ground pepper

Scatter the carrots over the bottom of the slow cooker and place the chicken in one layer on top. Add the drained artichokes and pour the marinated artichokes and oil evenly over all. Pour in the wine, squeeze the lemon over all and add the zest. Sprinkle salt and pepper over all and cook on high for 2 to 3 hours, or on low for 3 to 4 hours, until the chicken is cooked through.

YIELD: 4 to 6 servings

PER SERVING: Calories 257.2; Calories From Fat 19.4; Total Fat 1.6 g; Cholesterol 94.3 mg; Sodium 435.2 mg; Potassium 668.8 mg; Total Carbohydrates 16 g; Fiber 6.8 g; Sugar 3.1 g; Protein 41.2 g

CLEAN PEANUTTY THAI CHICKEN

INGREDIENTS

½ cup (130 g) smooth peanut butter

½ cup (120 ml) chicken broth

¼ cup (60 ml) low-sodium tamari sauce

Juice of 1 large lime

1 tablespoon (15 ml) rice wine vinegar

4 cloves garlic, crushed

1-inch (2.5 cm) chunk peeled fresh ginger

1 tablespoon (20 g) honey

½ teaspoon red pepper flakes

1 sweet onion, chopped

1 red bell pepper, cored, seeded, and chopped

1½ pounds (680 g) boneless, skinless chicken
   breast or thighs, cut into 1½-inch (3.8 cm)
   pieces

½ cup (8 g) chopped fresh cilantro

FROM DR. JONNY: Asian food can be really healthy, but unfortunately you might not know it if you've only eaten at the typical Asian fast-food restaurants found in every food court and mall around the country. Many restaurants rely on MSG for the flavor that's missing in the overcooked, overprocessed food they serve, and many use sauces that are made "tasty" not by the richness of the flavors, but by the addition of sugar and wheat starch (think "egg drop soup"). Our version of Thai chicken is much cleaner, lighter, and healthier than anything I've found in all but the very best Asian restaurants in Southern California. Remember to use chickens that were raised on pasture (the term being used these days is "pastured chickens," and they are superb—chemical- and steroid-free, with delicious meat and a higher content of omega-3 fats). We recommend using natural, organic peanut butter because many of the commercial brands have a ton of trans fats and added sugar.

In the bowl of a food processor, combine the peanut butter, broth, tamari, lime juice, vinegar, garlic, ginger, honey, and red pepper flakes. Process until smooth, scraping down the sides as necessary, and set aside.

Combine the onion, bell pepper, and chicken in the slow cooker and pour the sauce evenly over all. Stir gently to coat. Cover and cook on high for 3 to 4 hours, or on low for 5 to 6 hours, until the chicken is cooked through but still juicy. Stir in the cilantro just before serving.

YIELD: 4 servings

PER SERVING: Calories 469.5; Calories From Fat 165; Total Fat 18.2 g; Cholesterol 102 mg; Sodium 1,071.9 mg; Potassium 704.8 mg; Total Carbohydrates 24.4 g; Fiber 3.8 g; Sugar 13.5 g; Protein 52.6 g

LEAN DRIED APRICOT CHICKEN AND WILD RICE SOUP

INGREDIENTS

1 sweet onion, diced

1 sweet potato, peeled and cubed, or 2 cups (300 g) peeled, seeded, and cubed butternut squash (about 3/4-inch [2 cm] dice)

2 large chicken breasts, cut into chunks (about 2-inch [5 cm] dice)

1/2 cup (80 g) wild rice

6 cups (1,410 ml) chicken broth (or use our Lean and Clean Gingered Chicken Stock)

1 teaspoon organic chicken Better Than Bouillon

3 tablespoons (45 ml) mirin (or dry sherry)

1 teaspoon ground ginger

1/2 teaspoon ground allspice

1/2 teaspoon each salt and freshly ground pepper

1/3 cup (43 g) coarsely chopped dried apricots

1 1/2 cups (195 g) frozen corn

FROM DR. JONNY: Unusual and unexpected juxtapositions are at the heart of interesting fashion, art, and music, and unusual pairings are at the heart of interesting food. Before I tried this recipe I'd never tasted apricots with chicken, so it was unusual (at least for me), surprising, and delightful. If my taste buds could smile they'd be grinning from ear to ear. Lean breast meat has a lot going for it nutritionally but tends not to be as moist and juicy as the fatter cuts. But because it's immersed in liquid stock in the slow cooker, it will be as moist and tender when you eat it as you could possibly want it to be. Apricots are a tasty little bundle of nutrients that come in a sun-colored package, provide lots of vitamin A and beta-carotene, plus contain a special relative of beta-carotene called *beta-cryptoxanthin*, a powerful antioxidant that's associated with lower risk of both lung and colon cancer. This terrific pairing makes for a flavorful soup—slightly salty, slightly sweet, and very satisfying. The toothy "bite" from the wild rice adds a nice touch!

Combine the onion, sweet potato, chicken, and wild rice in a slow cooker. Pour the broth over all and stir in the Better Than Bouillon, mirin, ginger, allspice, salt, and pepper. Cover and cook on high for 2 to 3 hours, or on low for 3 to 4 hours, until the squash and rice are tender. Add the apricots and corn during last 20 minutes of cooking time.

YIELD: 6 servings

PER SERVING: Calories 282; Calories From Fat 27.1; Total Fat 2.7 g; Cholesterol 47.2 mg; Sodium 1,211.6 mg; Potassium 672.1 mg; Total Carbohydrates 36.8 g; Fiber 3.6 g; Sugar 12 g; Protein 28 g

EASY ASIAN SWEET CHILI CHICKEN

INGREDIENTS

1 sweet onion, chopped

1 red bell pepper, cored, seeded, and chopped

1 large summer squash, sliced into ³/₄-inch (2 cm) half-moons

3 pounds (1,362 g) boneless, skinless chicken pieces, dark or light meat

³/₄ cup (170 g) Thai sweet chili sauce

Juice of 1 lime

2 tablespoons (30 ml) low-sodium tamari sauce

2 tablespoons (30 ml) Thai fish sauce

4 cloves garlic, crushed and chopped

FROM DR. JONNY: This recipe is a great opportunity for me to introduce a term to you that I hope you will be hearing a lot in the coming years: pastured chicken. Pastured chickens are raised outside in fresh air and sunshine on fresh green growing pasture, in small groups, protected by large, bottomless pens that are moved regularly onto new ground. Grazing freely outdoors is the way chickens are supposed to be raised, and pastured chicken is the kind you should try to use in your cooking. Pastured chicken is actually preferable to free-range, though harder to find. Why? Because "free-range" often means the chickens have access to pasture, maybe only for limited times, and often the chickens don't even take advantage of that access, which sometimes consists of a little gate they can walk through if they like. Pastured chickens don't stand around in their own droppings, which naturally breaks the cycle of parasitic infections. In this recipe you can use dark meat or light meat, though the dark meat stays moister longer in the slow cooker. This dish is easy to prepare and has a sweet and satisfying "kicky" bite.

Arrange the sweet onion, bell pepper, and summer squash on the bottom of a slow cooker and place the chicken pieces on top.

In a small bowl, whisk together the chili sauce, lime juice, tamari, fish sauce, and garlic and pour it evenly over the chicken. Cover and cook on high for 2¹/₂ to 3 hours, or on low for 4 to 5 hours, until the chicken is cooked through but still juicy. Note: This dish makes great leftovers as the flavors continue to deepen over time.

YIELD: 6 servings

PER SERVING: Calories 301.4; Calories From Fat 35.4; Total Fat 3.9 g; Cholesterol 131.5 mg; Sodium 794.3 mg; Potassium 759.9 mg; Total Carbohydrates 8.4 g; Fiber 1.4 g; Sugar 4.5 g; Protein 55.2 g

VEGGIE-RICH ASIAN CHICKEN STEW

INGREDIENTS

1 large white onion, thinly sliced

2 carrots, peeled and thinly sliced on the diagonal

2 ribs celery, sliced on the diagonal

1 small red bell pepper, cored, seeded, and julienned

1 1/2 cups (135 g) thinly sliced napa cabbage

1 can (8 ounces, or 225 g) sliced water chestnuts, drained and rinsed

1 can (8 ounces, or 225 g) bamboo shoots, drained and rinsed

6 cups (1,410 ml) chicken broth

2 tablespoons (12 g) minced fresh ginger

3 cloves garlic, minced

1 1/2 tablespoons (23 ml) low-sodium tamari

1 tablespoon (15 ml) mirin

2 boneless, skinless chicken breasts, cut into 1 1/2-inch (3.8 cm) cubes

12 ounces (336 g) extra-firm tofu, cut into 1/2-inch (1.3 cm) cubes

1/2 cup (50 g) diagonally sliced scallion

1 tablespoon (8 g) black sesame seeds, for garnish (optional)

FROM DR. JONNY: If stews were basketball games, this one would be the national all-star team. The list of nutrients found in these ingredients—and all the benefits they provide—could fill a chapter of a nutrition textbook. How is this lean, low-cal veggie stew great for you? Let me count the ways! Sulfur compounds for your skin (onions), beta-carotene and vitamin A (carrots), vitamin K for heart health and bones (celery), vitamin C (red pepper), and cancer-fighting indoles (cabbage) and allicin (garlic). Though light on calories, this stew is anything but light on flavor and texture. Did I mention it's not exactly light on health benefits, either? (Just seeing if you're paying attention!)

Combine the onion, carrots, celery, bell pepper, cabbage, water chestnuts, bamboo shoots, broth, ginger, garlic, tamari, and mirin in the slow cooker. Cover and cook on low for 6 to 7 hours, until all the vegetables are tender. Add the chicken and tofu for the last half hour of cooking time. Garnish with the scallions and a sprinkle of sesame seeds, if desired.

YIELD: 6 servings

PER SERVING: Calories 245.2; Calories From Fat 47.4; Total Fat 4.8 g; Cholesterol 47.2 mg; Sodium 1,076.8 mg; Potassium 757.6 mg; Total Carbohydrates 18.4 g; Fiber 3.9 g; Sugar 7.5 g; Protein 30.6 g

LOW-CAL FIESTA MEXI-CHICKEN

FROM DR. JONNY: Here's a dish that's simple, flavorful, and a guar-anteed family-pleaser: lean, high-protein (and low-cal!) chicken breast, tenderized and "jucified" by a clever little sauce Chef Jeannette put to-gether from bell peppers, onions, tomato paste, and spices. Bell peppers are loaded with vitamin C, onions contain a fantastic anti-inflammatory called *quercetin* (so important to health that I take it as a supplement!), and cooked tomatoes have been associated with reduced risk of prostate cancer (probably because of the high lycopene content). This dish is a really nice variation on the traditional (and boring) grilled chicken breast. Did I mention that the whole family will love it? (I know I did— I just wanted to see if you were paying attention!)

INGREDIENTS

1 large red bell pepper, cored, seeded, and quartered

1 yellow onion, quartered

1 can (6 ounces, or 168 g) tomato paste

4 cloves garlic, crushed

1 teaspoon ground coriander

¾ teaspoon ground cumin

¾ teaspoon salt

¾ teaspoon chili powder

¼ teaspoon ground chipotle chile (or cayenne pepper)

Juice and zest of 1 lime (optional)

3 pounds (1.4 kg) bone-in, skinless chicken breasts

½ cup (8 g) chopped fresh cilantro

Combine the bell pepper, onion, tomato paste, garlic, coriander, cumin, salt, chili powder, ground chipotle, and lime zest, if using, in a food processor and process until smooth, scraping down the sides as necessary.

Place the chicken in a slow cooker and pour the sauce over all. Cover and cook on high for 2 to 3 hours, or on low for 4 to 6 hours, or until the chicken is very tender but still juicy. Sprinkle with the lime juice, if using, and the cilantro before serving.

YIELD: 6 servings

PER SERVING: Calories 309.3; Calories From Fat 30.2; Total Fat 2.5 g; Cholesterol 136 mg; Sodium 676.8 mg; Potassium 689.3 mg; Total Carbohydrates 11.2 g; Fiber 2.8 g; Sugar 5.8 g; Protein 56.1 g

FLAVORFUL, FIBER-FULL MOROCCAN CHICKEN

INGREDIENTS

1 cup (235 ml) chicken broth

1/2 cup (120 ml) dry white wine

Juice and zest of 1 navel orange

3 cloves garlic, minced

1 teaspoon ground cumin

1 teaspoon ground coriander

1 teaspoon ground ginger

1/2 teaspoon each salt and freshly cracked
   black pepper

3 pounds (1,362 g) skinless, bone-in chicken
   breast halves and thighs

2 cinnamon sticks

1 cup (175 g) pitted prunes, chopped

2 yellow onions, thinly sliced

1/3 cup (37 g) toasted sliced almonds, for
   garnish (optional)

FROM DR. JONNY: Just for fun, let's talk about prunes. Prunes, you say? The fruit you associate with elderly retirees in Miami Beach trying to get "regular"? Yep. The prune, despite its far-from-sexy reputation, is actually one of the most nutritionally dense foods around. U.S. Department of Agriculture scientists at Tufts University ranking various fruits on the basis of their antioxidant scores rated prunes among the highest fruits in overall antioxidant power. They're also loaded with good things like potassium (an amazing 796 mg per cup of pitted prunes, almost twice that of a banana) and have a fair amount of fiber as well (hence their reputation as an aid to "regularity"). And honestly, I love how they taste. Especially as part of this rich Moroccan recipe, which also features mineral- and fiber-rich almonds, high-protein chicken, and an assortment of delicious spices. The prunes add a fruity richness to the sauce that makes everything come together perfectly.

In a small bowl, whisk together the broth, wine, orange juice and zest, garlic, cumin, coriander, ginger, salt, and pepper and set aside.

Place the chicken pieces and cinnamon sticks in the slow cooker in an even layer. Add the prunes and onion slices, distributing evenly. Pour the broth mixture evenly over all. Cook on high for 2½ to 3 hours, or on low for 4 to 5 hours, until the chicken is cooked through but still juicy. Remove the cinnamon sticks and garnish with the almonds, if desired.

YIELD: 6 servings

PER SERVING: Calories 467.5; Calories From Fat 98.3; Total Fat 9.8 g; Cholesterol 136 mg; Sodium 482.4 mg; Potassium 697.6 mg; Total Carbohydrates 31.2 g; Fiber 6.9 g; Sugar 14.8 g; Protein 58.1 g

LEAN LEMON-APRICOT CHICKEN

FROM DR. JONNY: I have no idea why chicken and apricots go together so well, but they are clearly a match made in taste-combo heaven. Two medium apricots have more than 1,300 IUs of vitamin A, 766 IUs of beta-carotene, and a healthy dose of a plant chemical called *beta-cryptoxanthin*, which can reduce the risk for lung cancer by more than 30 percent and the risk for arthritis by 41 percent. This dish is on the leaner side because we used all white meat (slightly lower in calories and fat), but the natural sugars and acids in the juices help keep this divine dish as tender as you'd want it to be. Fun fact: Apricots originally hail from China, where they've been grown for more than 4,000 years; they were rumored to be introduced to the West by none other than Alexander the Great. Note: Health experts recommend unsulfured apricots. Sulfur dioxide is used to preserve the color, and is probably safe in tiny amounts, but in large amounts it is a potential carcinogen. And many people are allergic. If possible, get the unsulfured kind!

INGREDIENTS

1 large yellow onion, sliced

1 cup (110 g) grated carrot

6 boneless, skinless chicken breasts (or equivalent bone-in)

1/3 cup (80 ml) apricot nectar

2 tablespoons (30 ml) low-sodium tamari

1 tablespoon (15 ml) freshly squeezed lemon juice

2 tablespoons (22 g) Dijon mustard

1 tablespoon (6 g) lemon zest

1/2 cup (65 g) chopped dried apricots (unsulfured)

Scatter the onion slices and grated carrot on the bottom of the slow cooker. Place the chicken breasts on top.

In a small bowl, whisk the nectar, tamari, lemon juice, mustard, and zest together. Stir in the apricots and pour over the chicken. Cook on high for 2 to 3 hours, or on low for 3 to 4 hours, or until the chicken is cooked through but still juicy. Stir to baste before serving.

YIELD: 6 servings

PER SERVING: Calories 341; Calories From Fat 45.7; Total Fat 4 g; Cholesterol 141.5 mg; Sodium 472.2 mg; Potassium 507.8 mg; Total Carbohydrates 12.7 g; Fiber 1.9 g; Sugar 8.9 g; Protein 57.8 g

INGREDIENTS

8 ounces (225 g) sliced white cremini
    mushrooms
4 large shallots, quartered
⅓ cup (80 ml) chicken broth
4 boneless, skinless chicken breasts (or
    equivalent bone-in)
1 container (6 ounces, or 168 g) high-quality
    pesto

FROM CHEF JEANNETTE

Even Healthier: For a fresher taste and
higher nutritional impact, make your own
pesto from scratch by combining 1 cup
(40 g) fresh basil, ¼ cup (25 g) freshly grated
Parmesan, ¼ cup (34 g) toasted walnuts or
pine nuts, ¼ cup (60 ml) olive oil, 2 cloves
garlic, 2 teaspoons freshly squeezed lemon
juice, and ⅛ teaspoon each salt and freshly
ground pepper in a food processor and
process until mostly smooth, scraping
down the sides as necessary.

IN-A-PINCH PROTEIN PESTO CHICKEN AND MUSHROOMS

FROM DR. JONNY: I don't know about you, but I still get stuck from time to time figuring out what I can throw together quickly that still tastes great and provides world-class nourishment. This dish fits the bill. It's a basic five-ingredient mix. Lean, low-calorie chicken breasts provide the protein. Shallots are a member of the Allium vegetable family, along with onions and leeks; at least one study (published in the *Journal of the National Cancer Institute*) has shown that eating Allium vegetables significantly lowers the risk of prostate cancer. Pesto sauce offers the benefits of olive oil (heart healthy), basil (antioxidant, anticancer, antiviral, and antimicrobial!), and garlic (a natural antibiotic that's high in antioxidants). Best of all, the prep time for this is the same as it takes to brew a pot of coffee.

Combine the mushrooms and shallots in the slow cooker and pour the broth over all. Lay the chicken breasts on top and spoon the pesto evenly over them. Cook on high for 2 to 3 hours, or on low for 3 to 4 hours, or until the chicken is just cooked through.

YIELD: 4 servings
PER SERVING: Calories 530.3; Calories From Fat 228.7; Total Fat 23.4 g; Cholesterol 154.5 mg; Sodium 538.6 mg; Potassium 512.2 mg; Total Carbohydrates 9.6 g; Fiber 0.7 g; Sugar 0.3 g; Protein 67.3 g

FREE-RADICAL-FIGHTING KALAMATA CHICKEN

INGREDIENTS

2 ribs celery, sliced

4 skinless, bone-in chicken breasts

Salt and freshly ground pepper

1 teaspoon dried oregano

1 teaspoon dried basil

2 heirloom tomatoes, chopped

6 cloves garlic, crushed and chopped

1 cup (100 g) pitted kalamata olives

Zest and juice of 2 lemons

1/4 cup (38 g) feta cheese, crumbled

FROM DR. JONNY: Maybe you're asking yourself, "What the heck are free radicals and why should I care about fighting them?" Glad you asked, because there are three things you need to know. One, free radicals are everywhere. Two, free radicals age you. Three, they're actually weird little rogue molecules that attack our cells and DNA, literally aging us from within (and without, when they work their damage on our skin). This kind of damage is called *oxidative damage* and it's best combated with . . . what else? . . . *antioxidants!* Which this dish happens to be brimming with. Take the heirloom tomatoes, rich in one of the top antioxidants on the planet, vitamin C, as well as lesser-known ones such as lycopene, which also helps protect against certain cancers. And the olives—a rich source of plant substances called *polyphenols*, which are powerful antioxidants. Fun fact: Oregano's botanical name, *origanum*, is actually the contraction of two Greek words: *oros*, meaning "mountain," and *ganos*, meaning "joy." Some suggest that it was so named because of the beauty that oregano brings to the fields and hilltops on which it grows. According to Alan Gaby, M.D., a specialist in nutritional medicine, oregano was used extensively by the Greeks for conditions from convulsions to heart failure. Indeed, one popular book on oregano is called *The Cure Is in the Cupboard: How to Use Oregano for Better Health*.

Place the celery in the slow cooker and place the chicken on top in one layer. Sprinkle with salt and pepper to taste, then sprinkle with the oregano and basil. Add the tomatoes, garlic, kalamatas, and lemon zest and pour the lemon juice over all. Cover and cook on high for 3 to 4 hours, or on low for 6 to 7 hours, until the chicken is cooked through but still tender. Top with the feta just before serving.

YIELD: 4 servings

PER SERVING: Calories 396.7; Calories From Fat 115.2; Total Fat 11.1 g; Cholesterol 149.9 mg; Sodium 685.9 mg; Potassium 615.9 mg; Total Carbohydrates 13 g; Fiber 4.1 g; Sugar 2.9 g; Protein 59.3 g

SPINACH, BASIL, AND FETA–STUFFED CHICKEN ROLLS WITH PIGNOLI

INGREDIENTS

Olive oil cooking spray

6 boneless, skinless chicken breast halves

8 ounces (225 g) feta cheese, crumbled

4 cups (120 g) chopped baby spinach

¼ cup (10 g) chopped fresh basil

¼ cup (25 g) finely chopped pitted kalamata olives

4 cloves garlic, minced

2 teaspoons olive oil

½ teaspoon each salt and freshly ground pepper

1 can (14.5 ounces, or 406 g) diced tomatoes with garlic and basil, undrained

¼ cup (34 g) toasted pine nuts

FROM DR. JONNY: Pignoli are another name for pine nuts, those small, white, oval-shaped nuts that are actually the edible seeds of pines and are in demand because of the popularity of pesto. Here they add just a touch of flavor, texture, and visual interest to these delicious feta-stuffed chicken rolls, which boast a ton of nutrition from the spinach (iron, calcium, magnesium) and the kalamata olives (healthy plant chemicals called *polyphenols*). The lean chicken and feta cheese make this a high-protein dish. Fun fact: Kalamata olives are named after the city of Kalamata in Greece and are known for being jumbo size with a meaty taste. They enjoy PDO status (Protected Designation of Origin), which is a legal framework in the European Union designed to protect the names of regional foods.

Lightly spray the insert of a slow cooker with olive oil and set aside.

Place each chicken breast between two sheets of waxed paper and use a meat mallet to pound them to about ¼-inch (6 mm) thickness; lay them out flat. In a medium-size bowl, combine the feta, spinach, basil, olives, garlic, and olive oil and mix well.

Lightly and evenly sprinkle each chicken breast with salt and pepper. Dividing the spinach and feta mixture by 6, spoon an equal measure onto the wider end of each breast and roll it up. Lay the rolls close together, seam sides down, in the slow cooker insert and pour the diced tomatoes evenly over all. Cover and cook on high for about 4 hours, or on low for 5 to 6 hours, until the chicken is cooked through. Garnish with the pine nuts to serve.

YIELD: 6 servings

PER SERVING: Calories 327.5; Calories From Fat 149.8; Total Fat 15.8 g; Cholesterol 104.4 mg; Sodium 868.8 mg; Potassium 523 mg; Total Carbohydrates 9.1 g; Fiber 2.1 g; Sugar 2 g; Protein 36.1 g

THE SKINNY ON CHICKEN NUTRITION

	CHICKEN TENDERS	ROASTED DARK MEAT (MEAT ONLY)	ROASTED LIGHT MEAT (MEAT ONLY)	ROASTED, COMBINATION, MEAT AND SKIN
PROTEIN	15.78	23.25	27.13	17.15
CARBOHYDRATE	17	0	0	0
FAT	17.69	8.75	4.07	15.85
CALORIES	293	178	153	216
FIBER	1.3	0	0	0

	CHICKEN BREAST, MEAT AND SKIN, ROASTED	CHICKEN BREAST, MEAT ONLY, ROASTED	CHICKEN THIGH, MEAT AND SKIN, ROASTED	CHICKEN THIGH, MEAT ONLY, ROASTED
PROTEIN	30	31	25	26
CARBOHYDRATE	0	0	0	0
FAT	8	4	15	11
CALORIES	197	165	247	209
FIBER	0	0	0	0

	CHICKEN LEG, MEAT ONLY, ROASTED	CHICKEN LEG, MEAT AND SKIN, ROASTED
PROTEIN	27	26
CARBOHYDRATE	0	0
FAT	8	13
CALORIES	191	232
FIBER	0	0

Source: U.S. Department of Agriculture

SWEET AND SAUCY FREE-RANGE CHICKEN THIGHS

INGREDIENTS

3 tablespoons (45 ml) low-sodium tamari sauce

3 tablespoons (45 ml) Worcestershire sauce (use organic to avoid high-fructose corn syrup)

1 tablespoon (15 ml) freshly squeezed lemon juice

3 tablespoons (45 g) Sucanat

⅓ cup (80 g) high-quality, low-sugar ketchup

2 pounds (908 g) boneless, skinless chicken thighs

FROM DR. JONNY: Chicken thighs get a bad rap, but it's undeserved. Sure, they are slightly higher in calories and fat than breast meat, but they are hardly a distant second choice. First of all, they taste great. Second, a 3.5-ounce (98 g) portion delivers a very respectable 23 grams of protein, and most of the fat in the thighs is of the heart-healthy monounsaturated variety (the same kind of fat in olive oil. Surprised?). The thing of it is, the extra richness of the fat is just what the chef ordered for the longer cooking times required by the slow cooker. Go for free-range, organic chickens for the highest quality if you can. The tangy but sweet sauce is so good it'll have your family begging for more!

Combine the tamari, Worcestershire sauce, lemon juice, Sucanat, and ketchup in the slow cooker and mix well until thoroughly combined. Add the chicken and toss gently to coat. Cover and cook on high for 3 to 4 hours, or on low for 4 to 5 hours, or until the chicken is cooked through but still juicy.

YIELD: 6 to 8 servings

PER SERVING: Calories 155.9; Calories From Fat 40; Total Fat 4.5 g; Cholesterol 94.1 mg; Sodium 473.3 mg; Potassium 264.3 mg; Total Carbohydrates 4.2 g; Fiber 0 g; Sugar 3.7 g; Protein 23.1 g

SATISFYING, SPICY LEMON CHICKEN

INGREDIENTS

1 large yellow onion, chopped

12 ounces (336 g) baby carrots

3 pounds (1,362 g) skinless, bone-in chicken thighs

¾ cup (180 ml) dry white wine

Juice and zest of 1 medium-size lemon

1 tablespoon (15 ml) olive oil

1½ tablespoons (23 ml) hot pepper sauce

1 teaspoon salt

¼ teaspoon freshly ground pepper

6 cloves garlic, minced

1 tablespoon (14 g) unsalted butter, diced (optional)

FROM CHEF JEANNETTE

Serving Suggestion: This chicken is fabulous served over hot brown basmati rice.

FROM DR. JONNY: Did you scan the ingredient list of this recipe and recoil in horror when you saw chicken thighs? Many people are afraid of dark meat from chicken and turkey because they believe it to be so much higher in fat and calories. Actually, dark meat is a perfectly acceptable choice and has only minimally more calories than white meat. (There's only a measly 45-calorie difference between a 3.5-ounce [98 g] portion of stewed white meat chicken and the same size portion of dark meat. Not a big deal.) In this case, the slightly higher fat content makes for rich and juicy meat, especially when prepared in the slow cooker. Truth be told, we only removed the skin for aesthetic reasons, since we don't brown the chicken. And there's a modest amount of olive oil and butter—yes, *both* of them are perfectly healthy fats—to give the delicious flavors depth. You'll find this dish deeply satisfying: gently tangy with a nice mellow kick. Bonus points for the carrots, which absorb all the different flavors just beautifully and are a special treat all on their own!

Add the onion and carrots to the slow cooker. Arrange the thighs on top of the veggies.

In a medium-size bowl, whisk together the wine, lemon juice and zest, olive oil, pepper sauce, salt, pepper, and garlic and pour over the contents of the slow cooker. Scatter the diced butter pieces evenly over the top, if using. Cook on high for 2 to 4 hours, or on low for 4 to 5 hours, or until the chicken is cooked through but still very moist.

YIELD: 6 servings

PER SERVING: Calories 332.2; Calories From Fat 104.9; Total Fat 11.8 g; Cholesterol 162 mg; Sodium 623.9 mg; Potassium 702 mg; Total Carbohydrates 12.6 g; Fiber 3.1 g; Sugar 5.8 g; Protein 38.5 g

INDIAN SUPER-SPICE-RUBBED CHICKEN

INGREDIENTS

For Spice Rub

1 teaspoon salt

1 teaspoon freshly ground black pepper

1 teaspoon ground cumin

1 teaspoon ground coriander

1 teaspoon ground cardamom

½ teaspoon ground cinnamon

½ teaspoon ground cloves

½ teaspoon grond turmeric

For Chicken

4 boneless, skinless chicken thighs
(about 1 pound [454 g])

4 boneless, skinless chicken breasts
(about 2 pounds [908 g])

1 large sweet onion, sliced and separated
into rings

1 can (8 ounces, or 225 g) sliced water
chestnuts, drained

2 large sweet potatoes, peeled and sliced
into thick ¾-inch (2 cm) rounds, rounds
cut into quarters

3 medium carrots, thinly sliced into rounds

2 cups (470 ml) fat-free chicken broth

½ cup (120 ml) coconut milk

1 ½ tablespoons (9.5 g) curry powder, such
as Madras Hot Curry Powder

1 tablespoon (15 ml) freshly squeezed lemon
juice

1 teaspoon salt

½ teaspoon crushed red pepper flakes
(optional)

2 tablespoons (12 g) finely minced fresh ginger

1 clove garlic, minced

2 cups (142 g) broccoli florets, cut into bite-size
pieces

½ cup (115 g) plain low-fat yogurt

⅓ cup (5 g) chopped fresh cilantro (optional)

1 cup (145 g) dry-roasted peanuts or cashews

1 cup (145 g) regular or golden raisins

½ cup (43 g) unsweetened dried coconut flakes

FROM DR. JONNY: When people talk about making healthier food choices, they're usually referring to eating fruits, vegetables, and clean protein. But one class of "food" almost never gets the attention it deserves, and that class is spices. Spices are incredibly rich sources of antioxidants and plant compounds with enormous value to human health. Take the spice blend in this chicken dish, for example. Turmeric has phenomenal anti-inflammatory properties, and, precisely for that reason, one of its many traditional uses has been for the treatment of arthritis. It's also one of the most "liver-friendly" spices, largely through its strong antioxidant activity. In science jargon, curcumin—the most active of the ingredients in turmeric—inhibits *lipid peroxidation*. In English, that means it fights damage from iodating substances that age the body and contribute to disease. Cardamom is a *carminative* (a digestive tonic) that may be used to relieve symptoms of indigestion (especially when there's excessive gas). And both cloves and cinnamon rank among the top five spices as measured by something called the ORAC scale, which researchers use to rate foods and spices for overall antioxidant power. This recipe comes from my very first book with Chef Jeannette, *The Healthiest Meals on Earth.*

To make the spice rub: In a small bowl, combine all the spices. Set aside.

To make the chicken: Wash the chicken and pat dry. Place the chicken in a large bowl. Sprinkle the spices over the chicken and use your hands to thoroughly coat each piece. Cover the bowl and place in the refrigerator for 1 hour. Remove the chicken from the refrigerator.

Combine the onion, water chestnuts, sweet potatoes, and carrots in the slow cooker and place the chicken pieces on top.

In a small bowl, whisk together the broth, coconut milk, curry powder, lemon juice, salt, red pepper flakes (if using), ginger, and garlic. Pour the broth mixture gently over all. Cook on low for 4 to 5 hours, or until the chicken is cooked through. Place the broccoli on the top for the last 15 minutes of cooking time.

At the end of the cooking time, remove the chicken and place in a large bowl. Skim the fat from the surface of the broth. Gently stir in the yogurt and cilantro, if using. Pour the sauce over the chicken and serve with bowls of nuts, raisins, and coconut.

YIELD: 6 servings

PER SERVING: Calories 768.1; Calories From Fat 314.4; Total Fat 35.6 g; Cholesterol 133.8 mg; Sodium 1,184.5 mg; Potassium 1,401.3 mg; Total Carbohydrates 57.7 g; Fiber 11.9 g; Sugar 26.3 g; Protein 59.4 g

INGREDIENTS

¾ cup (180 ml) high-quality, low-sugar
   prepared teriyaki sauce
¼ cup (60 ml) water
1 teaspoon ground ginger
6 boneless, skinless chicken thighs
1 package (12 ounces, or 336 g) slaw mix
   (broccoli, carrots, and cabbage)
2 tablespoons (16 g) toasted sesame seeds
1 small head red-leaf or Bibb lettuce

QUICK SESAME TERIYAKI LOW-CARB LETTUCE WRAPS

FROM DR. JONNY: Chef Jeannette calls this recipe an example of "slow-cooked fast food," which I think is hysterical. But it's kind of true. The prep time is just a few minutes and the slow cooker does the rest. And yes, we did use a prepared teriyaki sauce (the tradeoff for such a short prep time), but that doesn't have to spell nutritional disaster. There are dozens of high-quality, all-natural options in the prepared teriyaki sauce department, so if you choose wisely you'll have the best of both worlds—convenience and nutrition. The most wonderful thing about this "slow-cooked fast food" is that it is absolutely loaded with nearly raw veggies. It's also wrapped in lettuce, the classic low-carb alternative to those stupid, doughy flour wraps that sometimes pass for "healthy" because they've got a tiny bit of green coloring in them. Go with the lettuce, get some vitamin K in the bargain, and save a bunch of useless calories. Enjoy!

In a small bowl, whisk together the teriyaki sauce, water, and ginger. Lay the chicken thighs in the bottom of the slow cooker and pour the sauce evenly over the top. Cover and cook on high for 2 to 3 hours, or on low for 3 to 4 hours, until the chicken is cooked through and very tender. Shred the chicken with two forks and add the slaw mix. Stir to combine, cover, and cook for 10 minutes. Stir in the sesame seeds and serve over individual lettuce leaves.

YIELD: 6 servings
PER SERVING: Calories 127.3; Calories From Fat 37.8; Total Fat 4.3 g; Cholesterol 57.3 mg; Sodium 671.8 mg; Potassium 336 mg; Total Carbohydrates 6.7 g; Fiber 2.1 g; Sugar 2.1 g; Protein 17.2 g

SAVORY SLOW COOKER TENDER TURKEY DRUMSTICKS

INGREDIENTS

3 turkey drumsticks

1 tablespoon (15 ml) olive oil

Salt and freshly cracked black pepper, to taste

1 large Vidalia onion, chopped

3 large carrots, peeled and sliced into thin coins

2 large cloves garlic, minced

½ teaspoon dried sage, crumbled

2 tablespoons (8 g) chopped fresh parsley

1 tablespoon (2.4 g) chopped fresh thyme
   (or 1 teaspoon dried)

1 lemon, halved

FROM DR. JONNY: You don't have to wait till the holidays to enjoy these tender turkey drumsticks, borrowed from one of our recent books, *The 150 Healthiest Comfort Foods on Earth*. This recipe is super easy and super fast, and when you use the slow cooker it cooks to a delicious tenderness in its own juices, with no added fat calories. The fat that's in there—perfectly healthy fat, mind you—replaces the conventional gravy or commercial cream of mushroom soup that generally smothers a dish like this. (Note: A can of commercial cream of mushroom soup has an astonishing 1,995 mg of sodium. Need I say more?) Onions are a rich source of sulfur, so good for the skin, not to mention that they are one of the best sources of a flavonoid called *quercetin*, which is one of the most anti-inflammatory plant compounds on the planet, and one that has been shown to have significant anticancer properties, to boot. Worth noting: Turkeys are frequently raised under horrific factory-farmed conditions, so if possible, get the free-range variety. They're better for you, anyway.

Coat the bottom of the slow cooker and the drumsticks with the olive oil. Sprinkle the drumsticks liberally with salt and pepper to taste. Place the onion and carrots in the bottom of the cooker and top with the prepared drumsticks.

In a small bowl, combine the garlic, sage, parsley, and thyme and sprinkle evenly over the drumsticks. Gently squeeze the lemon halves to release their juices into the vegetables and nestle them at the bottom of the pot. Cook on high for 4 to 5 hours, or on low for 8 to 10 hours, or until the meat is cooked through and the meat and veggies are very tender.

YIELD: 3 or 4 servings

PER SERVING: Calories 297.3; Calories From Fat 142.5; Total Fat 15.6 g; Cholesterol 97.2 mg; Sodium 143 mg; Potassium 661.9 mg; Total Carbohydrates 13.6 g; Fiber 4.2 g; Sugar 2.9 g; Protein 26.9 g

FLAVANOL-RICH COCOA CHICKEN MOLE

INGREDIENTS

2 ½ pounds (1,135 g) skinless, bone-in chicken
   pieces

½ sweet onion, quartered

3 cloves garlic, crushed

2 chipotle chiles in adobo sauce

1 can (4 ounces, or 112 g) diced green chiles

¼ cup (36 g) raisins

¼ cup (28 g) slivered almonds

2 tablespoons (14 g) high-quality dark cocoa
   powder

1 teaspoon chili powder

1 teaspoon ground cumin

¼ teaspoon ground cinnamon

Pinch of salt

1 can (14 ounces, or 392 g) fire-roasted diced
   tomatoes, undrained

2 tablespoons (30 g) quick-cooking tapioca

FROM DR. JONNY: Mole is a distinctly Mexican dish that has been called the "heart and soul of Mexican food and life." Its complex flavor, which often includes a hint of chocolate, makes it ideal for meat dishes, especially chicken. The ingredients in this chicken mole are great for you. There's iron in the raisins, monounsaturated fat and fiber in the almonds, lycopene (a powerful antioxidant) in the tomatoes, and allicin, a powerful medicinal compound, in the garlic. What's not to like? Cocoa powder is high in flavanols, which have been shown to have multiple health benefits, not the least of which is lowering blood pressure. And those chipotle chiles are chock-full of capsaicin, the compound that makes hot peppers so fiery and creates just the right amount of heat for this rich, delicious dish. Worth knowing: According to the American Association of Cancer Research, capsaicin is able to kill prostate cancer cells in animal studies, and several clinical studies conducted in Asia demonstrated that natural capsaicin directly inhibits the growth of leukemic cells.

Arrange the chicken pieces in the slow cooker.

Combine the onion, garlic, chipotles, green chiles, raisins, almonds, cocoa powder, chili powder, cumin, cinnamon, salt, and tomatoes and their juice in a food processor and process until the mixture forms a coarse purée. Stir in the tapioca. Pour the mixture evenly over the chicken, cover, and cook on high for 4 to 5 hours, or on low for 7 to 8 hours, until the chicken is cooked through but still juicy.

YIELD: 6 servings

PER SERVING: Calories 303.5; Calories From Fat 49.8; Total Fat 5 g; Cholesterol 90.7 mg; Sodium 258.1 mg; Potassium 715.4 mg; Total Carbohydrates 22.5 g; Fiber 5 g; Sugar 10 g; Protein 39.2 g

INGREDIENTS

For Jerk Seasoning

1/3 cup (80 ml) macadamia nut or olive oil
1 yellow onion, quartered
1 habanero or jalapeño pepper, seeded
1 1/2 tablespoons (9 g) minced fresh ginger
1 teaspoon dried thyme
3 cloves garlic, crushed
1/4 cup (60 ml) freshly squeezed orange juice
2 tablespoons (30 ml) raw apple cider vinegar
Juice of 1 Key lime (or regular lime)
2 tablespoons (30 g) Sucanat
1 1/2 teaspoons ground allspice
1/2 teaspoon crumbled sage
1/2 teaspoon ground cinnamon
1/4 teaspoon ground nutmeg

For Drumsticks

4 turkey drumsticks
Olive oil cooking spray
1 large Vidalia onion, sliced into rings

JAMAICAN JERKED TURKEY LEGS

FROM DR. JONNY: What gives jerk seasoning its terrific taste is the combination of spices. The spice list for this recipe is a virtual medicine cabinet! All of them are rich in antioxidants and anti-inflammatory agents. Cinnamon has been found to lower blood sugar; thyme contains an essential oil called *thymol*, which is both antibacterial and antiseptic; sage is anti-inflammatory and antimicrobial; and ginger contains chemicals called *shogaols* and *gingerols*, which help control the movements of the GI tract, making it a well-known treatment for nausea (and morning sickness!). The combination of the lime and orange juices add to the distinct Caribbean feel of this delicious recipe.

To make the jerk seasoning: Combine all the ingredients in a food processor and process until it forms a smooth paste, scraping down the sides as necessary.

Coat the turkey legs liberally with the jerk paste, cover, and marinate overnight. Before cooking, scrape off most of the marinade and discard. Spray a slow cooker insert with olive oil, layer with the onion slices, and top with the drumsticks. Cook on high for 4 to 5 hours, or on low for 8 to 10 hours, or until the meat is cooked through and still juicy.

YIELD: 4 servings
PER SERVING: Calories 335.8; Calories From Fat 171.5; Total Fat 18.6 g; Cholesterol 129.6 mg; Sodium 130.9 mg; Potassium 540.4 mg; Total Carbohydrates 5.7 g; Fiber 1 g; Sugar 1.4 g; Protein 34.5 g

LOW-CAL TROPICAL TURKEY BREAST

INGREDIENTS

1 tablespoon (15 ml) macadamia nut oil
    (or olive oil)
⅓ cup (80 ml) freshly squeezed lime juice
¼ cup (71 g) frozen orange juice concentrate,
    thawed
1½ teaspoons dried oregano
½ teaspoon ground cumin
8 cloves garlic, crushed
1 split, skinless turkey breast (about 4 pounds
    [1,816 g])
1 teaspoon sweet paprika
¾ teaspoon each salt and freshly cracked black
    pepper
6 thin slices lemon

FROM DR. JONNY: Here's another recipe that was clearly inspired by Chef Jeannette's annual trip to the Caribbean, where she takes a group of lucky people on one of her "healthy eating" retreats. This time she gave lean white turkey meat, one of the best sources of protein around, a tropical feel by using just the right combination of spices mixed with the citrus flavors of lime, orange, and lemon. And if you haven't tried macadamia nut oil before, you're in for a treat. Macadamia nut oil is just as high in omega-9s (monounsaturated fat) as olive oil, but stands up to heat a lot better and has a slightly nutty flavor. The lime juice marinade gives the turkey a Caribbean punch and a delightful zing!

In a small bowl, whisk together the oil, lime juice, concentrate, oregano, cumin, and garlic and set aside.

Sprinkle the turkey breast evenly all over with the paprika, salt, and pepper. Baste the turkey breast carefully with the marinade, cover, and refrigerate overnight, basting occasionally to recoat. Transfer to a slow cooker, basting again with the marinade. Lay the lemon slices over the surface of the turkey breast. Cover and cook on high for 4 to 5 hours, or on low 8 to 10 hours, until the turkey is cooked through and tender.

YIELD: 10 servings
PER SERVING: Calories 232.6; Calories From Fat 40.7; Total Fat 4.7 g; Cholesterol 78 mg; Sodium 2,019.1 mg; Potassium 721.4 mg; Total Carbohydrates 19.2 g; Fiber 4.3 g; Sugar 9.2 g; Protein 32.2 g

TURKEY AND FRUIT-SWEETENED CRANBERRY SAUCE SUPPER

INGREDIENTS

2 sweet baking apples, peeled, cored, and chopped

1 navel orange, peeled and quartered

1/2 cup (60 g) dried, juice-sweetened cranberries

1/2 cup (65 g) chopped unsulfured dried apples or apricots

1/2 cup (56 g) raw pecans

12 ounces (336 g) fresh cranberries

1 cup (235 ml) apple cider

1/3 cup (75 g) Sucanat (or 1/2 cup [120 g] xylitol)

1 tablespoon (15 g) minute tapioca

1/2 teaspoon ground cinnamon

1/2 teaspoon ground allspice

2 1/2- to 3-pound (1,135 to 1,362 g) turkey breast, bone-in

1/2 teaspoon each salt and freshly ground pepper

FROM DR. JONNY: I've never understood why some of the healthiest things on our holiday menus don't manage to make it into heavy rotation during the year. (For example, pumpkin is a fabulous vegetable that no one ever thinks of except during Halloween and Thanksgiving, but don't get me started.) Turkey with cranberry sauce is another perfect example. Turkey is a great source of high-quality, low-calorie protein. And studies presented at the 223rd national meeting of the American Chemical Society show that cranberries have some of the most potent antioxidants of any common fruit studied. Plant compounds in cranberries possess anticancer properties, inhibit the growth of common food-borne pathogens, and contain antibacterial properties to aid in the prevention of urinary tract infections. What Chef Jeannette has put together here is a relatively low-sugar version of a Thanksgiving meal in a pot! We use fresh and dried fruit plus nut purée to give the cranberry base sweetness and body. It's the perfect complement to lean, moist turkey breast. Enjoy!

Combine the apples, orange, dried cranberries, apples, and pecans in a food processor and process until mostly smooth, forming a paste, scraping down the sides as necessary.

Combine the fresh cranberries, cider, Sucanat, tapioca, cinnamon, allspice, and fruit paste in the slow cooker. Stir gently to thoroughly combine. Place the turkey on top of the mixture and season with salt and pepper. Cook on high for 3 1/2 to 4 hours, or on low for 6 to 7 hours, until the temperature reads 170°F (77°C) on an instant-read thermometer inserted into the thickest part of the breast meat (take care not to touch bone with the thermometer). Remove the turkey and stir the cranberry sauce well to combine.

Serve the turkey with the sauce drizzled over the top.

YIELD: Yield: 6 servings

PER SERVING: Calories 373.9; Calories From Fat 65.5; Total Fat 7.8 g; Cholesterol 80.6 mg; Sodium 274.1 mg; Potassium 658.3 mg; Total Carbohydrates 44.2 g; Fiber 5.1 g; Sugar 29.3 g; Protein 33.4 g

INGREDIENTS

4 large green bell peppers (or red bell peppers)

1 pound (454 g) leanest ground turkey

1/3 cup (38 g) shredded pepper Jack cheese

1/2 cup (50 g) chopped scallion, white and green parts

1 cup (165 g) cooked long-grain brown rice

1/2 cup (65 g) frozen corn

1 1/2 teaspoons chili powder

1 teaspoon garlic powder

1/2 teaspoon ground cumin

1/2 teaspoon each salt and freshly ground pepper

2 jars (16 ounces, or 454 g each) natural salsa

FROM CHEF JEANNETTE

Time-Saver Tip: Use uncooked, parboiled brown rice in place of the cooked long-grain rice and it will cook in the juices from the meat and salsa.

Stuffed peppers are typically labor-intensive because you have to cook the peppers, cook the meat, cook the rice, and then cook the final dish. The slow cooker can eliminate all the intermediary steps and make this dish super easy to prepare.

If your peppers are smaller and you have leftover filling, simply add it to the salsa.

LEAN AND GREEN STUFFED PEPPERS

FROM DR. JONNY: Bell peppers are an excellent source of vitamins C and A (beta-carotene) as well as potassium and vitamin K. You can use green or red peppers for this dish. We stuffed them with lean ground turkey and just a bit of cheese for a high-protein, very low-calorie dish. Fun fact: Many peppers start out as a green vegetable and then change color when they fully mature. Red is the sweetest of the bells and is actually a fully ripened green pepper with a milder flavor!

Slice off the tops of the peppers and remove all seeds and membranes.

In a medium-size bowl, combine the turkey, cheese, scallion, rice, corn, chili powder, garlic powder, cumin, salt, and pepper and mix well to combine. Stuff each pepper with an equal amount of the turkey mixture and place them, cut side up, in the slow cooker.

Pour the salsa evenly over the peppers, cover, and cook on low for 6 to 7 hours, or until the ground turkey is cooked through.

YIELD: 4 servings

PER SERVING: Calories 392.2; Calories From Fat 128.2; Total Fat 14.2 g; Cholesterol 89.6 mg; Sodium 2,064.3 mg; Potassium 1,399.4 mg; Total Carbohydrates 40.7 g; Fiber 8.9 g; Sugar 12.9 g; Protein 30 g

INGREDIENTS

2 teaspoons olive oil

1 pound (454 g) ground turkey

4 cloves garlic, minced

1 yellow onion, chopped

1 red or orange bell pepper, cored, seeded,
and chopped

1 can (15 ounces, or 420 g) kidney beans,
drained and rinsed

1 can (14.5 ounces, or 406 g) fire-roasted diced
tomatoes, undrained

1 can (4 ounces, or 112 g) chopped green chiles,
undrained

1 package (1 ounce, or 28 g) high-quality,
all-natural taco seasoning (such as Simply
Organic)

2 heads romaine lettuce, chopped

¾ cup (75 g) sliced scallion

1 heirloom tomato, chopped

FROM CHEF JEANNETTE

Even Healthier: To make your own taco
seasoning mix, combine 1 tablespoon chili
powder; 1 ½ teaspoons each onion powder,
garlic powder, and cumin; 1 teaspoon each
paprika and dried oregano; ¾ teaspoon each
arrowroot powder and salt; and ½ teaspoon
each Sucanat or xylitol and red pepper flakes.

LEAN AND EASY TACO SALAD

FROM DR. JONNY: It's hard to beat lean, low-cal ground turkey as a
source of high-quality protein. Frankly, I don't know why people don't
eat more turkey year-round; it's like we only remember how great it is
during Thanksgiving. But you can substitute turkey meat for all kinds
of recipes that call for beef. Turkey's not the only thing this taco salad
has going for it, though. Garlic lowers blood pressure and cholesterol
and reduces the risk for certain cancers. Kidney beans are an excellent
source of fiber, providing more than 11 grams per cup (not to mention
16 grams of protein and about double the potassium in a banana!). And
tomatoes and peppers have loads of antioxidants like vitamin C. Best of
all, our lean and easy taco does not come in an edible GMO (genetically
modified organism) corn chip bowl. Sorry! (Kidding.)

Heat the oil in large skillet over medium-high heat. Add the turkey and
cook, stirring frequently, until no pink remains, about 6 minutes. Stir in
the garlic and cook for 1 minute. Drain and add to the slow cooker. Add the
onion, bell pepper, beans, tomatoes, green chiles, and taco seasoning and
stir well to combine. Cover and cook on high for about 3 hours, or on low
for about 6 hours, until hot and bubbling.

Make 6 beds of romaine lettuce and mound the turkey mixture on top.
Top with the scallion and tomato.

YIELD: 6 servings

PER SERVING: Calories 305.1; Calories From Fat 78.9; Total Fat 8.8 g; Cholesterol
59.7 mg; Sodium 666.7 mg; Potassium 1,421.2 mg; Total Carbohydrates 35.4 g;
Fiber 13.1 g; Sugar 10.3 g; Protein 21.8 g

LOADED SPLIT PEA SWEET POTATO SOUP

INGREDIENTS

2 tablespoons (30 ml) olive oil

1 large Vidalia onion, diced

4 medium carrots, sliced into thin rounds

1 large rib celery, cut into thirds

2 cloves garlic, crushed and chopped

1 large sweet potato, peeled and cut into ½-inch
  (1.3 cm) cubes

½ teaspoon dried thyme

1 pound (454 g) split peas, sorted, rinsed, and
  drained

8 cups (1.9 L) vegetable broth (or chicken broth)

¼ to ½ teaspoon red pepper flakes, to taste

1 package (10 ounces, or 280 g) frozen spinach,
  thawed but not drained

½ teaspoon salt, or to taste

2 tablespoons (30 ml) cooking sherry

FROM CHEF JEANNETTE

Time-Saver Tip: Omit the sauté step and simply combine all the ingredients except the spinach, salt, and sherry in the slow cooker. Follow the rest of the instructions as written.

FROM DR. JONNY: My mother used to have a saying about any food she liked: "I could make a meal out of this." (Yes, folks, it did get to be annoying. But I digress.) I bring that up because it's actually true of this soup. In fact, not only did I make a meal of it, but I actually just about lived on it for two days after I made it! This version is way better than the usual pea soup fare for a number of reasons. Traditional split pea soup is made with ham, which I usually don't recommend because it's high in sodium and almost always from factory-farmed animals. We skip the ham, making this suitable for vegetarians. But even if you're not a vegetarian—and I'm certainly not—you won't miss the meat. This version is not only low fat (if you care about that) but also high in heart-friendly fiber and potassium—and that's something you don't often see in soup, especially soup that tastes this good. The mellow sweetness of the sweet potatoes compensates for the saltiness of the ham—you'll never miss it. And split peas are a great vegetarian source of protein.

Heat the oil in a large skillet over medium heat. Add the onion, carrots, and celery and sauté for about 6 minutes. Add the garlic and sauté for 1 minute.

Transfer the contents to a slow cooker and add the sweet potato, thyme, split peas, broth, and red pepper flakes. Cover and cook on high for 4 to 5 hours, or on low for 7 to 8 hours, or until everything is very tender. Remove the celery pieces, stir in the spinach and salt, and cook, uncovered, for 10 to 20 minutes, or until the spinach is hot. Stir in the sherry. Remove from the heat and purée partially with an immersion blender (or in a regular blender) to the desired consistency.

YIELD: 6 servings

PER SERVING: Calories 387.8; Calories From Fat 50.9; Total Fat 5.8 g; Cholesterol 0 mg; Sodium 1,550.9 mg; Potassium 1,214.7 mg; Total Carbohydrates 64.6 g; Fiber 23.5 g; Sugar 12.6 g; Protein 21.4 g

SWEET TOOTH–BUSTER SWEET POTATO APPLE SOUP

INGREDIENTS

1 Vidalia onion, chopped

2 ribs celery, halved

2 pounds (908 g) sweet potatoes (about 2 large), peeled and chopped

2 large baking apples, peeled, cored, and chopped (Jonagold or Mutsu work well)

4 cups (940 ml) low-sodium vegetable broth

1 clove garlic, minced

2 teaspoons minced fresh ginger

2 teaspoons honey, or to taste

½ teaspoon ground cinnamon

½ teaspoon salt, or to taste

¼ teaspoon ground chipotle chile or cayenne pepper (optional)

FROM DR. JONNY: I've been doing weight-loss coaching since 1990, and one thing I've found to be true is that you can trick a sweet tooth. Sure, that sweet tooth is whispering in your ear about how wonderful it would be to dive into a quart of Ben and Jerry's (at least that's my sweet tooth's idea of heaven), but you can pull the old bait and switch by feeding it nutritious fare that might tame the beast. Case in point: the delicious pairing of sweet potatoes and apples. Sweet potatoes are a tasty nutrient powerhouse and very high in potassium (which helps mitigate the negative impact of all the sodium hidden in our prepared foods), not to mention fiber and vitamin A. And apples, well, they're the original medicinal food—loaded with natural anti-inflammatory agents like the superstar nutrient quercetin. Plus, they're naturally juicy and sweet, to boot. Combine them and you're in for a major treat. This smooth, naturally sweet soup (with a little kick!) is super high in fiber, muting the impact on your blood sugar. Including sweet, fiber-rich dishes like this in your diet really helps calm those cravings!

Add the onion, celery, sweet potatoes, and apples to the slow cooker.

In a large bowl, whisk together the broth, garlic, ginger, honey, cinnamon, salt, and chipotle, if using, and pour over the fruit and veggies. Cook on high for 3 to 4 hours, or on low for 5 to 6 hours, or until the sweet potatoes are very tender.

Remove and discard the celery and purée the soup using an immersion blender. (Or cool and purée in batches in a blender or food processor.) Adjust the seasonings to taste and serve.

YIELD: 6 servings

PER SERVING: Calories 201.5; Calories From Fat 2.2; Total Fat 0.3 g; Cholesterol 0 mg; Sodium 381.8 mg; Potassium 669.9 mg; Total Carbohydrates 45.9 g; Fiber 7.2 g; Sugar 16.3 g; Protein 2.9 g

PINEAPPLE PEPPER CHILI

FROM DR. JONNY: Enzymes are biochemical catalysts. (Think of the enzymes in laundry detergent, dissolving dirt and stains.) In the body we need enzymes to digest food, making the nutrients within more digestible and available to us. One of the best sources is pineapple, rich in a special enzyme known as *bromelain*. Bromelain helps specifically with the digestion of protein, but it does much more. In Germany, bromelain is among the most popular supplements and is approved by the prestigious Commission E for the treatment of inflammation. Meanwhile, the other ingredients in this spectacular chili are not exactly nutritional lightweights. Peppers are loaded with vitamin C, and onions are one of the most healing foods on earth, with their generous amount of sulfur (for the skin) and quercetin (an important anticancer plant chemical). In a study of the antioxidant power of 100 different foods, beans came out on top—they're a superfood if there ever was one. Sweet tropical notes make this delicious chili stand out from the crowd.

INGREDIENTS

1 pound (454 g) navy beans, soaked overnight, rinsed, and drained

1 large sweet onion, chopped

1 red bell pepper, chopped

1 orange bell pepper, chopped

1 serrano chile, seeded and finely chopped

4 cups (940 ml) no-sodium vegetable broth (or water), or enough to cover

1 can (14.5 ounces, or 406 g) fire-roasted diced tomatoes, undrained

1 can (6 ounces, or 168 g) tomato paste

1 can (8 ounces, or 225 g) diced pineapple in juice or water, drained

2 tablespoons (15 g) chili powder

1 ½ teaspoons ground cumin

¾ teaspoon ground coriander

1 teaspoon salt

½ teaspoon freshly ground pepper

Add the soaked and drained beans, onion, bell peppers, and chile to the slow cooker. Pour the broth over all to cover and stir gently to combine. Cook on high for 3 to 4 hours, or on low for 6 to 7 hours, or until the beans are tender. Turn the heat to high, if necessary, and stir in the tomatoes, tomato paste, pineapple, chili powder, cumin, coriander, salt, and pepper. Cover and cook for 45 minutes longer.

YIELD: 8 to 10 servings

PER SERVING: Calories 217.9; Calories From Fat 9.9; Total Fat 1.2 g; Cholesterol 0 mg; Sodium 391.4 mg; Potassium 1,046.2 mg; Total Carbohydrates 42.3 g; Fiber 14.2 g; Sugar 11.8 g; Protein 11.4 g

FROM CHEF JEANNETTE

Time-Saver Tip: In lieu of soaking the beans overnight, you can also bring them to a rapid boil in water to cover. Cook for 10 minutes, remove from the heat, and let sit, covered, for 1 hour. Drain the cooking water and follow the recipe as directed.

MIGHTY MINESTRONE

INGREDIENTS

6 baby red potatoes, scrubbed, left unpeeled, and diced (or substitute 1 yam or sweet potato, peeled and chopped)

2 carrots, peeled and chopped

2 ribs celery, sliced

1 zucchini, coarsely chopped

½ sweet onion, chopped

1 can (15 ounces, or 420 g) chickpeas, drained and rinsed

1 can (15 ounces, or 420 g) kidney beans, drained and rinsed

4 cups (940 ml) vegetable broth (or replace half with organic beef broth)

2 cans (14.5 ounces, or 406 g each) diced tomatoes with basil, garlic, and oregano, undrained

¼ cup (60 ml) red wine

1 teaspoon dried basil

1 bay leaf

¾ teaspoon dried oregano

1 teaspoon salt

½ teaspoon freshly ground pepper, or to taste

1 package (10 ounces, or 280 g) frozen chopped spinach

1 tablespoon (15 ml) red wine vinegar

¼ cup (25 g) grated Parmesan cheese, for garnish (optional)

FROM DR. JONNY: Soups are all about "nutrient density," and if you're not familiar with that term, let me explain. It's actually very much like another term used to describe where people live: population density. Population density is basically a measure of how many people live in a designated area, be it a given number of square miles, a neighborhood, a city, or even a country. Bangladesh has the world's highest population density (2,200 people per square mile); the country of Mongolia has the least (4.3 people per square mile). Nutrient density is how many vitamins, minerals, phytochemicals, and other healthful compounds are found per calorie. Broccoli, for example, has a very high nutrient density (lots of nutrients, small number of calories); chocolate ice cream has the opposite—few nutrients at a very high caloric cost. Now let's turn to this nutritionally dense soup! For a very small number of calories you've got a nutritional powerhouse, brimming with fiber (beans), lycopene (tomatoes), beta-carotene (carrots), vitamin K (celery), sulfur compounds (onion), and from the zucchini, a truckload of heart-healthy potassium (okay, okay, 843 mg per large zucchini, if you want to get technical). Chef Jeannette threw in a little bit of Parmesan—the fat will help you feel satiated with fewer calories. And it makes the whole thing taste amazing!

Place the vegetables, beans, broth, tomatoes, red wine, basil, bay leaf, oregano, salt, and pepper in the slow cooker, stir gently to mix, cover, and cook on low for 4 to 5 hours, or until all the veggies are tender. Stir in the spinach and cook for 30 minutes, or until the spinach is hot. Add the red wine vinegar and stir. Stir to incorporate the spinach, garnish with the Parmesan, if using, and serve.

YIELD: 8 to 10 servings

PER SERVING: Calories 273; Calories From Fat 30.5; Total Fat 3.5 g; Cholesterol 3.2 mg; Sodium 1,367.5 mg; Potassium 1,175.9 mg; Total Carbohydrates 51.3 g; Fiber 9.8 g; Sugar 6.4 g; Protein 11.9 g

FROM CHEF JEANNETTE

Time-Saver Tip: To save chopping time, use 4 to 5 cups fresh prepared vegetables of your choice (corn, broccoli florets, cauliflower florets, colored bell pepper strips, sliced carrots, cut green beans, sliced zucchini, etc.).

LEAN GREEN CURRIED TOFU

FROM DR. JONNY: Tofu is the Forrest Gump of the food world. It has no real taste or flavor of its own but has this remarkable ability to absorb the flavors of whatever it's cooked with so that you wind up with an ingredient that can blend into and enhance almost any casserole, sauce, or dish. In this recipe, Chef Jeannette does tofu with a combination of fish sauce and green curry paste, lightly sweetened with honey and the natural sweetness of light coconut milk. The chickpeas make this a high-fiber dish, and the vegetables provide vitamin C, potassium, magnesium, iron, calcium, and a host of other nutrients.

INGREDIENTS

1 package (14 ounces, or 392 g) extra-firm tofu, drained
1 can (14.5 ounces, or 406 g) light coconut milk
1 ½ cups (353 ml) vegetable broth (try our recipe for Freshest Veggie Stock)
¼ cup (64 g) Thai green curry paste
¼ cup (60 ml) fish sauce (omit for vegan option)
3 tablespoons (45 ml) low-sodium tamari
1 tablespoon (20 g) honey or xylitol
Juice and zest of 1 lemon
1 can (15 ounces, or 420 g) chickpeas, drained and rinsed
4 shallots, chopped
1 red bell pepper, cored, seeded, and sliced into bite-size strips
1 small young eggplant, unpeeled, quartered, and thinly sliced
4 ounces (112 g) shiitake mushrooms, sliced
1 package (10 ounces, or 280 g) frozen chopped spinach, unthawed
¼ cup (10 g) slivered fresh basil

Place the drained tofu block between two large plates. Stack an unopened 28-ounce (784 g) can or two 15-ounce (420 g) cans on the top plate and press excess moisture out of the tofu for 15 to 20 minutes. Drain off the liquid and cut the tofu block into ½-inch (1.3 cm) cubes. Set aside.

Combine the coconut milk, broth, curry paste, fish sauce, tamari, honey, and lemon juice and zest in a slow cooker and whisk well to combine. Add the chickpeas, shallots, bell pepper, eggplant, and mushrooms and stir gently. Add the tofu and lay the spinach block on top. Cover and cook on low for 4 to 6 hours, or until all the veggies are tender. Stir gently to recombine and adjust the seasonings, if necessary. Garnish with the basil and serve.

YIELD: 6 servings
PER SERVING: Calories 344.6; Calories From Fat 60.7; Total Fat 7 g; Cholesterol 0.6 mg; Sodium 2,469.8 mg; Potassium 1,043.9 mg; Total Carbohydrates 59.1 g; Fiber 13 g; Sugar 7.4 g; Protein 17 g

LOW-CAL CARIBBEAN BLACK BEAN SOUP

INGREDIENTS

1 pound (454 g) dried black beans

1 ½ tablespoons (23 ml) olive oil

1 yellow onion, chopped

2 ribs celery, sliced

1 green or red bell pepper, cored, seeded, and chopped

8 cloves garlic, crushed and chopped

8 cups (1,880 ml) no-sodium vegetable broth

1 teaspoon dried oregano

1 teaspoon dried thyme

¾ teaspoon ground cumin

¾ teaspoon salt

½ teaspoon cracked black pepper

3 tablespoons (45 ml) apple cider vinegar

1 tablespoon (15 ml) hot pepper sauce

1 teaspoon Sucanat or xylitol

½ cup (8 g) chopped fresh cilantro (or basil)

FROM CHEF JEANNETTE

Time-Saver Tip: If you're in a hurry, omit the oil and veggie sautéing step and simply add all the ingredients directly to the slow cooker.

FROM DR. JONNY: There's a famous reggae singer in Anguilla named Bankie Banx who owns a legendary beach joint where they serve island food. This soup reminds me of just the kind of fare you'd expect to be served there, on checkered tablecloths overlooking the gorgeous calm turquoise water of the Caribbean. Black bean soup might not be the first thing you think of when you think of "diet food," but think again. Beans are the ultimate high-fiber food, meaning they fill you up and keep you full a long time. (One cup of black beans contains a whopping 15 grams of fiber.) They have about 227 calories per cup, contain more than 15 grams of satisfying, satiating protein, and feature 611 mg of potassium. And black beans are just about the only ingredient in this soup that contains any calories to speak of (other than the tiny bit of olive oil). The interesting combination of spices adds an island-y flavor to the whole shebang.

Soak the beans overnight in water to cover by 2 inches (5 cm). Drain and rinse the beans well. Transfer to a slow cooker.

Heat the oil in a large skillet over medium heat and add the onion, celery, and bell pepper. Cook for about 7 minutes, or until the vegetables are starting to soften. Add the garlic and cook for 1 minute. Transfer the contents to the slow cooker. Add the broth, oregano, thyme, cumin, salt, and pepper, stir well, cover, and cook on low for 7 to 8 hours, or until the beans are tender to the squeeze. Stir in the vinegar, hot pepper sauce, Sucanat, and cilantro just before serving.

YIELD: 8 servings

PER SERVING: Calories 265; Calories From Fat 44.1; Total Fat 4.7 g; Cholesterol 0 mg; Sodium 381.1 mg; Potassium 965.7 mg; Total Carbohydrates 39.7 g; Fiber 9.7 g; Sugar 2.7 g; Protein 13 g

SEEDED AND STUFFED CARNIVAL SQUASH

INGREDIENTS

⅓ cup (67 g) quick-cooking barley
      (or 1 cup [157 g] cooked barley)

1 cup (175 g) cooked small red beans
      (drained and rinsed if using canned)

¼ cup (40 g) minced onion

2 cloves garlic, minced

1½ tablespoons (23 ml) low-sodium tamari

¾ teaspoon dried oregano

¾ teaspoon dried basil

½ teaspoon ground cumin

⅛ teaspoon cayenne pepper

2 tablespoons (18 g) roasted sunflower seeds

2 large carnival squash, halved lengthwise and
      seeded

½ cup (120 ml) water, vegetable broth, or
      apple cider

FROM DR. JONNY: Even for a carnivore like myself, a vegetarian dish from time to time is a welcome addition to the menu. A vegetarian offering like the one below is not only high in fiber and nutrients, but it will also save you a little cash, because veggies are always cheaper than grass-fed meat or wild-caught fish. Carnival squash is a colorful, small, hard-skinned variety of winter squash that tastes somewhat similar to a sweet potato or butternut squash. This dish is especially rich in fiber from the red beans, squash, and barley. And speaking of fiber, a recent study published in the *Archives of Internal Medicine* investigated diet and the risk of death among 388,000 men and women who were followed over a nine-year period. Men and women consuming the most fiber in their diet (between 25 and 30 grams per day) were significantly less likely to die from cardiovascular, infectious, or respiratory disease, and were an impressive 22 percent less likely to die from any cause whatsoever. The Institute of Medicine recommends between 25 and 38 grams of fiber daily. This recipe is a delicious way to help get you to that target!

Cook the barley according to package directions. In a medium-size bowl, combine the barley, red beans, onion, garlic, tamari, oregano, basil, cumin, cayenne pepper, and sunnies and mix well.

Stuff each squash half with one-fourth of the mixture and arrange the filled halves in the slow cooker. Gently pour the liquid into the bottom of the cooker, cover, and cook on low for 2 to 3 hours, or until the squash is tender.

YIELD: 4 servings

PER SERVING: Calories 164.7; Calories From Fat 24.6; Total Fat 2.9 g; Cholesterol 0 mg; Sodium 432.5 mg; Potassium 381.7 mg; Total Carbohydrates 28.8 g; Fiber 7 g; Sugar 1.9 g; Protein 7.5 g

LIVER-LOVIN' ROOT AND CABBAGE STEW

INGREDIENTS

2-inch (5 cm) piece kombu

2 tablespoons (30 ml) olive oil

1 large onion, chopped

1 rib celery, sliced

2 carrots, peeled and thinly sliced on the diagonal (½ inch [1.3 cm] thick)

2 cloves garlic, minced

1 medium rutabaga (or yellow turnip), peeled and finely diced

½ green cabbage, cut in half lengthwise and sliced into thin ribbons

¾ cup (150 g) hato mugi (Job's Tears) or quick-cooking barley

1 can (15 ounces, or 420 g) chickpeas, drained and rinsed

6 cups (1,410 ml) vegetable broth (or chicken broth)

2 tablespoons (30 ml) tamari

1 tablespoon (15 ml) apple cider vinegar

½ teaspoon salt

½ teaspoon dried tarragon

½ teaspoon cracked black pepper

FROM CHEF JEANNETTE

Hato mugi is an Asian heirloom grain that looks like fat barley. Unlike barley, it is totally gluten free. It has a soft, chewy texture and is easy to digest. In the macrobiotic world, it is considered a mild detoxifier. Look for it in Asian markets (it is also called Job's Tears and yimi *in Chinese). I often add it to brown rice for extra texture. If you can't find it, in this recipe you can substitute quick-cooking pearl barley. Add the barley for the last 30 minutes of cooking time.*

FROM DR. JONNY: If vegetables were dogs, rutabagas would be a lovable mutt. They're actually believed to be a mutation of sorts, kind of a blend of wild cabbage and turnips, according to well-known plant and herbal expert Brigitte Mars. She calls rutabagas "liver stimulating," because they provide nutrients that the liver needs for detoxification. Kombu is a sea vegetable rich in minerals that the liver also needs to perform the myriad functions it carries out on a daily basis. And, of course, cabbage contains a wealth of nutrients, one of which provides chemicals that stimulate detoxifying pathways in the liver. Blend them together in a delicious stew like this one, and you've got a supper that supports liver function. On a personal note, one thing I particularly love about meals like this is that they are easy on my blood sugar. A stew like this satisfies for a long time without putting you in the kind of blood sugar hell that creates cravings and overeating. This is a hearty, creamy stew with an Eastern European feeling. Tip: It's even better the next day!

In a small bowl, soak the piece of kombu for 10 minutes in just enough water to cover.

In a large skillet, heat the oil over medium heat. Add the onion, celery, and carrots and sauté for 5 minutes. Add the garlic and sauté for 1 minute.

Transfer the contents to a slow cooker and add the rutabaga, cabbage, hato mugi, and chickpeas. Stir gently to combine. Pour the broth over all to cover generously. Add the tamari, vinegar, salt, tarragon, and pepper and mix well. When the kombu is soft, pour the soaking water into the stew, finely dice the kombu, and add to the stew.

Cover and cook for about 4 hours on high, or 6 to 7 hours on low, or until all the veggies and hato mugi are tender.

YIELD: 6 to 8 servings

PER SERVING: Calories 220.2; Calories From Fat 38.8; Total Fat 4.4 g; Cholesterol 0 mg; Sodium 1,312.9 mg; Potassium 523.3 mg; Total Carbohydrates 40.4 g; Fiber 9 g; Sugar 8 g; Protein 6.8 g

VITAMIN C–RICH, THREE-PEPPER 'N BEAN CHILI

INGREDIENTS

1 Vidalia onion, chopped

1 red bell pepper, cored, seeded, and chopped

1 green bell pepper, cored, seeded, and chopped

1 poblano chile pepper, seeded and chopped

1 can (15 ounces, or 420 g) black beans, drained and rinsed

1 can (15 ounces, or 420 g) kidney beans, drained and rinsed

2 cans (15 ounces, or 420 g each) fire-roasted diced tomatoes, undrained

1 cup (235 ml) vegetable broth

¼ cup (60 ml) dry red wine

1 can (6 ounces, or 168 g) tomato paste

1 cup (130 g) frozen corn

1 teaspoon salt

1 teaspoon chili powder

1 teaspoon ground chipotle chile (or use additional chili powder for less heat)

½ teaspoon ground cumin

½ teaspoon ground coriander

½ teaspoon dried oregano

FROM DR. JONNY: Every time I think about chili, I think about the time I was touring with the Andrew Lloyd Weber musical *Joseph and the Amazing Technicolor Dreamcoat*. We were in Denver for a week, and the company decided to have a chili-making contest. My roommate and I didn't cook, so we decided to go to the gourmet store and buy the finest canned chili we could get, heat it up in a pot, and pass it off as our own. (Okay, okay, I know.) We got second place, and the guilt has stayed with me all these decades. (Thanks for letting me confess.) The thing of it is, chili is one of those great dishes that has something for everyone. It's high in fiber from the beans, is loaded with antioxidants, and has an incredibly low impact on your blood sugar. This particular one is rich in vitamin C from the peppers, and rich in sulfur compounds from the Vidalia onion (good for the skin!). If we had had this recipe in the 1980s, we would've probably won first place and I wouldn't have had to feel guilty all these years for cheating!

Combine all the ingredients in the slow cooker, mix well, cover, and cook on high for 3 to 4 hours, or on low for 6 to 8 hours.

YIELD: 8 servings

PER SERVING: Calories 248.7; Calories From Fat 8.6; Total Fat 1 g; Cholesterol 0 mg; Sodium 746.9 mg; Potassium 1,276.9 mg; Total Carbohydrates 48 g; Fiber 14.9 g; Sugar 12.3 g; Protein 11.2 g

ITALIAN WHITE BEAN SOUP

FROM DR. JONNY: White beans are rich in protein and fiber. They are also chock-full of vitamins and minerals. One cup of white beans contains more than 1,000 mg of potassium, one of the most important minerals for heart health and for maintaining a healthy blood pressure. And the substantial amount of fiber—more than 11 grams per cup—offers all sorts of benefits, such as stabilizing blood sugar and keeping energy constant. When I lecture about food and blood sugar I often use this example: eat beans on a Tuesday morning and your blood sugar will go up slightly by Wednesday afternoon! It's an exaggeration, of course, but the point is that fiber slows the entrance of glucose (sugar) into the bloodstream, helping to prevent that crash and burn you get from eating foods that raise blood sugar quickly and then drop it precipitously. The slow cooker is perfect for this soup—prep time is a snap, so all you do is leave it and eat it. This really is "fast" slow food!

INGREDIENTS

1 pound (454 g) small dried white beans
    (navy or cannellini)
1 large yellow onion, chopped
2 large carrots, peeled and sliced into thin
    rounds
2 ribs celery, thinly sliced
4 cloves garlic, minced
7 cups (1,645 ml) no-sodium vegetable broth
1 can (28 ounces, or 784 g) crushed tomatoes
2 teaspoons lemon zest (optional)
1/4 cup (60 ml) dry red wine
1/2 teaspoon red pepper flakes
3/4 teaspoon salt, or to taste
1/2 teaspoon freshly ground pepper
3/4 cup (45 g) chopped fresh parsley

Soak the beans overnight in water to cover by 2 inches (5 cm). Drain the water and place the beans in a slow cooker. Add the onion, carrots, celery, garlic, broth, tomatoes, zest, if using, wine, and red pepper flakes. Stir gently to combine and cook on low for 7 to 8 hours, or until the beans are tender to the squeeze. Add the salt and pepper for the last 30 minutes of cooking time and stir in the parsley just before serving.

YIELD: 6 servings
PER SERVING: Calories 332.1; Calories From Fat 14.2; Total Fat 1.6 g; Cholesterol 0 mg; Sodium 662.9 mg; Potassium 1,429.6 mg; Total Carbohydrates 58.3 g; Fiber 21.2 g; Sugar 5.3 g; Protein 18.6 g

FROM CHEF JEANNETTE

Be sure to use sodium-free broth because salt added too early in the cooking process toughens beans and increases their cooking time.

NO-CREAM OF LEEK AND POTATO SOUP

INGREDIENTS

1 ½ tablespoons (23 ml) olive oil

3 small leeks, white and tender green parts only, washed well to remove all grit and chopped

4 cloves garlic, minced

1 pound (454 g) small baby red or new potatoes, well scrubbed, left unpeeled, and quartered

4 cups (940 ml) unsweetened plain soymilk

¾ teaspoon salt, or to taste

¼ teaspoon white pepper (optional)

½ teaspoon cracked black pepper, or to taste

1 to 2 tablespoons (16 to 32 g) mellow white miso, to taste

¼ cup (34 g) toasted pine nuts, for garnish (optional)

FROM CHEF JEANNETTE

When making a puréed soup, it's more typical to peel the potatoes for smoothness, but I encourage you to leave them—and their nutrients—intact for this healthier version. You can use baby red, new, or baby Yukon gold. Look for potatoes about the size of golf balls.

FROM DR. JONNY: The liver is command central for detoxification in the body, but like the engine in your car, the liver needs fuel to run on. That fuel comes in the form of vitamins and other liver-supporting nutrients and phytochemicals, and vegetables are just loaded with them. Vegetables such as leeks, for example, are like fuel injectors for the metabolic machinery of the liver, making it run as smoothly as a well-tuned Ferrari. Leeks contain vitamin K, which the liver needs to make factors necessary for proper blood clotting. And anything that strains or impairs liver function, like alcohol, can seriously deplete antioxidants. You'll find a ton of antioxidants in the leeks. This is a creamy and satisfying leek and potato soup without the cream!

Heat the oil in a large skillet over medium heat. Add the leeks and sauté until tender, 5 to 7 minutes. Add the garlic and cook for 1 minute. Transfer the contents to a slow cooker and add the potatoes, soymilk, salt, and peppers. Cover and cook on low for about 4 hours, or until the potatoes are tender. Using an immersion or countertop blender, purée the soup until nearly smooth. Stir in the miso, blending lightly with an immersion wand or spoon to get it to disperse and mix. Adjust the seasonings to taste. Serve garnished with the pine nuts, if using.

YIELD: 4 to 6 servings

PER SERVING: Calories 217.7; Calories From Fat 89; Total Fat 10.2 g; Cholesterol 0 mg; Sodium 471.7 mg; Potassium 735.7 mg; Total Carbohydrates 25.1 g; Fiber 3.3 g; Sugar 2.8 g; Protein 8.1 g

RICH AND CREAMY HIGH-FIBER SWEET POTATO PEANUT BISQUE

INGREDIENTS

1 tablespoon (15 g) coconut oil

1 large yellow onion, chopped

1 cup (110 g) grated carrot

2 tablespoons (12 g) minced fresh ginger

3 cloves garlic, minced

1 can (14.5 ounces, or 406 g) diced tomatoes, drained

2 pounds (908 g) sweet potatoes or yams, peeled and chopped

6 cups (1,410 ml) low-sodium vegetable broth

1/3 cup (87 g) natural unsalted peanut butter (no additives)

1 very ripe mango, peeled, pitted, and chopped (or 1/2 cup [120 ml] mango nectar)

Juice of 3 limes, divided

1 1/2 teaspoons ground cumin

1 tablespoon (6 g) ground coriander

3/4 teaspoon salt, or to taste

3/4 teaspoon red pepper flakes

1 cup (230 g) puréed soft silken tofu (optional)

1 bunch fresh cilantro, chopped

1/2 cup (50 g) sliced scallion

Hot pepper sauce, to taste

FROM CHEF JEANNETTE

Variation: For a different flavor twist and to save peeling and chopping time, replace the fresh sweet potatoes with 3 cups (735 g) canned or fresh pumpkin purée.

FROM DR. JONNY: Back in the day when I was a gym rat, I used to bake up about a half dozen sweet potatoes every Sunday and take them with me to the gym in Tupperware containers. (Don't knock it 'til you try it; sweet potatoes taste even better cold, when they just ooze sweetness and richness. Really.) So what could make one of nature's greatest foods taste even better? Peanuts. Sweet potatoes are a high-fiber food—one large potato has nearly 6 grams of the stuff—and are rich in plant chemicals known as *carotenoids*. (You've probably heard of the most famous carotenoid—beta-carotene—but there are about 600 others!) What's more, sweet potatoes are a potassium heavyweight, and potassium is one of the nutrients that most protects the blood vessels and cardiovascular system. This creamy, rich sweet potato dish will light a gentle fire in your taste buds with its lime bite and red pepper kick—warming and satisfying. Silken high-protein tofu replaces calorie-rich conventional cream, enriching this flavorful bisque and adding a nice protein "pop." Fun fact: Resveratrol, the famous anti-aging nutrient found in red wine and the skin of dark grapes, is also found in peanuts.

Heat the oil in a large skillet over medium-high heat. Add the onion and carrot and sauté for 4 minutes, or until the onion begins to soften. Add the ginger and garlic and cook for 1 minute, stirring constantly. Add the contents to a slow cooker.

Add the tomatoes, sweet potatoes, broth, peanut butter, mango, juice of 2 limes, cumin, coriander, salt, and red pepper flakes, and stir to combine.

Cook on high for 3 to 4 hours, or on low for 6 to 7 hours, or until the vegetables are tender. Purée the cooked soup with an immersion blender (or carefully, in batches, in a blender or food processor).

Return the soup to the slow cooker and set to high. Whisk in the tofu and cook for 5 minutes. Stir in the cilantro and scallion and season to taste with the juice of the remaining 1 lime and hot pepper sauce.

YIELD: 6 servings

PER SERVING: Calories 384; Calories From Fat 47.1; Total Fat 5.1 g; Cholesterol 0 mg; Sodium 647.5 mg; Potassium 1,096.8 mg; Total Carbohydrates 54.7 g; Fiber 9.9 g; Sugar 15.4 g; Protein 13.6 g

CURRIED SPINACH AND LENTILS

FROM DR. JONNY: Those who read my book *The 150 Healthiest Foods on Earth* may remember my rhapsodic waxing about a super-spice called *turmeric*. In case you missed it, or need a reminder, here's a short list of the wonderful things it does. One, it's among the most anti-inflammatory foods on the planet, which matters because inflammation is a major part of every degenerative disease we know of. Two, it's extremely good for the liver, that poor, overworked organ that has to rid your body of all the toxins it's exposed to on a daily basis. And three, it's got significant anticancer activity. The thing of it is, turmeric goes beautifully with all sorts of dishes (besides, of course, the Indian food it's best known for). This dish is a perfect example. Rich in fiber from the lentils, and with a ton of nutrients like iron, potassium, calcium, and magnesium from the spinach, the dish goes together beautifully. A rich, fragrant vegetarian curry with warming, complex flavor notes. You'll love it.

INGREDIENTS

2 ½ teaspoons cumin seeds

1 ½ teaspoons coriander seeds

1 tablespoon (15 ml) olive oil

2 medium sweet onions, diced

5 medium carrots, peeled and thinly sliced

5 medium parsnips, peeled and thinly sliced

5 cloves garlic, minced

2 tablespoons (12 g) finely minced fresh ginger

2 ½ teaspoons ground turmeric

1 cinnamon stick

½ teaspoon cracked black or mixed peppercorns

2 ½ cups (588 ml) vegetable stock

Salt, to taste

3 medium-size sweet potatoes, peeled and thinly sliced

1 ¼ cups (240 ml) brown lentils, rinsed thoroughly

1 red chile, seeded and minced

1 pound (454 g) fresh spinach, stemmed and coarsely chopped

1 cup (235 ml) reduced-fat coconut milk

¼ cup (4 g) chopped fresh cilantro (optional)

In a dry cast-iron skillet over medium heat, toast the cumin and coriander seeds for a couple of minutes, stirring often, until they just begin to brown. Grind the toasted seeds to a powder in a spice grinder or designated coffee grinder and set aside.

In the same skillet, heat the olive oil over medium heat and add the onions, carrots, and parsnips. Cook until tender, about 6 minutes. Add the garlic, ginger, turmeric, cinnamon stick, peppercorns, and ground cumin and coriander seeds. Cook for 1 minute, stirring constantly. Add the vegetable stock and bring to a boil. Remove from the heat, add salt to taste, and carefully transfer the contents to a slow cooker. Add the sweet potatoes and lentils and stir well. Cover and cook on high for 3 hours, or on low for 4 to 5 hours, until the vegetables and lentils are tender.

Add the chile pepper and stir well to incorporate. Add the fresh spinach in handfuls, stirring each handful into the curry. Add the coconut milk and stir until incorporated. Cook on high for 20 more minutes.

Remove the cinnamon stick and discard before serving. Garnish with the cilantro, if using.

YIELD: 6 to 8 servings

PER SERVING: Calories 387; Calories From Fat 41.1; Total Fat 4.8 g; Cholesterol 0 mg; Sodium 441.7 mg; Potassium 1,727.4 mg; Total Carbohydrates 77.2 g; Fiber 24.1 g; Sugar 18.5 g; Protein 13.8 g

FROM CHEF JEANNETTE

The concept for this recipe comes from my friend, Mary Weaver, owner of the gourmet cooking school Newport Cooks in Newport, Rhode Island. She is a vegetarian and always on the lookout for hearty meatless meals that taste delicious and provide a great balance of macronutrients.

Serving Suggestions: This curry is delicious served over brown basmati rice or Thai-style rice noodles. To cool the heat a bit and add more protein, spoon a dollop of plain, low-fat Greek yogurt into each bowl.

GIFTS FROM THE SEA CHOWDER

FROM DR. JONNY: Many cookbooks will tell you how bad cream is for you (saturated fat! oh my God!), but I don't agree. Even though I don't think there's anything wrong with a bit of saturated fat, I like to cut calories whenever possible and cream is anything but a low-cal ingredient. Chef Jeannette made this rich seafood chowder with a tomato base to reduce the calories, but I'm telling you, you'll never miss the cream. This is a high-protein soup loaded with some of the lowest-calorie, richest protein sources in the sea—oysters, scallops, and shrimp. The spinach adds texture, color, and a heap of calcium and iron. And the skin of new potatoes is flakier and thinner than the kind found on the "old" kind. Fun fact: "New potatoes" are immature potatoes harvested during the summer or spring. They're not actually a separate variety of potato, but younger versions of other varieties.

INGREDIENTS

1 tablespoon (14 g) unsalted butter

½ tablespoon (8 ml) olive oil

1 yellow onion, chopped

1 carrot, thinly sliced

2 ribs celery, thinly sliced

6 baby Yukon gold potatoes, scrubbed, left unpeeled, and quartered (or use red new potatoes, about the size of golf balls)

1 package (10 ounces, or 280 g) frozen chopped spinach, unthawed

1 can (28 ounces, or 784 g) tomato purée

2 cups (470 ml) chicken or vegetable broth

2 cups (470 ml) clam juice

¾ cup (180 ml) dry white wine

1 tablespoon (2.4 g) chopped fresh thyme (or 1 teaspoon dried)

¾ teaspoon salt

½ teaspoon freshly ground black pepper

2 cans (8 ounces, or 225 g each) whole oysters, drained and rinsed

8 ounces (225 g) peeled, frozen shrimp (uncooked, unthawed)

12 ounces (336 g) fresh bay scallops

½ cup (30 g) chopped fresh flat-leaf parsley

6 to 8 thin slices lemon, for garnish

Heat the butter and oil in a large skillet over medium heat. Add the onion, carrot, and celery and cook for about 8 minutes, or until beginning to soften.

Transfer the contents to a slow cooker. Add the potatoes, spinach, tomato purée, broth, clam juice, wine, thyme, salt, and pepper. Cover and cook on low for 6 to 7 hours, or until the vegetables are tender. Stir well to incorporate the spinach and add the oysters, shrimp, and scallops. Cook for 10 to 15 minutes longer, or until the seafood is cooked through but still tender. Stir in the parsley and float a lemon slice in each individual bowl to serve.

YIELD: 6 to 8 servings

FOR ENTIRE RECIPE: Calories 311.4; Calories From Fat 43.9; Total Fat 5.1 g; Cholesterol 86.4 mg; Sodium 1,443.9 mg; Potassium 1,473.5 mg; Total Carbohydrates 49.8 g; Fiber 10 g; Sugar 11.1 g; Protein 23.7 g

PUNGENT, LIGHT, AND CLEAR THAI SEAFOOD STEW

INGREDIENTS

1 large red onion, chopped

8 baby red potatoes, scrubbed, left unpeeled, and halved

6 stalks lemongrass, trimmed and cut into 1-inch (2.5 cm) pieces

6 cups (1,410 ml) chicken broth

15 kaffir lime leaves (or 2 teaspoons fresh lime zest)

1/3 cup (80 ml) Thai fish sauce

Juice of 2 limes, divided

2 teaspoons low-sodium tamari

3 red chiles, seeded and minced, or to taste

2 tablespoons (30 g) Sucanat (or brown sugar)

12 ounces (340 g) medium shrimp, shelled and deveined

8 ounces (225 g) halibut, sliced into 1 1/2-inch (4 cm) pieces

1/3 cup (5 g) chopped fresh cilantro

FROM DR. JONNY: The magic ingredient in this delicious and exotic Thai-inspired seafood stew is *capsaicin*. Found in hot peppers, capsaicin helps tone down a compound called *substance P*, which is associated with inflammatory processes in the joints and contributes mightily to various pain syndromes (such as fibromyalgia, low-back pain, and arthritis). According to WebMD, capsaicin may even help prevent heart disease by stimulating the cardiovascular system and lowering blood pressure. (It also improves digestion!) This light and fresh-tasting seafood stew will clear out your sinuses and may even leave you feeling mildly stimulated. Fun fact: During the 2008 presidential primary, Hillary Clinton told interviewers that she owed her indefatigable energy to eating hot peppers!

Place the onion, potatoes, and lemongrass in the bottom of the slow cooker. Pour the chicken broth over all. Stir in the lime leaves, fish sauce, juice of 1 lime, tamari, chiles, and Sucanat. Cook on high for 2 to 3 hours, or on low for 3 to 4 hours, or until the vegetables are tender.

Add the shrimp and halibut and cook for 10 to 15 minutes, or until the seafood is just cooked through. Stir in the cilantro and the remaining juice of 1 lime, to taste, and adjust the seasonings.

YIELD: 6 servings

PER SERVING: Calories 313.4; Calories From Fat 32.2; Total Fat 3.5 g; Cholesterol 98.3 mg; Sodium 2,070.9 mg; Potassium 1,429.1 mg; Total Carbohydrates 40.9 g; Fiber 3.9 g; Sugar 5.1 g; Protein 30.2 g

SHELLFISH JAMBALAYA

FROM DR. JONNY: Shrimp is the most popular shellfish in the world and probably one of the most popular varieties of seafood, period. And I don't know where scallops rank, but they're sure up there in my book of favorites. Both are rich in an essential nutrient from the B-vitamin family, *choline*. (Choline helps form an important neurotransmitter in the brain called *acetylcholine*, which is necessary for memory and motor activity. No wonder fish is known as brain food!) Put this crustacean-mollusk mixture together with some antioxidant-rich tomatoes, peppers, and onions, season with essence of New Orleans, and presto, you've got jambalaya. Typical jambalaya has fatty, poor-quality sausage and chicken, but ours is pure soul of the sea with that New Orleans flair. This is a fabulous lean, high-protein, nutrient-rich recipe that will make you think you're eating in an outdoor café deep in the heart of Tremé.

INGREDIENTS

- 1 can (28 ounces, or 784 g) diced tomatoes, undrained
- 1 can (14.5 ounces, or 406 g) crushed tomatoes
- 1 large yellow onion, chopped
- 2 colored bell peppers, cored, seeded, and chopped (red, yellow, orange, or green)
- 3 ribs celery, thinly sliced
- 6 cloves garlic, chopped
- Juice and zest of 1 lemon
- 1 bay leaf
- 1 teaspoon sweet paprika
- 1 teaspoon dried oregano
- ¾ teaspoon dried thyme
- ¾ teaspoon salt
- ½ teaspoon cracked black pepper
- ½ teaspoon cayenne pepper
- ½ teaspoon hot pepper sauce, or more to taste
- Pinch of Sucanat or xylitol
- 1 pound (454 g) fresh shrimp, shelled and deveined
- 1 pound (454 g) fresh bay scallops
- ½ cup (30 g) chopped fresh parsley
- 2 to 3 cups (330 to 495 g) cooked long-grain brown rice, for serving

In a slow cooker, combine the tomatoes, onion, peppers, celery, garlic, lemon zest, bay leaf, paprika, oregano, thyme, salt, peppers, hot sauce, and Sucanat. Cover and cook on high for 3 to 4 hours, or on low for 7 to 8 hours. Increase the heat to high, if necessary, add the shrimp and scallops, and cook for 10 to 15 minutes, or until the seafood is just cooked through but still tender. Stir in the lemon juice and parsley and serve over hot rice.

YIELD: 6 to 8 servings

PER SERVING: Calories 236.9; Calories From Fat 21.8; Total Fat 2.5 g; Cholesterol 105.1 mg; Sodium 736.2 mg; Potassium 694.5 mg; Total Carbohydrates 30.7 g; Fiber 5.4 g; Sugar 6.2 g; Protein 25.3 g

INGREDIENTS

1 ½ tablespoons (23 ml) olive oil

6 large shallots, chopped (or 1 yellow onion, chopped)

2 ribs celery, thinly sliced

2 cloves garlic, minced

1 can (14.5 ounces, or 406 g) peeled tomatoes, drained

1 can (14.5 ounces, or 406 g) tomato purée

1 can (6 ounces, or 168 g) tomato paste

⅓ cup (80 ml) dry white wine

1 teaspoon dried oregano

1 teaspoon dried basil

½ teaspoon each salt and freshly ground black pepper

1 ½ pounds (680 g) fresh sea scallops

2 ounces (56 g) feta cheese, crumbled

½ cup (30 g) chopped fresh parsley

Lemon wedges, for garnish (optional)

SEA SCALLOPS MEDITERRANEAN

FROM DR. JONNY: In addition to being delicious, scallops are a low-calorie source of high-quality protein from the sea. They're more than 80 percent protein, providing a rich 15 grams per 3-ounce (84 g) serving, plus trace amounts of at least eighteen vitamins and minerals. This Mediterranean sauce is a perfect way to serve them. Rich in tomatoes—which are swimming in antioxidants such as lycopene, a nutrient that has been associated with lower rates of prostate cancer—this cheesy, spicy sauce is the perfect accompaniment for the light, chewy scallops. This dish would be right at home served by the pool in the Greek Isles. Fun fact: The volatile oils in both oregano and basil have been shown in research to have both antimicrobial and antiviral activity.

Heat the oil in a large skillet over medium heat. Add the shallots and celery and cook for about 5 minutes, or until the shallots are beginning to soften. Add the garlic and cook for 30 seconds. Transfer the contents to a slow cooker.

Add the tomatoes, tomato purée, tomato paste, wine, oregano, basil, salt, and pepper, and stir gently to combine. Cover and cook on low for 5 to 6 hours. Fold in the scallops and cook to desired doneness; they are best when they are very tender with a bit of pink in the center—about 10 to 15 minutes. Stir in the feta and parsley and serve with the lemon wedges, if using.

YIELD: 6 servings

PER SERVING: Calories 248.3; Calories From Fat 59.6; Total Fat 6.7 g; Cholesterol 46.2 mg; Sodium 1,201 mg; Potassium 896.1 mg; Total Carbohydrates 22.5 g; Fiber 4.2 g; Sugar 7.5 g; Protein 24.5 g

LIGHT LOUISIANA CREOLE SHRIMP SOUP

INGREDIENTS

1 large yellow onion, chopped

1 red bell pepper, cored, seeded, and chopped

1 green bell pepper, cored, seeded, and chopped

$\frac{1}{2}$ jalapeño pepper, seeded and minced

3 ribs celery, thinly sliced

1 bottle (32 ounces, 940 ml) high-quality tomato-based vegetable juice (we like Knudsen's Very Veggie)

$\frac{1}{2}$ cup (120 ml) clam juice

2 tablespoons (30 ml) Worcestershire sauce (use organic to avoid high-fructose corn syrup)

1 teaspoon paprika

1 teaspoon dried oregano

$\frac{3}{4}$ teaspoon cracked black pepper

$\frac{1}{2}$ teaspoon celery salt

$\frac{1}{4}$ teaspoon cayenne pepper

1 bay leaf

1 $\frac{1}{2}$ pounds (680 g) medium shrimp, peeled and deveined

$\frac{1}{2}$ cup (30 g) chopped fresh parsley

4 to 6 slices lemon, for garnish (optional)

FROM DR. JONNY: Shrimp Creole is a classic Louisiana dish of cooked shrimp in a mixture of tomatoes, celery, and peppers traditionally served over boiled or steamed rice. Here, Chef Jeannette has taken the basic template and turned it into a light, delicious soup. I've sung the praises of soup for weight loss for a long time now, and this dish is a perfect example of why. First, it's low in calories. Second, it's high in volume. According to Barbara Rolls, Ph.D., of the University of Pennsylvania, "high-volume" foods are those that take up a lot of space in the tummy but are relatively low in calories. They're also "nutrient dense," which means that there is also a lot of nutrition packed into very few calories (the opposite of a food that has a ton of calories and not so much nutrition—like most desserts!). Rolls's research shows that eating a bowl of low-calorie soup before dinner actually causes people to spontaneously eat fewer calories during the actual meal, an effortless weight-loss strategy if there every was one. In any event, this soup is meal-worthy. Loaded with nutrients from the vegetables and protein from the shrimp, it's just about perfect.

Combine the onion, peppers, celery, juices, Worcestershire, paprika, oregano, black pepper, celery salt, cayenne pepper, and bay leaf in a slow cooker and stir well to combine. Cover and cook on high for 3 to 4 hours, or on low for 6 to 7 hours, until the vegetables are soft.

Increase the heat to high, if necessary, add the shrimp, and cook for 15 to 20 minutes, or until they are cooked through but still tender. Stir in the parsley just before serving and garnish each bowl with a lemon slice, if using.

YIELD: 4 to 6 servings

PER SERVING: Calories 194.9; Calories From Fat 21.1; Total Fat 2.4 g; Cholesterol 172.4 mg; Sodium 682.6 mg; Potassium 906.3 mg; Total Carbohydrates 18.7 g; Fiber 4.3 g; Sugar 8.7 g; Protein 25.8 g

PIQUANT HOT TUNA AND CANNELLINI STEW

INGREDIENTS

6 shallots, chopped (or 1 red onion, chopped, and 2 cloves garlic, minced)

2 ribs celery, thinly sliced

6 anchovy fillets, chopped

⅓ cup (33 g) niçoise olives, pitted and chopped

1 tablespoon (8.6 g) capers, drained

1 can (15 ounces, or 420 g) cannellini beans, drained and rinsed

1 can (28 ounces, or 784 g) peeled tomatoes, undrained, tomatoes chopped

1 cup (235 ml) clam juice or fish stock

1 cup (235 ml) dry white wine

Juice and zest of 1 small lemon

½ teaspoon salt

½ teaspoon cracked black pepper

12 ounces (336 g) fresh green beans, trimmed and cut into 1-inch (2.5 cm) pieces (or use frozen)

2 cans (6.5 ounces, or 182 g each) tuna, drained and flaked (we like Vital Choice)

FROM DR. JONNY: What would bodybuilders do without tuna? For as long as I can remember, gym rats and trainers have been bringing Tupperware containers full of the stuff to the gym so they can be sure to have a nice, high-protein meal after their workout. And why not? Tuna has about 42 grams of protein per 6-ounce (168 g) can, has relatively few calories (less than 200 for the same amount), and is rich in B vitamins, especially niacin and B$_{12}$. Tuna is also high in *choline*, a member of the B-vitamin family, which is an essential component of an important neurotransmitter necessary for attention and memory. The only thing "lacking" in a high-protein food like tuna is fiber, but there's plenty of it in this dish courtesy of the white beans, which also up the nutrition with their high concentration of antioxidants. The anchovies are an additional source of both protein and omega-3 fats, and give the dish a nice flavor undertone.

Combine the shallots, celery, anchovies, olives, capers, beans, tomatoes, clam juice, wine, lemon zest and juice, salt, and cracked pepper in a slow cooker and stir gently to combine. Cover and cook on high for 3 to 4 hours, or on low for 6 to 7 hours. Increase the heat to high, if necessary, and add the green beans and tuna for the last 20 minutes of cooking time.

YIELD: 6 servings

PER SERVING: Calories 274.9; Calories From Fat 21.6; Total Fat 3.4 g; Cholesterol 27.5 mg; Sodium 1,118.7 mg; Potassium 695 mg; Total Carbohydrates 34 g; Fiber 8.4 g; Sugar 2.8 g; Protein 21.7 g

TANGY TOMATO-SOUSED SALMON PATTIES WITH PINEAPPLE AND MISO

INGREDIENTS

Olive oil cooking spray

2 eggs

2 cans (7.5 ounces, or 210 g each) wild Alaskan salmon, bones and skin removed (we like Vital Choice)

⅓ cup (27 g) rolled oats (not instant) or ⅓ cup (38 g) whole wheat bread crumbs

3 tablespoons (30 g) crushed or minced pineapple

2 teaspoons mellow white miso paste

½ cup (50 g) chopped scallion, divided

2 tablespoons (30 ml) white wine

1 can (14.5 ounces, or 406 g) diced tomatoes, undrained

¼ cup (4 g) chopped fresh cilantro

6 lemon wedges (optional)

FROM DR. JONNY: Most people know that salmon is one of the world's great health foods. (Did you forget why? Let me list the reasons: high-quality protein, a ton of those "wellness molecules" known as omega-3 fats, and *astaxanthin*, a superstar antioxidant that gives salmon its pinkish red color.) But, you say, there are only so many ways to cook salmon! Ah, grasshopper, *au contraire*. Here's one way I'll bet you never thought of featuring canned wild Alaskan salmon that, by the way, tastes remarkable. Chef Jeannette gussied it up with rolled oats (fiber), pineapple (enzymes, potassium, vitamin C), tomatoes (lycopene, an antioxidant associated with lower rates of prostate cancer), and mineral-rich miso. The pineapple really sets off the salmon flavor, much like it does for ham but even better. Fun fact: Cilantro, also known as coriander, is a rich source of vitamin C, calcium, magnesium, potassium, and iron.

Spray the insert of a slow cooker lightly with olive oil. In a medium-size bowl, lightly beat the eggs. Add the salmon, oats, pineapple, and miso, and ¼ cup (25 g) of the scallion. Mix well to thoroughly combine and form into 6 patties—the patties will be a little wet. Lay the patties in the slow cooker.

Add the wine to the open can of tomatoes and stir gently with a fork to incorporate. Pour the tomatoes over the salmon patties, cover, and cook on low for 2½ to 3½ hours, or until the patties are cooked through (an instant-read meat thermometer should read 160°F [71°C]).

Transfer the patties to 6 plates. Stir the remaining ¼ cup (25 g) scallion and the cilantro into the tomatoes, spoon some of the sauce over each patty, and garnish each serving with a lemon wedge, if using.

YIELD: 6 servings

PER SERVING: Calories 172.7; Calories From Fat 48.9; Total Fat 5.7 g; Cholesterol 128.6 mg; Sodium 470.7 mg; Potassium 489.4 mg; Total Carbohydrates 38 g; Fiber 2.2 g; Sugar 1.1 g; Protein 20.6 g

INGREDIENTS

4 fillets (6 ounces, or 168 g each) tilapia

Salt and freshly ground pepper

4 small cloves garlic, minced

4 small shallots, peeled and thinly sliced

1 tablespoon (15 ml) plus 2 teaspoons (10 ml)
    olive oil, divided

Juice and zest of 2 lemons

1 tablespoon (15 ml) tamari

8 ounces (225 g) shiitake mushrooms, stems
    removed and caps thinly sliced (about
    ⅓ inch [8 mm])

FROM CHEF JEANNETTE

This shiitake presentation comes from the
genius concept of chef and author Myra
Kornfeld (www.myrakornfeld.com). I like to
double the recipe and keep leftovers in the
fridge to add later to salads or sandwiches, or
to top a cup of miso or winter squash soup.

To save time, omit the shiitakes and serve the
tilapia as is—it's still delicious!

ZESTED AND LIGHT LEMON-GARLIC TILAPIA WITH ROASTED SHIITAKES

FROM DR. JONNY: One reason I'm known as "the Rogue Nutritionist"
is that I am comfortable busting many of the biggest misconceptions in
health and nutrition. So I'm going to tell you the truth: when it comes
to fish, tilapia isn't at the very top of the "must-eat" list. Unlike salmon,
for example, it has almost no omega-3s (in fact, it has a vanishingly
low amount of fat of any kind!). But what it does offer is an awful lot
of protein for a very small number of calories. (If you're counting,
roughly 3.5 ounces [98 g] provide a whopping 26-plus grams of protein
for a measly 128 calories. That's a bargain!) It also provides a hefty dose
of selenium, one of the most important cancer-fighting trace minerals,
and one that most of us don't get nearly enough of. Bonus points for the
shallots, which are rich in sulfur compounds that help make your skin
look great, and for the shiitake mushrooms, one of the great medicinal
foods of all time.

Preheat the oven to 375°F (190°C, or gas mark 5).

Lay out two sections of foil on your countertop in a cross shape. Place
the fillets in one layer in the center of each piece of foil and sprinkle to
taste with salt and pepper. Top each fillet evenly with 1 clove minced garlic
and 1 sliced shallot (in a single layer). Drizzle ½ teaspoon olive oil over
each fillet. Squeeze ½ lemon over each fillet and top each with the zest
from ½ lemon. Fold the foil up and over the sides of the fillets and pinch
or crimp the edges together to make a good seal on the packet. Using a large
spatula, carefully place the packet in a dry 6- or 7-quart (5.7 or 6.6 L) slow
cooker. Cover and cook on low for about 2 hours, or until fish is tender
and flakes easily.

While the fish is cooking, in a large bowl, whisk together the remaining
1 tablespoon (15 ml) olive oil and tamari. Add the shiitakes and toss to coat.

Spread the shiitakes out in a single layer on a parchment-lined baking
sheet and roast for about 35 minutes, turning after 15 minutes, until the
mushrooms have browned and are starting to crisp but have not scorched.
Remove them from the oven and set aside.

To serve, carefully remove the fish from the foil and top each fillet with
a generous portion of roasted shiitakes.

YIELD: 4 servings

PER SERVING: Calories 409.6; Calories From Fat 81.4; Total Fat 9.3 g; Cholesterol
85.1 mg; Sodium 351.2 mg; Potassium 1,533.5 mg; Total Carbohydrates 52.3 g;
Fiber 9.2 g; Sugar 1.4 g; Protein 41.3 g

OMEGA-RICH DILLED SALMON DIJON

INGREDIENTS

4 fillets (4 to 6 ounces, or 112 to 168 g each)
skinless wild-caught Alaskan salmon
2 tablespoons (22 g) Dijon mustard
1 ½ teaspoons honey
8 short sprigs fresh dill (or 1 tablespoon
[3 g] dried)
½ sweet onion, thinly sliced into rings

FROM DR. JONNY: I don't remember a lot of Hebrew from my very lax and Reform Jewish upbringing, but I do remember the first question on the first night of the Passover Seder: "Why is this night different from all other nights?" The first syllables of that phrase in Hebrew—*mah nishtana*—have come to be a shorthand in some circles (like my family!) for "So what's so different about this?" I get asked a form of that question about wild salmon—what's so different? And here's the answer: wild salmon, unlike its farmed brethren, actually swim in rivers and eat their natural diet of crustaceans like krill rather than the grain pellets they're fed in salmon pens. The wild kind come by their red color naturally, by ingesting a powerful antioxidant called *astaxanthin*, found in their food. Farmed salmon get their color from a color wheel of artificial shades. And according to the Environmental Working Group, farmed salmon are one of the biggest sources of PCBs in our diet. So we like wild salmon, and, shameless plug for a business in which we have no financial interest, we get it from Vital Choice, a terrific company of third-generation Alaskan fishermen who are all about the environment, sustainable fishing, high-quality product, and careful testing for toxic metals and contaminants. They ship everything right to my door in dry ice, and I love every piece of fish I get from them!

Lay out two sections of foil on your countertop in a cross shape. Place the fillets in one layer in the center of the foil cross. In a small bowl, whisk together the mustard and honey until well incorporated. Spread the top of each fillet with one-fourth of the mustard mixture in an even layer. Lay 2 dill sprigs over the top of each fillet and cover with an even layer of one-fourth of the onion rings. Fold the foil up and over the sides of the fillets and pinch or crimp the edges together to make a good seal on the packet. Using a large spatula, carefully place the packet in a dry, 6- or 7-quart (5.7 or 6.6 L) slow cooker. Cover and cook on low for about 2 hours, or until the fish is tender and flakes easily.

YIELD: 4 servings

PER SERVING: Calories 188; Calories From Fat 67.9; Total Fat 7.6 g; Cholesterol 62.4 mg; Sodium 147.4 mg; Potassium 618.8 mg; Total Carbohydrates 5.8 g; Fiber 0.6 g; Sugar 4.2 g; Protein 23.2 g

Stocks, Sauces, Purées, and Infusions

Stocks, sauces, purees, and infusions made in the slow cooker are like fine wines—aged just to perfection so the flavors can ripen. And nothing beats the slow cooker for infusing liquids with a rich blend of subtle flavors and without the added sodium you find in commercial offerings. You'll never want to make them any other way.

STOCKS
Mushroom Madness Stock

Lean and Clean Gingered Chicken Stock

Bone-Strengthening Beef Stock

Hearty, Rich Roasted Veggie Stock

Freshest Veggie Stock

Flavorful and Nourishing Turkey Stock

Capsaicin-Kickin' Fiery Fish Stock

SAUCES
Lower-Sugar Curried Mango Nectarine Chutney

Low-Cal Herbed Lemon Sauce

Slow-Cooked Two-Tomato and Spicy Turkey Sausage Sauce

Mega Omega Piquant Artichoke, Olive, and Anchovy Sauce

Immune-Boostin', Gut-Bustin', Fiery BBQ Sauce

Happy, Healthier Homemade Ketchup

Memorable Gingered Peach and Blues Sauce

Alkalizing Coconut Lemon Curd

All-Fruit Pear Apple Molasses

PURÉES
Luscious, High-Fiber Raspberry Purée

Potassium Powerhouse: Fresh Pumpkin Purée

INFUSIONS
Fresh Thai Oil Infusion

Heart-Healthy Spiced Citrus Oil Infusion

MUSHROOM MADNESS STOCK

FROM DR. JONNY: Mushrooms, along with garlic and a few other foods, have been used medicinally for thousands of years. And while many people are aware of the health benefits of shiitake mushrooms (more on that in a moment), less well known is the fact that the ordinary, everyday button mushroom (cremini) and its bigger cousin portobello are not exactly nutritional lightweights. A mere ½ cup (35 g) of those common button mushrooms provide more than 50 percent of the Daily Value for the cancer-fighting trace mineral selenium, not to mention double digit percentages of the Daily Value for riboflavin, copper, niacin, pantothenic acid, phosphorus, and zinc. And shiitakes are a great source of a special plant chemical called *beta 1,3 glucan*, which has potent immune-stimulating effects—the beta-glucan basically hooks up with immune system cells and acts as a turbocharger, getting them all stimulated and active so they can do a better job of protecting your body from foreign invaders! This is a great broth to use for soups and stews when your immune system could use a goosing—like during cold and flu season!

INGREDIENTS

1 tablespoon (15 ml) olive oil

2 portobello mushrooms, stems and caps sliced

8 shallots, peeled and halved (reserve skins for stock)

2 carrots, unpeeled and chopped

4 cloves garlic, peeled and crushed (reserve skins for stock)

½ cup (120 ml) dry white wine

2 ounces (56 g) dried shiitake mushrooms (Donko, if possible)

12 ounces (336 g) cremini mushrooms, sliced

2 tablespoons (12 g) fresh marjoram (or 2 teaspoons dried)

1 teaspoon black peppercorns

4 quarts (3.7 L) water

Heat the oil in a large skillet over medium heat. Add the portobellos, shallots, and carrots. Cook for about 6 minutes, stirring occasionally. Add the garlic and cook for 30 seconds. Add the wine and cook for a few minutes longer, until it is reduced by half. Transfer the cooked vegetable mixture to a 6-quart (5.7 L) slow cooker. Add the reserved shallot and garlic skins, dried shiitakes, creminis, marjoram, peppercorns, and water. Cook on low for about 8 hours.

Optional step for more concentrated flavor: Increase the temperature to high, remove the cover, and cook, uncovered, for 30 to 45 minutes longer.

Cool slightly and strain through a double-mesh sieve, discarding the solids. Store the broth in the fridge or in pint-size containers in the freezer for later use (place a layer of microwave-safe plastic wrap on the surface of the cold soup and under the lid before freezing to keep it airtight).

YIELD: 3½ to 4 quarts (3.3 to 3.7 L)
PER SERVING: Calories 114.1; Calories From Fat 20.4; Total Fat 2.3 g; Cholesterol 0 mg; Sodium 44.8 mg; Potassium 553.9 mg; Total Carbohydrates 19.1 g; Fiber 2.6 g; Sugar 2.4 g; Protein 5.6 g

LEAN AND CLEAN GINGERED CHICKEN STOCK

INGREDIENTS

1 large chicken carcass

2 whole chicken legs and thighs

4 carrots, unpeeled and quartered (with greens attached, if possible)

4 ribs celery with leaves, quartered

1 large sweet onion, unpeeled and quartered

$\frac{1}{2}$ medium-size turnip, peeled and halved

6 cloves garlic, unpeeled and crushed

8 quarter-size slices peeled fresh ginger

2 teaspoons orange zest (optional)

$\frac{1}{4}$ teaspoon red pepper flakes

Salt and black pepper, to taste

FROM CHEF JEANNETTE

For a more neutral stock, omit the ginger and substitute your favorite fresh herbs, such as three 6-inch (15 cm) stalks fresh thyme, two 4-inch (10 cm) stalks fresh rosemary, three 5-inch (12.5 cm) stalks fresh dill, or a combination.

FROM DR. JONNY: My grandma Blanche was an acknowledged master when it came to chicken soup. She lived in Brooklyn (with her nine kids, one of whom was my dad) and was of Eastern European peasant stock, and when she decided to make chicken soup you could be sure you were getting the "urtext" version—rich, wholesome, aromatic, and brimming with fresh vegetables. So I have high standards for chicken stock, and this recipe more than lives up to them. It's important, though, that you use quality chicken. Where Grandma Blanche came from, there were no factory feedlot operations like there are now, so chickens came from actual farms, where they ran around and pecked for food (we call that "free-range"). In addition, the chickens had no antibiotics or extra hormones in them, and because they ate their natural diet their meat and eggs were higher in omega-3s. As much as possible, that's the kind of chicken you want to use for this stock, which distills all the wonderful nutrients in chicken right out of the tissues and concentrates them in the broth. Chilling the stock overnight in the fridge allows you to remove most of the fat if you like, resulting in a clear (and lower-calorie) stock. Enjoy!

Combine the carcass, legs and thighs, carrots, celery, onion, turnip, garlic, ginger, zest, if using, and red pepper flakes in a 6- or 7-quart (5.7 or 6.6 L) slow cooker. Cover with water nearly to the top of the cooker insert (leave about $1\frac{1}{2}$ inches [3.8 cm] to prevent overflow). Cover and cook on low for 9 to 10 hours (overnight works well). Add salt and pepper to taste (omit salt for a no-sodium broth).

Let the mixture cool slightly and remove the chicken carcass and legs. Carefully pour the stock through a large, double-mesh sieve into one or two large storage containers to strain out the solids. Discard all the solids, or pull the meat from the legs and thighs to use in a soup. Cover and refrigerate the stock until completely chilled (overnight works well for this). Carefully remove any congealed fat from the surface of the stock and discard.

Store stock in the refrigerator or freeze in pint-size containers for later use (place a layer of microwave-safe plastic wrap on the surface of the cold soup and under the lid before freezing to keep it airtight).

YIELD: $2\frac{1}{2}$ to $3\frac{1}{2}$ quarts (2.4 to 3.3 L)

PER SERVING: Calories 110.4; Calories From Fat 26.6; Total Fat 3 g; Cholesterol 34.9 mg; Sodium 105 mg; Potassium 426.1 mg; Total Carbohydrates 11.6 g; Fiber 2.7 g; Sugar 5.9 g; Protein 9.7 g

BONE-STRENGTHENING BEEF STOCK

INGREDIENTS

4 to 6 high-quality marrow-filled beef bones (about 3 pounds [1,362 g]), preferably not completely stripped of meat

3 carrots, unpeeled and quartered (with greens attached, if possible)

3 ribs celery with leaves, quartered

6 large shallots, unpeeled and halved

1 1/2 tablespoons (23 ml) balsamic vinegar

4 cloves garlic, unpeeled and crushed

3 stalks fresh thyme (or 2 teaspoons dried)

3 stalks fresh oregano (or 2 teaspoons dried)

3 bay leaves

2 teaspoons lemon zest

1 teaspoon dried basil

3/4 teaspoon black peppercorns

FROM CHEF JEANNETTE

For a richer flavor and color to your stock, roast the raw bones on a broiler pan at 400°F (200°C, or gas mark 6) for 30 to 40 minutes until lightly browned before adding to the stock.

FROM DR. JONNY: People often comment on how good my skin looks and ask me how I do it. The obvious answer is that I eat really well and nourish my skin from within. But I have another trick that many people don't know about. My secret weapon—revealed here for the first time, ladies and gentleman!—is a powdered drink mix called "Anti-Aging," which was developed by my colleague, the brilliant naturopathic physician Sally Byrd, N.D. And why, you ask, am I telling you this in the middle of an introduction to a recipe for beef stock? Because the main ingredient in that drink—in fact the only active ingredient—is *collagen*, the exact same ingredient found in this beef stock. Collagen is the major element of skin, as well as bones (hence the eponymous "bone-strengthening"), tendons, and cartilage. In fact, collagen fibers are a big part of the reason your skin stays strong and elastic. When collagen degrades, the result is wrinkles. In this recipe, use the cleanest beef possible for the highest nutritional content—and that means grass-fed whenever possible. Fun fact: The word *collagen* means "glue producer" (*kola* means "glue" in Greek). In early times, glue was made by boiling animal hooves and sinew.

Combine all the ingredients in a 6- or 7-quart (5.7 to 6.6 L) slow cooker. Cover with water nearly to the top of the cooker insert (leave about 1 1/2 inches [3.8 cm] to prevent overflow). Cover and cook on low for 9 to 10 hours (overnight works well). Once it is simmering, occasionally skim off any scum that rises to the surface. Let the mixture cool slightly and line a double-mesh sieve with two layers of moistened cheesecloth. Remove the bones and carefully pour the stock through the lined sieve into one or two large storage containers to strain out and discard the solids.

Optional step: Return the strained stock to the slow cooker and cook, uncovered, on high for 30 minutes to 1 hour to concentrate flavors. Cover and refrigerate the stock until completely chilled (overnight works well). Carefully remove any congealed fat from the surface of the stock and discard.

Store stock in the refrigerator or freeze it in pint-size containers for later use (place a layer of microwave-safe plastic wrap on the surface of the cold soup and under the lid before freezing to keep it airtight).

YIELD: 2 1/2 to 3 1/2 quarts (2.4 to 3.3 L)
PER SERVING: Calories 230.3; Calories From Fat 127.4; Total Fat 13.8 g; Cholesterol 56.6 mg; Sodium 265.3 mg; Potassium 400.9 mg; Total Carbohydrates 9.2 g; Fiber 1.9 g; Sugar 2.7 g; Protein 16.9 g

HEARTY, RICH ROASTED VEGGIE STOCK

INGREDIENTS

4 carrots, unpeeled and quartered (reserve the greens for stock, if possible)

2 sweet onions, peeled, seeded, and quartered (reserve skins for stock)

2 heirloom tomatoes, halved

1 cup (150 g) peeled and chopped butternut squash

1 red bell pepper, cored, seeded, and halved

1 green bell pepper, cored, seeded, and halved

1 large turnip, coarsely chopped

1 head garlic, unpeeled, cloves separated

1 tablespoon (15 ml) olive oil

2 bay leaves

½ teaspoon whole cloves

½ teaspoon black peppercorns

2 cardamom pods

FROM DR. JONNY: You can think of this hearty veggie stock as a multiple vitamin on steroids. Actually, it's even better because multiple vitamins—even the best ones—don't contain cancer-fighting phytochemicals such as lycopene (from the tomatoes) and quercetin (from the onions). The peppers and tomatoes add vitamin C, the turnips provide generous amounts of calcium and potassium (not to mention fiber), and garlic is the ultimate medicinal food, helping to lower blood pressure and the risk of certain cancers. Fun fact: In test tube studies, garlic has been shown to have antibacterial, antiviral, and antifungal activity. And human population studies suggest that regular garlic consumption reduces the risk of esophageal, stomach, and colon cancer. According to Alan Gaby, M.D., a specialist in nutritional medicine, this may be partially because of garlic's ability to reduce the formation of carcinogenic (cancer-causing) compounds.

Preheat the oven to 425°F (220°C, or gas mark 7).

In a large bowl, combine the carrots, onions, tomatoes, squash, bell peppers, turnip, and garlic cloves in a large bowl, drizzle with the olive oil, and toss gently to lightly coat. Lay the veggies out in a single layer in a large roasting pan. Roast for 30 to 45 minutes, turning occasionally, until many of the vegetables have lightly browned.

Transfer the roasted veggies to a 6- or 7-quart (5.7 to 6.6 L) slow cooker and cover with water to about 2 inches (5 cm) from the top of the insert. Stir in the reserved carrot greens, reserved onion skins, bay leaves, cloves, peppercorns, and cardamom pods. Cover and cook on low for 8 to 9 hours. Stir well, cool slightly, and strain the mixture through a colander into one or two large storage containers. It will be a little thick; use it as is or thin with a little water. Reserve the veggies for another use or discard.

Store the broth in the fridge or in pint-size containers in the freezer for later use (place a layer of microwave-safe plastic wrap on the surface of the cold soup and under the lid before freezing to keep it airtight).

YIELD: 4 to 5 quarts (3.8 to 4.7 L)

PER SERVING: Calories 144.7; Calories From Fat 27.6; Total Fat 3.2 g; Cholesterol 0 mg; Sodium 68.3 mg; Potassium 621.7 mg; Total Carbohydrates 29 g; Fiber 7.3 g; Sugar 11.4 g; Protein 3 g

FRESHEST VEGGIE STOCK

INGREDIENTS

4 ribs celery with leaves, quartered

4 carrots, unpeeled and quartered (with greens, if possible)

3 parsnips, unpeeled and quartered

1 large yellow onion, unpeeled and quartered

1 large leek, well rinsed and coarsely chopped

2 portobello mushrooms, including stems (use 6 or 8 cremini mushrooms if you prefer a lighter-colored broth)

1 small zucchini, coarsely chopped

2 cabbage leaves (optional)

1 bunch Italian parsley, thicker stems removed

4 cloves garlic, unpeeled and crushed

2 star anise (optional)

$\frac{1}{2}$ teaspoon green peppercorns (or $\frac{1}{2}$ teaspoon freshly ground pepper)

FROM CHEF JEANNETTE

An easy and economical way to make vegetable stock is to hang on to all the peels, cores, and ends of your vegetables from the week and use them over the weekend to make stock. Just keep them fresh in a container in the refrigerator. Different herbs and veggies lend different qualities to your stocks. Many peels, such as onion skins, tend to darken the color. You can also sweat chopped veggies in a skillet on the stove for 5 to 10 minutes before adding to the slow cooker to further concentrate their flavors.

FROM DR. JONNY: Whenever nutritionists talk about detox diets, they'll often mention the low-tech version, which works just fine: eat clean. That can mean eating raw foods for a week, going off sugar and caffeine for a week, or consuming the standard "juice and broth" program with steamed vegetables and high-quality protein. Why broth? Because it's a highly concentrated form of nutrients, distilling everything wonderful from the vegetables into a nice rich liquid, perfect for providing your liver with everything it needs to do its natural job of detoxifying the body. Homemade stock is the best. It's fresher tasting, it doesn't have added sodium, and you control the quality of the ingredients. The slow cooker is absolutely the best tool ever for making perfect stock because all you do is prep it and leave it. Note: We leave the skins on all the veggies because of their concentration of nutrients, but the skins are also where pesticides and chemicals tend to accumulate, so we strongly recommend you use organic veggies for this recipe. Or at the very least, wash them in a high-quality vegetable wash.

Combine all the ingredients in a 6-quart (5.7 L) slow cooker and cover with water to about 2 inches (5 cm) from the top of the insert. Cover and cook on low for 9 to 10 hours (or overnight). Cool slightly and strain the mixture through a double-mesh sieve into one or two large storage containers. Reserve the veggies for another use or discard. Store in the fridge or in pint-size containers in the freezer for later use (place a layer of microwave-safe plastic wrap on the surface of the cold soup and under the lid before freezing to keep it airtight).

YIELD: 3 to 4 quarts (2.8 to 3.7 L)
PER SERVING: Calories 143.4; Calories From Fat 6.3; Total Fat 0.8 g; Cholesterol 0 mg; Sodium 74.3 mg; Potassium 844.2 mg; Total Carbohydrates 33.6 g; Fiber 8.9 g; Sugar 10.4 g; Protein 3.2 g

FLAVORFUL AND NOURISHING TURKEY STOCK

INGREDIENTS

1 turkey carcass with leftover skin and cartilage

3 large ribs celery, halved

2 large carrots, unpeeled and chopped

2 sweet onions, unpeeled and quartered

2 bay leaves

1 cinnamon stick

4 whole cloves

1 teaspoon black peppercorns

2 tablespoons (30 ml) mirin (or sherry)

FROM DR. JONNY: Reading through these recipes for stock and broths reminded me of just what an untapped nutritional resource homemade stock can be. After all, think about it. You throw nothing but terrific veggies into a pot, add some protein (like turkey), and let the ingredients simmer in water, creating a rich mixture of vitamins, minerals, and phytochemicals. You can sip it all day (a great idea, actually) or use it as a base for all kinds of tasty dishes. The point to remember is that stock, when it's homemade like this with fine ingredients, is really a health food. In this case, it contains beta-carotene and vitamin A from the carrots, sulfur compounds and quercetin from the onions, and some interesting compounds in celery called *phthalides*, which help relax the muscle tissue in artery walls and thus increase blood flow. Any way you choose to use it, this stock is great for you!

Strip away as much of the remaining meat from the bones if you can, reserving it for your soup later, if desired. Break the carcass bones into large pieces and place in a 6- or 7-quart (5.7 or 6.6 L) slow cooker with the skin and cartilage. Add the celery, carrots, onions, bay leaves, cinnamon, cloves, and peppercorns and cover with cold water to within 2 inches (5 cm) of the rim of the cooker (starting with cold water will help to extract more of the collagen). Cover and cook on low for 8 to 10 hours, periodically skimming any "scum" that rises to the surface. Add the mirin during the last hour of cooking time.

Optional step for more concentrated flavor: Increase the temperature to high, remove the cover, and cook, uncovered, for 30 to 45 minutes longer.

Cool slightly and strain the stock through a fine-mesh sieve into one or two large storage containers, discarding all solid materials. Refrigerate overnight, then skim off any fat solids from the surface.

Store the broth in the fridge or in pint-size containers in the freezer for later use (place a layer of microwave-safe plastic wrap on the surface of the cold soup and under the lid before freezing to keep it airtight).

YIELD: 2 to 3 quarts (1.9 to 2.8 L)

PER SERVING: Calories 87.2; Calories From Fat 21.6; Total Fat 4.3 g; Cholesterol 13.1 mg; Sodium 87.1 mg; Potassium 273.7 mg; Total Carbohydrates 14.6 g; Fiber 3.2 g; Sugar 7.7 g; Protein 3.2 g

CAPSAICIN-KICKIN' FIERY FISH STOCK

INGREDIENTS

Heads, tails, and bones from 4 white fish, or
    8 fish heads, or 4 pounds (1.8 kg) fish bones
    (or substitute 2 pounds [908 g] shrimp or
    lobster shells for 2 of the fish)

2 ribs celery, quartered

2 yellow onions, unpeeled and quartered

5 dried Thai chile peppers

5 dried red chile peppers

2 cloves garlic, crushed

4 quarts (3.7 L) pure water

Juice of 1 lemon

FROM DR. JONNY: This slightly smoky, spicy fish base is just perfect for a fish stew or a Thai fish soup. All you do is add seafood, leafy greens, and other veggies, and voilà! Restaurant-quality main dish! But the real beauty here is that you totally get to control the quality of the ingredients. No mystery fish, no canned garlic, no unpronounceable ingredients, nada. Celery and onions blend beautifully together in terms of both visuals and texture. Celery is a good source of vitamin K, while onions are wonderfully anti-inflammatory because of their concentration of quercetin. Onions also contain all sorts of sulfur compounds that make your skin feel and look wonderful. And you know that hot spicy taste that comes from the peppers? It's because of a wonderful pain-relieving, metabolism-stimulating ingredient called *capsaicin*. Note: Don't tell Chef Jeannette, but I think you could easily throw in a handful of spinach or kale to this recipe without harming the delicate flavor in the slightest—and adding even more nutritional benefits (such as calcium, magnesium, potassium, and cancer-fighting indoles).

Pulverize the bones or shells with a meat hammer or pulse them in the food processor—this will help them release their juices. Combine all the ingredients in a 6- or 7-quart (5.7 or 6.6 L) slow cooker, cover, and cook on low for 8 to 10 hours. Strain out and discard all the solids. Refrigerate the stock until well chilled (5 hours to overnight) and remove any foam or fat that's risen to the surface.

Store the broth in the fridge or in pint-size containers in the freezer for later use (place a layer of microwave-safe plastic wrap on the surface of the cold soup and under the lid before freezing to keep it airtight).

YIELD: 4 quarts (3.7 L)
PER SERVING: Calories 47.4; Calories From Fat 3.1; Total Fat 0.4 g; Cholesterol 0 mg; Sodium 35.7 mg; Potassium 326.3 mg; Total Carbohydrates 10.8 g; Fiber 1.9 g; Sugar 5.6 g; Protein 1.9 g

LOWER-SUGAR CURRIED MANGO NECTARINE CHUTNEY

INGREDIENTS

2 ripe mangoes, peeled, pitted, and chopped

2 large, firm nectarines, unpeeled, pitted, and chopped

1 large Vidalia onion, chopped

¼ cup (36 g) golden raisins

½ cup (120 ml) apple cider vinegar

½ cup (120 g) Sucanat

1 tablespoon (8 g) finely grated fresh ginger

1 cinnamon stick

1 teaspoon ground turmeric

1 teaspoon ground coriander

1 teaspoon ground cumin

½ teaspoon mustard seeds

½ teaspoon red pepper flakes

½ teaspoon salt

FROM CHEF JEANNETTE

Serving Suggestions: This chutney makes an excellent accompaniment to grilled chicken or fish dishes. Or try mixing a few teaspoons into cold chopped chicken or salmon for an instant Indian salad or wrap. It's also nice served cold with sharp cheeses.

FROM DR. JONNY: How can the four words "curried mango nectarine chutney" not make your mouth water? I can see no possible way. These are three of my favorite tastes that go together so perfectly you'd think nature grew them this way, complete with the curry seasoning. If you haven't read my many raves on the subject of curry before, let me repeat the main point: curry is yellow because of an almost miraculous spice called turmeric, which has been shown to have anticancer activity, be an incredible tonic for the liver, and act as a powerful anti-inflammatory (in some cases working as well as over-the-counter pain relievers). So we love turmeric, which means we love curry, and which, I guarantee you, means you will love the artful way Chef Jeannette threw this chutney together, combining the distinct curry taste with a fruity richness from the hydrating, sweet fruits. And for those who are counting, ours is much lower in sugar than most commercially prepared chutneys. Bonus points for the nice bite courtesy of the mustard seeds and red pepper flakes!

Combine all the ingredients in a slow cooker and stir well to combine. Cover and cook for 3 to 4 hours on high or 5 to 6 hours on low, or to the desired texture. To speed thickening, remove the lid and increase the temperature to high for the last 30 minutes of cooking time.

Remove the cinnamon stick, cool completely, and store in clean jars in the refrigerator for up to 3 weeks.

YIELD: about 5 cups (1200 g)

FOR ENTIRE RECIPE: Calories 1,030; Calories From Fat 34.6; Total Fat 4.2 g; Cholesterol 0 mg; Sodium 1,200.8 mg; Potassium 1,982.9 mg; Total Carbohydrates 259.1 g; Fiber 26.2 g; Sugar 204.2 g; Protein 9.5 g

LOW-CAL HERBED LEMON SAUCE

FROM DR. JONNY: Lemons are a great source of vitamin C, which by now you probably know is a powerful antioxidant (not to mention an anti-inflammatory agent), protecting your cells against damage from free radicals. But lemons also have other good things in them—healthy plant chemicals called *limonoids*. One in particular, called *limonene*, has anticancer properties and has been shown in studies to be chemoprotective against breast, liver, lung, and skin cancer. (Limonene is found in the peel, but you can still get some in your diet by throwing a slice of lemon, complete with peel, into your tea!) And the health benefits of garlic are legion. It's antihypertensive and works as an anticoagulant. And studies show a decreased risk of at least two types of cancer in areas where consumption of garlic (and its relatives in the Allium family) is high. Plus, it wards off vampires. (Okay, just testing to see if you were paying attention!) This sauce is rich in tangy, garlicky flavor but very light on calories—enjoy to your heart's content!

INGREDIENTS

4 cups (940 ml) high-quality chicken broth (or use our Lean and Clean Gingered Chicken Stock)

1 cup (235 ml) freshly squeezed lemon juice

4 cloves garlic, minced

1 teaspoon dried oregano

1 teaspoon dried basil

2 teaspoons unsalted butter

¼ teaspoon black peppercorns

2 tablespoons (8 g) minced fresh parsley (optional)

2 teaspoons capers, drained

Combine the broth, lemon juice, garlic, oregano, basil, butter, and peppercorns in the slow cooker. Cook on high, uncovered, for 2 to 4 hours, until the sauce reduces by about 1½ cups (353 ml). Remove the peppercorns and stir in the parsley and capers just before serving.

YIELD: 6 to 8 servings

PER SERVING: Calories 39.2; Calories From Fat 15.4; Total Fat 1.7 g; Cholesterol 2.5 mg; Sodium 404.2 mg; Potassium 162.8 mg; Total Carbohydrates 4 g; Fiber 0.4 g; Sugar 1.1 g; Protein 2.7 g

FROM CHEF JEANNETTE

Serving Suggestions: This thin, flavorful sauce will enliven all sorts of plain foods. Try stirring it into mashed potatoes, tossing it with green beans or roasted asparagus, and pouring it over grilled chicken or almost any kind of fish.

SLOW-COOKED TWO-TOMATO AND SPICY TURKEY SAUSAGE SAUCE

FROM DR. JONNY: If you're new to the pleasures of slow cooking, you'll be a convert after you make this sauce. The slow cooking brings out the subtle flavors in a way no other kind of cooking can, and even has some salutatory health benefits—for example, increasing the availability of lycopene, an important plant chemical that has been linked to a lower risk of prostate cancer. But the real flavor breakthrough comes from the turkey sausage. The better organic turkey sausages are way lower in calories than traditional sausage and the ingredients tend to be "cleaner" than with commercial pork sausage. The ½ cup (55 g) sun-dried tomatoes adds a nice 3.5 grams of fiber and a surprising 4 grams of protein. Plus, the artist in me loves how the color of the tomatoes subtly blends with the colors of the red peppers and carrots! A nutritionist might call it "a regular carotenoid festival!"

INGREDIENTS

½ cup (55 g) sun-dried tomato strips in olive oil, drained, oil reserved

2 yellow onions, chopped

2 ribs celery, finely chopped

1 cup (110 g) grated carrot

1 red bell pepper, cored, seeded, and finely chopped

4 cloves garlic, minced

4 links (4 ounces, or 112 g each) spicy Italian turkey sausage, chopped or skinned and crumbled

2 cans (28 ounces, or 784 g each) crushed tomatoes

1 teaspoon dried oregano

¾ teaspoon Sucanat

¾ teaspoon salt

½ teaspoon cracked black pepper

½ teaspoon dried thyme

½ teaspoon ground fennel

Heat 1½ tablespoons (23 ml) of the reserved olive oil from the sun-dried tomatoes in a large skillet over medium heat. Add the onions, celery, carrot, and bell pepper and cook for 6 to 8 minutes, until the onions are softened but not browned. Add the garlic and cook for 30 seconds.

Transfer the mixture to the slow cooker and add the sun-dried tomatoes, sausage, crushed tomatoes, oregano, Sucanat, salt, pepper, thyme, and fennel and stir gently to combine. Cook on low for 6 to 8 hours to the desired consistency. To thicken the sauce, remove the lid, increase the temperature to high, and cook for 30 minutes longer.

YIELD: 6 to 8 servings

PER SERVING: Calories 132.3; Calories From Fat 35.4; Total Fat 4.1 g; Cholesterol 22.4 mg; Sodium 853.2 mg; Potassium 748.2 mg; Total Carbohydrates 21.9 g; Fiber 4.1 g; Sugar 10.8 g; Protein 5.3 g

FROM CHEF JEANNETTE

Serving Suggestions: This sauce is great over traditional whole-grain pasta, or, for a low-carb option, serve over zucchini "noodles": thinly slice 4 to 6 zucchinis lengthwise using a vegetable peeler or mandoline and sauté in a little olive oil until just tender.

MEGA OMEGA PIQUANT ARTICHOKE, OLIVE, AND ANCHOVY SAUCE

INGREDIENTS

1 tablespoon (15 ml) olive oil

1 large yellow onion, finely chopped

1 jar or can (12 or 14 ounces, 336 or 392 g) artichoke hearts in water, drained and chopped

4 cloves garlic, minced

1 can (28 ounces, or 784 g) crushed tomatoes

4 anchovy fillets, minced

⅓ cup (33 g) pitted and sliced black olives

1 tablespoon (8.6 g) capers, drained

1 teaspoon dried thyme

½ teaspoon each salt and cracked black pepper

FROM CHEF JEANNETTE

Serving Suggestions: This sauce is great over grilled white fish for a Mediterranean main dish, tossed with whole-grain pasta (we like Barilla Plus), or over baked chicken.

FROM DR. JONNY: This pungent sauce has "Greek" written all over it. Or at least it does to me. We all know anchovies from the local pizzeria, but this lowly little fish delivers a knockout nutritional punch. One 3-ounce (84 g) portion delivers an incredible 24.5 grams of protein and more than 1,600 mg of combined EPA and DHA, the critically important omega-3 fats found in fish and fish oil. Black olives are a rich source of important polyphenols, plant chemicals with multiple health benefits, including the ability to help fight certain pathogens. And they're loaded with heart-healthy monounsaturated fat. Add some liver-cleansing artichokes—rich in the plant chemical silymarin, which is enormously supportive to the liver—and you're in business. The tomato base is rich in lycopene, a powerful antioxidant that has also been linked to a reduced risk of prostate cancer. I love this tangy sauce! So will you.

Heat the oil in a large skillet over medium heat. Add the onion and artichokes and cook for 6 to 7 minutes, or until the onion is tender. Add the garlic and cook for 1 minute.

Transfer the mixture to a slow cooker. Add the tomatoes, anchovies, olives, capers, thyme, salt, and pepper and stir gently to combine. Cook on high for 3 to 4 hours, or on low for 7 to 8 hours.

YIELD: 4 to 6 servings

PER SERVING: Calories 117.3; Calories From Fat 33.1; Total Fat 3.8 g; Cholesterol 2.3 mg; Sodium 628.9 mg; Potassium 646 mg; Total Carbohydrates 19.3 g; Fiber 6.4 g; Sugar 0.9 g; Protein 5.4 g

IMMUNE-BOOSTIN', GUT-BUSTIN', FIERY BBQ SAUCE

INGREDIENTS

1 tablespoon (15 g) coconut oil

1 large yellow onion, finely diced

6 cloves garlic, minced

1 or 2 habanero peppers, seeded and minced, to taste

1/2 cup (120 ml) malt vinegar (or raw apple cider vinegar)

1/2 cup (120 ml) freshly squeezed lime juice

1/2 cup (120 ml) water or vegetable broth

1 can (6 ounces, or 168 g) tomato paste

3 tablespoons (45 ml) dark rum

1 tablespoon (11 g) Dijon mustard

1 tablespoon (15 ml) Worcestershire sauce (use organic to avoid high-fructose corn syrup)

1/4 cup (60 g) Sucanat

3/4 teaspoon salt

1/2 teaspoon dried thyme

FROM DR. JONNY: Hey, if you think Chef Jeannette is kidding about the title, let me alert you: she's not. This is fiery stuff, largely thanks to the intense flavor and spice of the habanero pepper, one of the strongest species of chile peppers. Chile peppers are themselves a member of the *Capsicum* genus, which means they're filled with *capsaicin*, the painkilling, metabolism-boosting ingredient that makes these peppers so fiery (and so good for you!). The thing about making your own barbecue sauce as opposed to getting it out of a jar is that you can control the ingredients. No artificial ingredients, no added sugar (especially high-fructose corn syrup, which most commercial BBQ sauces are loaded with), and only top-quality, high-flavor fresh ingredients. This sauce, in Chef Jeannette's words, is "kickin'"—use caution. Only the brave need apply!

Heat the oil in a medium-size skillet over medium-high heat. Add the onion and cook for about 4 minutes, until the onion is starting to soften. Add the garlic and cook for 30 seconds. Remove from the heat and transfer the contents to a 1- or 1½-quart (1 or 1.4 L) slow cooker.

Stir in all the remaining ingredients and mix well. Cover and cook on high for 1½ to 2 hours, until the mixture comes to a simmer. Remove the insert from the cooker, stir well, recover, and let sit for about 1 hour. Leave as is for a chunkier sauce or purée with an immersion wand or in a blender or food processor for a smoother sauce.

Transfer to a storage container and keep refrigerated. Will keep for up to 2 weeks.

YIELD: 2½ cups (625 g)

FOR ENTIRE RECIPE: Calories 714.2; Calories From Fat 139.3; Total Fat 16.5 g; Cholesterol 1.2 mg; Sodium 3,687.5 mg; Potassium 2,387.7 mg; Total Carbohydrates 123.5 g; Fiber 11.8 g; Sugar 77.6 g; Protein 12.8 g

HAPPY, HEALTHIER HOMEMADE KETCHUP

INGREDIENTS

10 pounds (4.5 kg) ripe red heirloom tomatoes, chopped

1 large sweet onion, chopped

1 cup (235 ml) apple cider vinegar

²/₃ cup (160 g) Sucanat

2 tablespoons (40 g) blackstrap molasses (or replace with 2 tablespoons [30 g] additional Sucanat for redder ketchup because molasses darkens the color)

1 tablespoon (18 g) high-quality salt, such as Himalayan pink

1 teaspoon baking soda

1 teaspoon ground mustard

1 teaspoon ground cinnamon

1 teaspoon ground allspice

¹/₂ teaspoon cayenne pepper

¹/₂ teaspoon black pepper

¹/₂ teaspoon ground nutmeg

¹/₄ teaspoon ground cloves

FROM DR. JONNY: I remember the days when ketchup was considered a vegetable, one of the most consumed "vegetables" in the American diet. Pretty sad, especially since the only ketchup most of us knew was a heavily seasoned mix containing a few tomatoes and a lot of sugar, salt, and food coloring. But tomatoes, the basic stock of ketchup, are great vegetables. Chef Jeannette has created a ketchup that will make you forget about that gelatinous paste that gets stuck in the bottle and passes for seasoning. Using rich, low-acid heirloom tomatoes in the slow cooker allows all the terrific nutrients, like the powerful antioxidant lycopene, to be retained, not to mention the rich, complex flavors so often missing in the tasteless, uniform, pale tomatoes that line the grocery store shelves. And because the flavor is so naturally rich we can use a lot less sugar and salt in the recipe. We sweeten with the granddaddy of nutritious natural sweeteners, iron-rich molasses, rather than high-fructose corn syrup (a staple ingredient in commercial ketchups). Even your kids will think this ketchup tastes sensational. You *certainly* will.

Combine the tomatoes and onion in a slow cooker and cook on high for about 2 hours, or until all the veggies are soft. Remove the insert from the slow cooker, cool slightly, and pour the cooked veggies into a large, double-mesh sieve to strain out the solids. Press and mash the mixture through the sieve to extract as much juice and pulp as possible. Discard the remaining solids and return the strained pulpy sauce to the insert.

Replace the insert in the slow cooker and stir in all the remaining ingredients. Cook the mixture, uncovered, on high for 2 to 4 hours, or until the desired thickness. Stir a couple of times per hour. Cool and pour into clean or sterilized jars to store in the refrigerator for up to 1 month.

YIELD: 4 to 6 cups (960 to 1,440 g)

FOR ENTIRE RECIPE: Calories 1,575; Calories From Fat 88.18; Total Fat 40.5 g; Cholesterol 0 mg; Sodium 8,588 mg; Potassium 12,395.4 mg; Total Carbohydrates 363.3 g; Fiber 60.3 g; Sugar 265.4 g; Protein 43.3 g

MEMORABLE GINGERED PEACH AND BLUES SAUCE

INGREDIENTS

4 medium fresh, ripe peaches, peeled, pitted, and chopped

8 ounces (225 g) fresh blueberries

¼ cup (60 ml) pear nectar (or apple juice concentrate or water)

2 teaspoons ginger juice

¾ teaspoon dried ginger

2 tablespoons (30 g) minute tapioca

FROM CHEF JEANNETTE

Use prepared ginger juice, run fresh ginger through a juicer, or simply grate a large handful of shavings and squeeze.

Serving Suggestions: This fruity sauce is great in the morning over pancakes or French toast, mixed into cottage cheese for a tasty snack, or served over low-sugar vanilla ice cream or Rice Dream for dessert.

FROM DR. JONNY: So I was thinking to myself, what's the one food that I really do eat on a daily basis that I couldn't imagine living without? I didn't have to look far for the answer: blueberries. I have at least one bowl of frozen blueberries right out of the freezer sprinkled with coconut flakes and tamari almonds and covered with almond milk every single day. It's my ultimate treat, and I love it more than even ice cream. Blueberries are a true "memory" food. Animal studies have demonstrated that daily consumption of blueberries dramatically slows impairments in motor coordination and memory. And they have one of the highest "ORAC" scores of all time, meaning they score high on a standardized test for antioxidant power. This peachy-blue sauce is all fruit, with no added sweeteners. It doesn't need them! Enjoy!

Combine all the ingredients in a slow cooker and stir gently until well mixed. Cook, uncovered, on low for 4 to 5 hours, stirring occasionally, until the sauce reaches the desired consistency.

YIELD: 3 to 4 cups (720 to 960 g)

PER SERVING: Calories 474.9; Calories From Fat 16.6; Total Fat 2 g; Cholesterol 0 mg; Sodium 21.5 mg; Potassium 1,283.7 mg; Total Carbohydrates 117.8 g; Fiber 11.7 g; Sugar 83.5 g; Protein 5.8 g

INGREDIENTS

½ cup (120 g) unrefined coconut oil

Juice and zest of 4 lemons

½ cup (120 g) erythritol

½ cup (120 g) Sucanat (or replace with erythritol for brighter lemon color)

4 eggs, beaten

FROM CHEF JEANNETTE

To sterilize, run the jars and lids through the hottest cycle of your dishwasher, or submerge in a pot of boiling water for at least 2 minutes and allow to air-dry.

Serving Suggestions: Lemon curd is wonderful on light, whole-grain toast with a little butter; stirred into yogurt, cottage cheese, or fresh ricotta cheese; or drizzled over berries.

ALKALIZING COCONUT LEMON CURD

FROM DR. JONNY: Though considered an "acid" fruit, lemons actually have the exact opposite effect on the body, acting more like an alkalizing agent. Because our standard diet tends to be pretty acidic, we can use all the help we can get to reach a more balanced state, and lemons do the job nicely. (One of the countless reasons why vegetables and fruits are so good for you is that virtually all of them are highly alkalizing to the body.) As far as the other ingredients go, well, I've been raving about coconut oil since I wrote *The 150 Healthiest Foods on Earth*. It hits the trifecta for cooking oils: tastes terrific, stands up well to heat, and is good for you. (We particularly like the Barlean's brand of coconut oil, which is widely available and of superb quality.) Coconut oil contains particular fatty acids (like lauric acid) that are antimicrobial, thus supporting the immune system. The fat in coconut oil is a kind of fat known as medium-chain triglycerides, or MCTs, which the body prefers to use for energy rather than turning it into a spare tire. Just for good measure we reduced the sugar to about half that in a classic curd. You'll love this!

In a small pan over low heat, melt the coconut oil. Remove from the heat and whisk in the lemon juice, zest, erythritol, and Sucanat, and allow the mixture to cool. Whisk in the eggs until well combined and pour into a small, shallow casserole dish with a lid (or make one out of aluminum foil). Cover and place the casserole in a 6- or 7-quart (5.7 or 6.6 L) slow cooker and add water to come halfway up the sides of the casserole.

Cover the slow cooker and cook on low for 4 to 4½ hours, whisking very well once at about 2 hours. Unplug the slow cooker and remove the covers to cool enough to remove the casserole dish from the hot water. Whisk well, cool completely, and store in sterilized jars in the fridge for up to 4 weeks.

YIELD: about 3 cups (960 g)

FOR ENTIRE RECIPE: Calories 1,644.7; Calories From Fat 1,118.7; Total Fat 128.9 g; Cholesterol 846 mg; Sodium 282.4 mg; Potassium 561.3 mg; Total Carbohydrates 118 g; Fiber 1 g; Sugar 103.2 g; Protein 26.1

ALL-FRUIT PEAR APPLE MOLASSES

INGREDIENTS

1 pound (454 g) ripe pears

3 pounds (1.4 kg) ripe apples

FROM DR. JONNY: Want a healthier, more flavorful substitute for those crummy, sugar-laden "pancake syrups" lining the supermarket aisles? Look no further. Use this rich, fruity, sweet, concentrated "molasses" sparingly because it's so concentrated—a dab of it is absolutely incredible on pancakes. Or peanut butter sandwiches. Or as a sweetener in baked goods when the recipe calls for syrup. In my bachelor days in Manhattan I used to do a "low-tech" version of this by mashing up apples and warming them in a skillet, then spooning the "butter" onto whole-grain French toast. This version's even better. And it's a great way to get the multiple benefits of apples and pears—with their myriad anti-inflammatory, antioxidant plant compounds and fiber—into your diet. Try making this at the height of fall so that you get fruit with peak nutrition and flavor.

Cut the whole, unpeeled fruit into pieces to fit into a juicer. Run them through the juicer to extract the juice. Pour the juice into the slow cooker and heat on high, uncovered, for 2 to 4 hours, stirring occasionally, until most of the watery liquid has evaporated and you are left with a thick syrup. Watch closely starting at 2 hours to make sure that it doesn't dry out too much and make pear apple brown sugar!

YIELD: about 1 cup (320 g)

FOR ENTIRE RECIPE: Calories 970.7; Calories From Fat 23.9; Total Fat 2.9 g; Cholesterol 0 mg; Sodium 18.1 mg; Potassium 1,995.8 mg; Total Carbohydrates 258.1 g; Fiber 46.7 g; Sugar 185.8 g; Protein 5.3 g

LUSCIOUS, HIGH-FIBER RASPBERRY PURÉE

FROM DR. JONNY: Raspberries are one of my favorite foods, and they're also the food I use to make a point about net carbs. (Those of you who read Fran McCullough's *Living Low-Carb* know that net carbs are the carbs in food that remain after you subtract the fiber, which has zero effect on blood sugar. In the case of raspberries, there are about 15 grams of carbs in a cup, but 8 of them are fiber, so 1 cup [125 g] of raspberries is basically a low-carb treat containing only 7 grams of net carbs—the ones that can actually have an impact on your blood sugar.) And just for the record, raspberries are one of the best sources in the world of a plant chemical called *ellagic acid*, which, according to the American Cancer Society, is a very promising natural compound because it causes apoptosis (cell death) of cancer cells in the lab. In this purée, the flavor of tart berries is nicely rounded off by the taste of the red wine. (And don't worry about the alcohol content—it evaporates.)

INGREDIENTS

1 pound (454 g) fresh, ripe raspberries

3 tablespoons (45 ml) dry red wine

3 to 4 tablespoons (45 to 60 g) Sucanat, to taste

Combine the raspberries, wine, and Sucanat in the slow cooker. Stir well to combine and smash them gently with a potato masher or the bottom of a wide glass. Cook, uncovered, on low for 4 to 5 hours, or until the desired consistency.

YIELD: about 3 cups (720 g)

FOR ENTIRE RECIPE: Calories 407.9; Calories From Fat 24.5; Total Fat 3 g; Cholesterol 0 mg; Sodium 6.3 mg; Potassium 740.2 mg; Total Carbohydrates 91.3 g; Fiber 29.5 g; Sugar 56.3 g; Protein 5.5 g

FROM CHEF JEANNETTE

If your berries are tart, add more sweetener; if they are sweeter, add less. Because we are cooking such a delicate fruit over time in the slow cooker, there is no need to actually purée this purée: the berries become so tender that they fall apart when you stir them at the end.

Serving Suggestions: This seedy, high-fiber purée is delicious served over waffles, pancakes, Greek yogurt, or roasted chicken, or spooned into roasted or puréed butternut squash.

POTASSIUM POWERHOUSE: FRESH PUMPKIN PURÉE

INGREDIENTS

3- to 4-pound (1.4 to 1.8 kg) sugar pumpkin
¼ cup (60 ml) water, chicken or vegetable
    broth, or apple cider

FROM DR. JONNY: Here's a *Jeopardy!* question for you: is pumpkin a fruit or a vegetable? If you're not sure, you're not alone. Botanists classify it as a fruit because it has seeds, but culinarians define it as a vegetable. Regardless, pumpkin is one of the unsung heroes of the plant community. It has considerably more potassium than a banana, and here's why that matters: several large epidemiological studies suggest that increased potassium intake is associated with decreased risk of stroke. And four other studies have reported significant positive associations between dietary potassium intake and bone mineral density. Potassium is also one of the best nutrients for heart health. But it's not just potassium that makes pumpkin such a winner—it's also the fact that a mere cup (245 g) of the stuff provides more than 5,000 mcg of beta-carotene and more than 3,500 mcg of beta-cryptoxanthin, a member of the carotenoid family that lowers the risk of lung and colon cancer. This is a simple purée, easy to make, inexpensive, and delicious. Cook a couple of pumpkins this way in October when they are cheap and plentiful—extras last a long time in the freezer! Note: Feel free to use canned pumpkin, though you may find fresh is better for the ultimate in flavor.

FROM CHEF JEANNETTE

Use water if you want to keep the flavor neutral; use broth for savory dishes; and use cider for pies, puddings, or other sweet treats.

Very occasionally a sugar pumpkin will be watery. Usually it is drier and fleshier than traditional carving pumpkins, but if you get a "juicy" one, simply drain the cooked flesh in a double-mesh sieve for about 20 minutes before mashing or puréeing.

Serving Suggestions: Use this fresh purée in any dish that calls for fresh or canned pumpkin, such as pumpkin pie, pumpkin hummus, or our own Lower-Sugar Raisin-Orange Pumpkin Pie Pudding.

Using a sharp cleaver or heavy chef's knife, remove the stem and slice the pumpkin in half. Scoop out the seeds with a heavy spoon and discard or clean and roast. Using a sharp, heavy chef's knife, cut away the peels and discard. Cut the flesh into large chunks, place in the slow cooker, and pour the liquid into the bottom. Cook on low for 5 to 7 hours, or until soft.

    Mash with a potato masher or purée with an immersion blender, cool, and it's ready for use. Store in the fridge or cool completely in the fridge, seal in an airtight, freezer-safe container, and store in the freezer.

YIELD: 2 to 3 cups (490 to 735 g)
PER SERVING: Calories 353.8; Calories From Fat 11.2; Total Fat 1.4 g; Cholesterol 0 mg; Sodium 15.4 mg; Potassium 4,627.3 mg; Total Carbohydrates 88.5 g; Fiber 6.8 g; Sugar 18.5 g; Protein 13.6 g

FRESH THAI OIL INFUSION

FROM DR. JONNY: Working with Chef Jeannette over the years, I've discovered a basic truth about mastery and it's this: the best masters reinvent their tools. In this case, the "tool" is plain old cooking oil. Rather than use the same old out-of-the-bottle stuff, Chef Jeannette created the cooking oil version of a "mix tape." Starting with equal amounts peanut and sesame oil—both excellent for their ability to withstand high temperatures and being eminently suited for stir-fries—she then infused the oil mix with a fabulous amalgamation of flavors, textures, and aromas. The fresh scent and taste of lemongrass permeates the oil, which is also enriched with chile peppers, garlic, and ginger. Fun fact: The active ingredient in chile peppers that makes them so tongue-burning hot is a chemical called *capsaicin*. At least one study (published in *Cancer Research*) found that capsaicin causes cancer cells to commit suicide. "Capsaicin inhibits the growth of human prostate cells in Petri dishes and mice," said lead researcher H. Phillip Koeffler, M.D., director of hematology and oncology at Cedars-Sinai Medical Center.

INGREDIENTS

1 cup (235 ml) peanut oil

1 cup (235 ml) sesame oil

1 stalk lemongrass, coarsely chopped

½ sweet onion, coarsely chopped

1 or 2 dried Thai chile peppers, to taste

8 quarter-size slices peeled fresh ginger

6 cloves garlic, crushed

¾ teaspoon coriander seeds

¼ teaspoon cumin seeds

Combine all the ingredients in a 1-, 1½-, or 2-quart (1, 1.4, or 1.9 L) slow cooker. Cook on low for 1 to 2 hours, or to the desired strength (cool a teaspoon of oil carefully before tasting). Remove the insert from the cooker and allow to cool to room temperature. Slowly pour the oil through a paper coffee filter into a sterilized jar to strain out all solids. Seal the jar and keep refrigerated for up to 1 month.

YIELD: 2 cups (470 ml)

FOR ENTIRE RECIPE: Calories 3,942.6; Calories From Fat 3,843.3; Total Fat 434.8 g; Cholesterol 0 mg; Sodium 22.1 mg; Potassium 452.1 mg; Total Carbohydrates 23.9 g; Fiber 3.2 g; Sugar 10.9 g; Protein 3.6 g

FROM CHEF JEANNETTE

When making oil infusions, use sterilized jars to prevent any bacterial growth. To sterilize, run the jars and lids through the hottest cycle of your dishwasher, or submerge in a pot of boiling water for at least 2 minutes and allow to air-dry. To strain, place the coffee filter into a sterile funnel.

Serving Suggestions: The slow cooker is an ideal tool for making herbal infusions because it keeps the temperature low and steady. Try this oil sprinkled on cooked brown rice or veggies. Or use it to cook Thai stir-fries or lean beef or chicken strips and veggies. Thai cuisine relies on a balance of heat, sweet, sour, and salty flavors, so add pinches of salt (or a dash of fish sauce) and Sucanat (or a little sliced tropical fruit, such as mango) to your dish to round out the flavors.

INGREDIENTS

2 cups (470 ml) almond oil

6 quarter-size slices peeled fresh ginger

Zest of ½ lemon

Zest of ½ orange

15 whole allspice berries

6 whole cloves

6 cardamom pods

2 (4-inch, or 10-cm) cinnamon sticks

FROM CHEF JEANNETTE

When making oil infusions, use sterilized jars to prevent any bacterial growth. To sterilize, run the jars and lids through the hottest cycle of your dishwasher, or submerge in a pot of boiling water for at least 2 minutes and allow to air-dry.

Serving Suggestions: The slow cooker is perfect for making herbal infusions because it keeps the temperature low and constant. Try using this oil to sauté different vegetables, such as matchstick carrots, broccoli florets, or sliced sweet onions. It also makes an interesting base oil for salad dressing.

HEART-HEALTHY SPICED CITRUS OIL INFUSION

FROM DR. JONNY: What do you get when you take one of the healthiest oils on the planet and cross it with an interesting mix of citrus flavors, spices, and cinnamon? Give up? Well, it's a supercharged almond oil, infused with so much richness and flavor that you'll find you need far less salt, sweetener, and additional fat to bring out the flavor of your dish. Almond oil, the basis for this recipe, is extremely high in heart-healthy monounsaturated fat, the same kind found in olive oil and in large amounts in the Mediterranean diet, which is associated with substantially lower rates of heart disease and which some research suggests may be protective against Alzheimer's. Fun fact: Although most people know that ginger is great for an upset stomach, it has historically been used for arthritis and rheumatism.

Combine all the ingredients in a 1-, 1 ½-, or 2-quart (1, 1.4, or 1.9 L) slow cooker. Cover and cook on low for 2 to 3 hours, or to the desired strength (cool a teaspoon of oil carefully before tasting). Remove the insert from the cooker and allow the oil to cool to room temperature. Strain the oil through a double layer of cheesecloth into a sterile glass jar and discard the solids. Seal the jar and store in the refrigerator for up to 1 month.

YIELD: 6 to 7 servings

FOR ENTIRE RECIPE: Calories 4,475.7; Calories From Fat 3,966.1; Total Fat 449.8 g; Cholesterol 0 mg; Sodium 49.3 mg; Potassium 112 mg; Total Carbohydrates 141.8 g; Fiber 65.1 g; Sugar 0.4 g; Protein 1.6 g

Side Dishes

Here's a great mantra for you: "slow cook the rainbow." Choose vegetables rich in color and you'll be sure to get a wide range of antioxidants, vitamins, minerals, and other healthful members of the plant kingdom. The sides in this section are not only flavorful and visually appealing, they're highly nutritious.

LOWER-CAL EASY CHEESY PEPPER CORN

INGREDIENTS

2 pounds (908 g) high-quality frozen corn (preferably organic)

1 red bell pepper, cored, seeded, and finely diced

1 can (4 ounces, or 112 g) chopped green chiles, drained

1 fresh serrano or jalapeño pepper, seeded and finely diced

1/4 cup (60 ml) vegetable broth or water

2 packages (8 ounces, or 225 g each) Neufchâtel cheese, each cut in half

1/2 cup (58 g) shredded sharp Cheddar or Jack cheese

1 teaspoon Sucanat or xylitol

1/2 teaspoon salt

FROM DR. JONNY: I'll be honest with you, cheesy corn isn't a dish that's in heavy rotation on my menu, so I decided to do a little digging and see what the conventional recipes for this American favorite actually look like. Woo-boy. Tons of cream cheese, milk, sugar, and cheese "foods"—not exactly a nutritionist's dream. So how do you get that fabulous taste and still do damage control? Simple. First, we use Neufchâtel cheese instead of the much higher-calorie cream cheese. Second, we dump the sugar and use Sucanat or xylitol, both of which are an improvement over regular sugar. (Sucanat retains its molasses content, making it a healthier option than sugar, and xylitol, a healthy sugar alcohol, has virtually no calories and a negligible impact on blood sugar.) We used vegetable broth or water (you'll never miss the milk), and boosted the nutritional value of the whole shebang by adding peppers and chiles. Capsaicin, the ingredient that makes peppers and chiles so hot, also provides a number of health benefits, such as lowering inflammation (and pain!). This is one cheesy corn you'll never have to feel guilty about enjoying!

Combine the corn, bell pepper, chiles, and serrano pepper in the slow cooker. Pour the broth over all. Place the 4 halves of Neufchâtel cheese on top of the veggies. Sprinkle the grated cheese, Sucanat, and salt evenly over all. Cover and cook on low for 5 to 6 hours, until melted and well incorporated. Stir well and serve.

YIELD: 8 servings

PER SERVING: Calories 289.2; Calories From Fat 146.2; Total Fat 16.7 g; Cholesterol 50.6 mg; Sodium 500.9 mg; Potassium 373.7 mg; Total Carbohydrates 28.1 g; Fiber 3.5 g; Sugar 5.2 g; Protein 11.2 g

SHALLOT APPLE BRUSSELS SPROUTS

INGREDIENTS

1 pound (454 g) brussels sprouts, trimmed

6 shallots, peeled and sliced

¼ cup (60 ml) apple cider

1½ tablespoons (21 g) unsalted butter, melted

2 teaspoons Dijon mustard

½ teaspoon each salt and freshly ground
   pepper

FROM DR. JONNY: Brussels sprouts are members of the cruciferous vegetable family and have many of the same nutritional benefits of other cabbages, namely cancer-fighting nutrients that are so powerful the American Cancer Society recommends consumption of cruciferous vegetables on a regular basis. Brussels sprouts contain a special chemical called *sinigrin*, which actually suppresses the development of precancerous cells. They are also high in a particularly powerful antioxidant called *sulforaphane*, which has the added benefit of helping to neutralize potentially carcinogenic toxins. What's really cool about this dish is the juxtaposition of the sprouts with sweetness from the apple cider and a mild bite from the Dijon. It's like a taste trifecta. Just a bit of butter provides a nice richness to finish it off perfectly.

Combine the brussels sprouts and shallots in a 2-quart (1.9 L) slow cooker. In a small bowl, whisk together the cider, melted butter, mustard, salt, and pepper and pour evenly over the veggies. Stir gently to coat. Cover and cook on high for 2 to 3 hours, or on low for 4 to 5 hours, until the brussels sprouts reach the desired tenderness.

YIELD: 4 to 6 servings

PER SERVING: Calories 78.9; Calories From Fat 28.1; Total Fat 3.2 g; Cholesterol 7.6 mg; Sodium 236.7 mg; Potassium 378.4 mg; Total Carbohydrates 11.6 g; Fiber 3 g; Sugar 1.7 g; Protein 3.2 g

NOT YOUR GRANDMA'S GREEN BEANS

INGREDIENTS

1 pound (454 g) fresh green beans, trimmed

Juice and zest of ½ lemon

2 tablespoons (30 ml) water

2 teaspoons low-sodium tamari

2 cloves garlic, minced

2 anchovy fillets, minced

1 tablespoon (15 ml) olive oil

2 tablespoons (10 g) grated Parmesan cheese

¼ cup (30 g) toasted, chopped walnuts

FROM DR. JONNY: When I was a kid, we called these beans "string beans" because there really was a kind of fibrous string running through the length of the pod seam that had to be removed from each bean before cooking. As you can imagine, this didn't exactly make them a breeze to prepare. But that was then and this is now. Today's green beans have been conveniently bred to be stringless, a boon to cooks every-where. Now, let me be honest—green beans aren't at the top of the list of superstar vegetables. They still have small but decent amounts of a lot of nutrients, including folate, calcium, potassium, manganese, vita-min A, and half the daily requirement of heart-healthy bone-building vitamin K. (They also contain about 4 grams of fiber per cup, nothing to sneeze at!) This recipe is more about the sum of its parts, both nutrition-ally and taste-wise. The Parmesan adds a kick, the walnuts add crunch and monounsaturated fat (the same kind found in olive oil), and the anchovies add protein and omega-3 fats. Sure beats the stuff we used to get out of a can!

Combine green beans, lemon juice and zest, water, tamari, and garlic in a slow cooker and toss to coat. Cover and cook on low for 1½ hours, or until tender.

In a serving bowl, whisk together the anchovy fillets and olive oil. Add the hot beans and Parmesan and toss to coat. Garnish with the walnuts before serving.

YIELD: 4 servings

PER SERVING: Calories 135.2; Calories From Fat 79.1; Total Fat 9.2 g; Cholesterol 3.9 mg; Sodium 236.1 mg; Potassium 309 mg; Total Carbohydrates 11.3 g; Fiber 5 g; Sugar 1.8 g; Protein 5.3 g

FRESH CHILI LIME COB CORN

FROM DR. JONNY: I'll be the first to admit that I have not been a cheerleader for corn. It is the source of some of the unhealthiest things in the American diet, like high-fructose corn syrup, and it's a starchy, high-glycemic vegetable that—along with potatoes—we eat way too much of. That said, real fresh corn right off the cob is a wonderful vegetable, especially if you don't eat a ton of it every day. Each ear has a couple grams of fiber, some potassium and vitamin A, and a nice amount of lutein and zeaxanthin, two important nutrients for the eyes. Plus, who doesn't love corn on the cob at the peak of the season? (Personally, it reminds me of outdoor barbecues and family summer vacations in upstate New York.) The heat and tang of chili lime are the perfect complement to corn's natural sweetness.

INGREDIENTS

4 teaspoons (20 ml) olive oil (or melted unsalted butter)

$\frac{1}{2}$ teaspoon cayenne pepper

$\frac{1}{2}$ teaspoon garlic salt, or more to taste

1 teaspoon lime zest

3 tablespoons (3 g) minced fresh cilantro, divided

4 ears freshest corn, husks and silks removed

Juice of $\frac{1}{2}$ lime

In a small bowl, whisk together the olive oil, cayenne pepper, garlic salt, zest, and 1$\frac{1}{2}$ tablespoons (1.5 g) of the cilantro.

Place the cleaned corn in a large mixing bowl and pour the oil mixture over all, rubbing gently to thoroughly coat. Wrap each ear tightly in a piece of aluminum foil and lay them all horizontally in the slow cooker. Add water to about $\frac{1}{2}$ inch (1.3 cm), cover, and cook on high for 2 hours, or on low for 4 to 5 hours, until cooked through. Carefully unwrap the packs, squeeze the lime over all, and sprinkle with the remaining 1$\frac{1}{2}$ tablespoons (1.5 g) minced cilantro.

YIELD: 4 servings

PER SERVING: Calories 198.6; Calories From Fat 67.2; Total Fat 8 g; Cholesterol 6 mg; Sodium 287.5 mg; Potassium 30.2 mg; Total Carbohydrates 32.9 g; Fiber 0.4 g; Sugar 0.1 g; Protein 4.6 g

FRAGRANT FALL RUTABAGA MASH: POTASSIUM POWERHOUSE

INGREDIENTS

1 medium rutabaga (about 2 pounds [908 g]),
    peeled and chopped

Olive oil cooking spray

2 eggs, beaten

½ cup (120 ml) evaporated skim milk

½ cup (60 g) shredded Gruyère cheese

¼ cup (20 g) shredded Parmesan cheese

¼ cup (28 g) toasted wheat germ

¾ teaspoon salt

½ teaspoon cayenne pepper

FROM DR. JONNY: Okay, admit it: you're not 100 percent sure what a rutabaga is. If you're not, you're hardly alone. Rutabagas are weird-looking root vegetables that look like a cross between a cabbage and a turnip. They're an important part of Scandinavian cuisine and are sometimes referred to as "Swedes" for just that reason. They're an amazing source of potassium, weighing in at 782 mg per cup (compared to, say, 422 mg in a medium banana). They also contain 115 mg of calcium, 55 mg of magnesium, 45 mg of vitamin C, and a little more than 4 grams of fiber. Now that's a powerful combo! But it wouldn't mean anything if they didn't taste great. This recipe pairs the natural flavor of the rutabagas with the richness of an exquisite mix of Gruyère and Parmesan cheeses, coupled with the creaminess of evaporated milk. My mouth is already watering.

Boil the prepared rutabaga in a large pot of water for 15 to 20 minutes, or until tender. While the rutabaga is cooking, spray the insert of a slow cooker lightly with olive oil and set aside. Drain the cooked rutabaga well, mash (by hand with a potato masher or use an immersion blender) and transfer to a double-mesh sieve to drain off excess liquid for 5 minutes. Transfer to the slow cooker and stir in the eggs, evaporated milk, cheeses, wheat germ, salt, and cayenne pepper to thoroughly mix. Cover and cook on high for 2 to 3 hours, or on low for 4 to 5 hours, until set.

YIELD: 4 servings

PER SERVING: Calories 204.7; Calories From Fat 86.1; Total Fat 9.6 g; Cholesterol 127.4 mg; Sodium 669 mg; Potassium 541.5 mg; Total Carbohydrates 15.8 g; Fiber 3.4 g; Sugar 9.3 g; Protein 14.8 g

LIVER-LOVIN' RED CABBAGE, GREEN APPLE, AND SWEET ONION

INGREDIENTS

1 small Vidalia onion, halved and sliced into
   ¼-inch (6 mm) slices
1 head red cabbage, cored, quartered, and sliced
   into ¼-inch (6 mm) strips
2 green apples, unpeeled, cored, and chopped
¾ teaspoon salt
Freshly ground pepper, to taste
1 teaspoon caraway seeds (optional)
3 cups (705 ml) low-sodium chicken or
   vegetable broth
1 tablespoon (15 ml) apple cider vinegar

FROM DR. JONNY: Decades ago, researchers wondered why Eastern European women had such low rates of breast cancer and looked to their diet for an explanation. They found it in one of the staples of Eastern European cooking: cabbage. Compounds in the Brassica vegetable family, of which cabbage is the paterfamilias, help modify the metabolism of hormones in the body, making them less likely to contribute to cancer. And with detox diets all the rage, it's worth noting that cabbage—along with onions, a great source of the natural anti-inflammatory flavonoid quercetin—is wonderful for the liver, the organ that is "detox central" in the body. The sweetness of the apples and onions together mellows the edgy taste of the cabbage, creating a simply perfect side dish for any meal.

Add the onion to the slow cooker. Top with the cabbage, and then the apples. Sprinkle with the salt, pepper, and caraway seeds, if using. Pour the broth and vinegar over all, cover, and cook on high for about 2 hours, or on low for 3 to 4 hours, until the cabbage and onion are tender.

YIELD: 8 servings
PER SERVING: Calories 70.4; Calories From Fat 6.3; Total Fat 0.8 g; Cholesterol 0 mg; Sodium 266.8 mg; Potassium 386.6 mg; Total Carbohydrates 14.6 g; Fiber 4.3 g; Sugar 4.4 g; Protein 3.4 g

SULFUR-RICH CAYENNE CARAMELIZED ONIONS

INGREDIENTS

9 Vidalia onions (about 3 pounds [1.4 kg]),
   thinly sliced
2 ½ tablespoons (35 g) unsalted butter, melted
1 ½ tablespoons (23 g) Sucanat
1 teaspoon cayenne pepper

FROM CHEF JEANNETTE

Serving Suggestions: These are delicious over roasted or grilled red meats, on salads or sandwiches, or mixed with low-fat Greek yogurt or low-fat sour cream to make a quick, spicy onion dip. They will keep for about 2 weeks in the refrigerator, and they also freeze beautifully.

FROM DR. JONNY: Onions are such a fixture on the menu of fast food joints and large chain restaurants that it's easy to overlook the fact that they are one of the world's healthiest foods. In Vidalia, Georgia, where the Vidalia onion comes from and where onions are consumed in large quantities, the death rate from stomach cancer is about 50 percent lower than the national mortality rate from that same disease. One theory: onions contain *diallyl sulfide*, which increases the body's production of an important cancer-fighting enzyme. Onions also benefit your bones and contain powerful antioxidants as well as compounds that are anti-inflammatory, antibiotic, and antiviral. And best of all, they are a great source of a superstar flavonoid known as *quercetin*, which has been shown to have anticancer activity as well as being a powerful anti-inflammatory. Slow cooking allows you to caramelize the onions using the barest minimum of added sugar, and draws out the natural sweetness of the Vidalias—the perfect counterpoint to the bite of cayenne pepper! Enjoy!

Scatter the onions in an even layer in the slow cooker. Whisk the butter, Sucanat, and cayenne pepper together and drizzle it evenly over the onions. Toss to coat. Cover and cook on low for 8 to 9 hours. For the last half hour, remove the cover and turn the temperature to high to reduce any remaining moisture.

YIELD: about 3 cups (735 g)
FOR ENTIRE RECIPE: Calories 872.1; Calories From Fat 255.8; Total Fat 29.1 g; Cholesterol 76.3 mg; Sodium 95.2 mg; Potassium 1,859.2 mg; Total Carbohydrates 146.1 g; Fiber 25.9 g; Sugar 18.2 g; Protein 9.6 g

EARTHY HIGH-FIBER WILD RICE AND VEGGIES

INGREDIENTS

Olive oil cooking spray

1 ¹/₂ tablespoons (23 ml) olive oil

4 large shallots, finely chopped

2 ribs celery, thinly sliced

8 ounces (225 g) cremini mushrooms, thinly sliced

1 tablespoon (2.4 g) minced fresh thyme (or 1 teaspoon dried)

3 cloves garlic, minced

2 tablespoons (28 g) unsalted butter

2 tablespoons (8 g) unbleached wheat flour

1 can (12 ounces, or 353 ml) evaporated skim milk

³/₄ teaspoon salt

2 cups (230 g) shredded Swiss cheese

2 cups (330 g) cooked wild rice (or a combination of brown and wild rice)

1 can (14 ounces, or 392 g) diced tomatoes, drained

¹/₄ cup (30 g) chopped toasted hazelnuts or pine nuts, for garnish (optional)

FROM DR. JONNY: Wild rice is a chewier, richer-tasting alternative to brown rice, with a nice bite, 3 grams of fiber per cup, and a relatively low glycemic impact, measuring a moderate 16 on the glycemic-load scale. (For those who are wondering, less than 10 is very low; more than 20 is high.) In any case, this recipe won't play havoc with your blood sugar because the small amount of healthy fat from the cheese, butter, and hazelnuts will lower the glycemic impact even further. Also worth mentioning is the surprising amount of nutrition provided by those ordinary, innocuous white button mushrooms, which are actually pretty rich in nutrients, especially potassium. This recipe does involve a few cooking steps, but the result is worth it: an earthy, cheesy, and delicious casserole that's just perfect for a holiday meal!

Spray the insert of a slow cooker with olive oil and set aside.

Heat the oil in a large skillet over medium heat. Add the shallots, celery, mushrooms, and thyme and cook for 5 to 6 minutes, or until the shallots are tender but not browned. Add the garlic and cook for 30 seconds longer. Transfer the contents to a large bowl.

Add the butter to the same pan. When it melts, whisk in the flour and cook, stirring frequently, until lightly browned, 4 to 5 minutes. Whisk in the evaporated milk, increase the heat to medium-high, and bring the mixture to a boil, whisking constantly. Season with the salt. Whisk in the cheese until melted and well incorporated. Pour the mixture over the vegetables, add the rice and tomatoes, and stir gently to combine well. Transfer the contents to the slow cooker, cover, and cook on high for 2 to 3 hours, or on low for 4 to 5 hours. Garnish with the nuts, if using, before serving.

YIELD: 6 servings

PER SERVING: Calories 407.4; Calories From Fat 194.5; Total Fat 22.4 g; Cholesterol 45.9 mg; Sodium 538.6 mg; Potassium 639.6 mg; Total Carbohydrates 34.1 g; Fiber 3.3 g; Sugar 8.8 g; Protein 21.6 g

CURRIED LIME BETA-CARROTS-TENE

INGREDIENTS

2 teaspoons curry powder

¼ teaspoon salt

3 tablespoons (45 ml) lime juice

¼ cup (80 g) honey

1 tablespoon (15 ml) ghee

2 pounds (908 g) baby carrots

FROM DR. JONNY: A fast story about flavor pairings and genius chefs. I was having dinner with my friend Amber Linder, a private chef in the Los Angeles area, at my favorite restaurant in the world, Inn of the Seventh Ray, right near my home in the hills of Topanga (in the San Fernando Valley of Southern California). One of their famous appetizers is this amazing plate of artisan cheeses accompanied by all kinds of weird little sweet pastes and gourmet honeys. Amber took one look at the plate and immediately mixed a forkful of blue cheese with one of the darker honeys. "Try this," she said. To say it was heavenly is an understatement—it was more like transcendental. And I would no more have thought of putting just that cheese with just that honey than I would have thought to translate Dante into Portuguese. But that's the point. Unusual flavor pairing is the heart and soul of the chef's talent, and Chef Jeannette has demonstrated it perfectly in this dish, using the sweetness of the honey to mellow the citrus tang of the lime, all warmed up by the hints of curry. Who'da thunk it? Gorgeous and delicious. Fun fact: In Ayurvedic medicine, ghee is believed to strengthen the *ojas*, the essential energy of the body thought to be at the root of well-being and immunity.

In a small bowl, whisk the curry powder and salt into the lime juice. Add the honey and whisk to combine. Set aside.

Place the ghee and carrots in the slow cooker and pour the honey juice mixture over the top. Cook on low for 3 to 4 hours, or until the carrots are tender-crisp. Stir gently before serving.

YIELD: 6 servings

PER SERVING: Calories 116.6; Calories From Fat 19.1; Total Fat 2.2 g; Cholesterol 5 mg; Sodium 216.1 mg; Potassium 385 mg; Total Carbohydrates 25.1 g; Fiber 4.7 g; Sugar 18.9 g; Protein 1.1 g

AUTUMNAL RICH-ROOTS MEDLEY: SWEET POTATOES, PARSNIPS, AND CELERIAC

INGREDIENTS

2 sweet potatoes, peeled and chopped into
    ½-inch (1.3 cm) dice

3 parsnips, peeled and chopped into ½-inch
    (1.3 cm) dice

1 small celery root, peeled and chopped into
    ½-inch (1.3 cm) dice

2 red cooking apples, peeled, cored, and sliced

1 ½ cups (353 ml) vegetable or chicken broth

½ cup (120 ml) apple cider

½ teaspoon ground nutmeg

½ teaspoon salt

FROM DR. JONNY: Parsnips are one of the most underappreciated vegetables, and when you taste them in this recipe you'll instantly know why. They're as sweet as sugar, beautifully complement the flavor and texture of celery and apples, and happen to be extraordinarily low in calories while providing a nice blend of fiber (2.8 grams per ½ cup [112 g]), potassium (286 mg), and folate (45 mcg). Sweet potatoes are the best the potato family has to offer, rich in the carotenoids (like beta-carotene) that give it that deep orange-red color, fairly high in fiber (slightly less than 6 grams per large potato), and with almost twice the potassium of a banana. This recipe comes together as a warming, cold-weather medley that deliciously accompanies any roasted meat dish.

Combine the sweet potatoes, parsnips, celery root, and apples in the slow cooker.

In a small bowl, whisk together the broth, cider, nutmeg, and salt and pour over all. Cover and cook on high for 4 to 5 hours, or on low for 6 to 7 hours, or until the vegetables are tender. Partially purée with an immersion wand and adjust the seasonings to taste. The celery root will be firmer than the other veggies, but it should not be crunchy.

YIELD: 8 to 10 servings

PER SERVING: Calories 109.7; Calories From Fat 5; Total Fat 0.6 g; Cholesterol 0 mg; Sodium 257.3 mg; Potassium 475.4 mg; Total Carbohydrates 25.2 g; Fiber 5.5 g; Sugar 8 g; Protein 2.2 g

C-RICH LEMONY LEEK AND FENNEL POTATOES

INGREDIENTS

¾ cup (180 ml) chicken or vegetable broth

⅓ cup (80 ml) freshly squeezed lemon juice, divided

1 tablespoon (11 g) Dijon mustard

2 teaspoons olive oil (or melted unsalted butter)

2 teaspoons lemon zest

2 teaspoons minced fresh rosemary (or 1 teaspoon dried, crumbled) (optional)

½ each teaspoon salt and freshly ground pepper

1 large leek, well cleaned and chopped into ½-inch (1.3 cm) pieces

3 Yukon gold potatoes, unpeeled and chopped into ½-inch (1.3 cm) dice

1 head fennel, chopped into ½-inch (1.3 cm) dice

FROM DR. JONNY: Back in the days when I was a struggling jazz musician living on the Upper West Side of Manhattan, I used to make a nightly stir-fry out of the cheapest veggies I could find in the markets up on Broadway. During this time I discovered leeks—a bachelor's dream. You simply can't screw them up. Chop, chop, plunk them in the stir-fry, and voilà, you've got this rich, sweet, melt-in-your-mouth veggie. But I digress. The thing that sets this recipe apart isn't the leeks but the fennel. In addition to imparting its distinct flavor, which blends so beautifully with both leeks and potatoes, it's used in several cultures to prevent gas and upset stomach. And speaking of potatoes, we used Yukon gold potatoes because they're lower in starch than either Idaho or russet potatoes, plus they have the extra advantage of having a light, clean skin that allows you to preserve all the nutrients. The lemon juice adds a nice dollop of vitamin C to the mix. Fun fact: According to the Greek legend of Prometheus, fennel was thought to bestow immortality. And fennel was formerly a drug in the United States used for indigestion.

In a small bowl, whisk together the broth, ¼ cup (60 ml) of the lemon juice, mustard, olive oil, zest, rosemary, salt, and pepper.

Combine the leek, potatoes, and fennel in the slow cooker and pour the liquid evenly over all. Cover and cook on high for 2 to 3 hours or on low for 3½ to 4 hours, until the vegetables are tender, stirring once during the cooking time if possible. Adjust the seasonings to taste, adding the remaining 1½ tablespoons (20 ml) lemon juice if desired.

YIELD: 4 to 6 servings

PER SERVING: Calories 217.5; Calories From Fat 64.8; Total Fat 7.6 g; Cholesterol 0 mg; Sodium 358 mg; Potassium 1,095.9 mg; Total Carbohydrates 37.1 g; Fiber 17.5 g; Sugar 2.5 g; Protein 9.2 g

TENDER AND TANGY "BAKED" YAMS WITH COCONUT LIME "BUTTER"

INGREDIENTS

6 small garnet yams, unpeeled (or very small sweet potatoes)

2 tablespoons (30 g) coconut oil, melted (or melted unsalted butter)

1 tablespoon (15 ml) freshly squeezed lime juice

FROM DR. JONNY: When I was deeply into the gym culture and working as a personal trainer, sweet potatoes were one of my basic "pack and carry" meals. I used to cook up about a half dozen of them every Sunday afternoon and then put them in the fridge to cool. Then I'd mash one up with a can of tuna, put it in Tupperware, and carry it with me to the gym. (Some people find the combination disgusting when they hear about it, but those people have never tried it. It's actually delicious.) Sweet potatoes are much more nutritionally rich than their poor white cousins. A single medium sweet potato is only 105 calories but provides almost 4 grams of fiber, way more potassium than a banana (542 mg compared to 422 mg), some calcium, vitamin C, and even a couple of grams of protein. This is a simple, delicious way to cook faux "baked" sweet potatoes, and unleash their perfect moist tenderness and flavor. Chef Jeannette whimsically topped the whole shebang with a small amount of real coconut and lime (got to love that!) for an unusual twist that "pops" the naturally sweet flavor.

Scrub the sweet potatoes clean and do not pat them dry. Place them in a single layer in the slow cooker, cover, and cook on low for 4 to 6 hours, or until the potatoes are tender.

Just before serving, in a small bowl, whisk together the coconut oil and lime juice.

To serve, slice each potato open and drizzle 1½ teaspoons of the coconut lime into the flesh of each one and gently mix. Serve piping hot.

YIELD: 6 servings

PER SERVING: Calories 151.5; Calories From Fat 39.6; Total Fat 4.6 g; Cholesterol 0 mg; Sodium 71.6 mg; Potassium 441.1 mg; Total Carbohydrates 26.4 g; Fiber 3.9 g; Sugar 5.5 g; Protein 2.1 g

CRAN-ORANGE SWEET POTATO CUSTARD

FROM DR. JONNY: Can we just talk about the title of this recipe for a second? Sweet potato custard? Is your mouth watering? Mine is. Sweet potatoes are such a versatile food, working great by themselves but also enriching all sorts of dishes from pies to custards. They're rich in carotenoids, a family of plant chemicals with multiple health benefits, and of course they're a prime source of vitamin A. They also contain a decent amount of fiber. The one thing they don't have much of is protein, but worry not—the eggs in this recipe provide about 3 grams per custard serving and when combined with the potatoes, they create a lightly sweet, orange-scented dish with a tart cranberry "pop" that is fit to grace any fall or cold-season holiday meal. Word to the wise: this dish doubles as an ultra-healthy dessert. Seriously.

INGREDIENTS

1 can (15 ounces, or 420 g) high-quality sweet potato purée (we like Farmer's Market Organic)

1 can (12 ounces, or 353 ml) evaporated skim milk

2 tablespoons (30 ml) freshly squeezed orange juice

2 eggs

1 teaspoon orange zest

¾ teaspoon orange extract

3 tablespoons (8 g) juice-sweetened dried cranberries

Combine the purée, skim milk, juice, eggs, zest, and orange extract in a food processor and process until smooth, scraping down the sides as necessary. Gently fold in the cranberries. Spoon the mixture into a 6-cup (1.5 L) shallow glass baking dish and place it in the center of a 6-quart (5.7 L) slow cooker. Using a spouted 4-cup (1 L) liquid measuring glass, slowly pour water into the cooker, being careful not to splash it into the potatoes, until the level reaches halfway up the baking dish. Cover and cook on high for about 3 hours, or until set. Remove the cover, turn off the heat, and let cool until you are able to remove the baking dish from the cooker (at least 30 minutes).

YIELD: 4 servings

PER SERVING: Calories 245.5; Calories From Fat 27.1; Total Fat 3 g; Cholesterol 109.6 mg; Sodium 227.7 mg; Potassium 607.2 mg; Total Carbohydrates 41.3 g; Fiber 2.2 g; Sugar 21 g; Protein 12.5 g

FROM CHEF JEANNETTE

Even Healthier: If you have the time, make your own nutrient-rich sweet potato purée. Choose 2 or 3 garnet yams (depending on the size, you'll need about 2 cups [490 g] purée), scrub them well, and then roast on a baking sheet for 1 hour at 400°F (200°C, or gas mark 6) until very tender. Let cool until warm, not hot, and then scoop the purée out of the skins and proceed with the recipe as directed.

FRESH SWEET 'N SOUR BEETS

FROM DR. JONNY: I grew up eating beets, largely because of two reasons. One, I had an Eastern European Jewish grandmother and they make beets in the most spectacularly delicious ways—it's in their DNA. And two, we used to spend family vacations in what is affectionately known as "the Borscht Belt," an area of upstate New York popular among Jewish families and singles, where beets (and borscht) are not considered exotic cuisine. So I never quite got why so many people dislike this amazing vegetable. These slow-cooked beets are tangy and sweet with a citrus-y bite. And beets are not exactly nutritional lightweights. They're an important dietary source of *betaine*, a nutrient known for its role in bringing down high levels of a toxic inflammatory compound in our bodies known as *homocysteine*. (High homocysteine levels are a risk factor for heart disease and stroke.) Beets are also loaded with potassium, a vitally important mineral for heart health. Enjoy!

INGREDIENTS

1 pound (454 g) fresh, young beets, peeled and
　　halved

¼ cup (60 g) Sucanat

1 tablespoon (8 g) enriched wheat flour

2 tablespoons (30 ml) apple cider vinegar

2 tablespoons (30 ml) freshly squeezed
　　lemon juice

Place the beets in a slow cooker. In a small bowl, whisk together the Sucanat and flour. Add the vinegar and lemon juice and whisk to combine. Pour the sauce over the beets, cover, and cook on low for 2 to 3 hours, or until the beets are tender. Baste before serving.

YIELD: 4 servings

PER SERVING: Calories 104.3; Calories From Fat 1.8; Total Fat 0.2 g; Cholesterol 0 mg; Sodium 88.9 mg; Potassium 385.5 mg; Total Carbohydrates 25.1 g; Fiber 3.3 g; Sugar 19.9 g; Protein 2.1 g

INGREDIENTS

4 medium zucchini, sliced

1 large Vidalia onion, thinly sliced into rings

1 large red bell pepper, julienned

1 can (14.5 ounces, or 406 g) roasted diced tomatoes, undrained

1 teaspoon dried basil

1 teaspoon dried thyme

3 cloves garlic, minced

¾ teaspoon salt

½ teaspoon cracked black pepper

½ cup (75 g) crumbled feta cheese

FRESH AND LIGHT SUMMER MEDLEY WITH FETA: ZUCCHINI, BELL PEPPERS, AND ONION

FROM DR. JONNY: Nutritionally speaking, it's just about impossible to go wrong with any kind of vegetable stew, and this one is no exception. After all, what's not to like? Red bell peppers are rich in vitamin C and beta-carotene, onions are a great source of sulfur compounds, which give your skin a healthy, glowing look, and zucchinis are a better source of potassium than bananas! (Sharp-eyed readers and my beloved editor Cara Connors will ask, "How much better?" And the answer is: a medium-size banana has 105 calories and 422 mg of potassium while a medium-size zucchini has only 33 calories and 512 mg of potassium!) This low-cal recipe even has a bit of protein from the flavorful cheese. It's slow cooked to tender perfection and topped with tangy feta. As I said, what's not to like?

Layer the zucchini, onion, and bell pepper in the bottom of a slow cooker. In a small bowl, combine the tomatoes, basil, thyme, garlic, salt, and pepper and mix. Pour the tomatoes evenly over the vegetables, cover, and cook on low for 1 to 2 hours, or until the veggies are tender. Sprinkle individual servings with the feta before serving.

YIELD: 6 servings

PER SERVING: Calories 98.3; Calories From Fat 28; Total Fat 3.2 g; Cholesterol 11.1 mg; Sodium 537.6 mg; Potassium 671.4 mg; Total Carbohydrates 14.8 g; Fiber 4 g; Sugar 3.9 g; Protein 5.1 g

CURRIED COCONUT CREAM OF CAULIFLOWER SOUP

INGREDIENTS

2 ¹/₂-pound (1.1 kg) cauliflower, stemmed and
   chopped (or use precut florets)
1 tablespoon (15 ml) olive oil
2 large Vidalia onions, chopped
2 ¹/₂ teaspoons curry powder
³/₄ teaspoon ground turmeric
¹/₂ teaspoon ground cardamom
¹/₄ teaspoon ground cloves
¹/₄ teaspoon cayenne pepper
2 cups (470 ml) chicken or vegetable broth
³/₄ teaspoon salt
1 can (15 ounces, or 420 g) light coconut milk
1 ¹/₂ cups (195 g) frozen peas (optional)
¹/₂ cup (8 g) chopped fresh cilantro

FROM DR. JONNY: When people ask me to summarize my diet philosophy in 6 seconds or less, I usually quip, "Don't eat anything white." Of course, God is in the details, and there are a few exceptions to the rule, one of which is cauliflower. Another of which is coconut (and coconut milk). A third is chicken and turkey, but hey, let's not be picky; you get the idea. Cauliflower gets a pass on the "no white stuff" rule because it's a member of the Brassica family of vegetable royalty; loaded with cancer-fighting chemicals called *indoles*; low in calories (ridiculously low, actually, at 29 calories per cup!); high in fiber; and brimming with nutrients like calcium, potassium, vitamin C, and folate. And coconut milk is the perfect bath for this wonderful vegetable, especially flavored with the super-spice turmeric. Turmeric is responsible for the yellow color of curry, and is one of the healthiest foods on the planet—anti-inflammatory, anticancer, and liver-protective. What a combo! The cardamom adds a nice finishing touch, a hint of unexpected fresh spice.

Place the cauliflower in the slow cooker and set aside.

Heat the oil in a large skillet over medium heat. Add the onions and cook for about 5 minutes, or until just softened. Stir in the curry powder, turmeric, cardamom, cloves, and cayenne pepper and cook for 1 minute. Add the broth and salt and stir to incorporate the spices.

Pour the mixture into the slow cooker over the cauliflower, being careful to get everything from the pan. Stir in the coconut milk. Cook on high for about 3 hours or on low for about 6 hours, or until the cauliflower is very tender. Purée, using an immersion wand (or carefully in batches in a blender), to the desired consistency. Stir in the peas, if using, adjust the seasonings, if necessary, and cook for 10 minutes longer on low. Stir in the cilantro just before serving.

YIELD: 6 to 8 servings
PER SERVING: Calories 123.5; Calories From Fat 39.1; Total Fat 4.5 g; Cholesterol 0 mg; Sodium 551.6 mg; Potassium 552.6 mg; Total Carbohydrates 18.7 g; Fiber 6.4 g; Sugar 5.4 g; Protein 4.6 g

FRUIT-STUFFED ACORN SQUASH

INGREDIENTS

2 teaspoons Sucanat or xylitol

1 teaspoon ground cinnamon

1/2 teaspoon ground nutmeg

1/2 teaspoon ground cardamom

1/4 teaspoon salt

1 sweet apple, such as Jonagold, unpeeled and finely chopped

1/2 cup (75 g) raisins

1/4 cup (26 g) chopped pecans

2 acorn squash, halved and seeded

4 teaspoons (18 g) unsalted butter or coconut oil, melted

1/2 cup (120 ml) apple cider or water

FROM DR. JONNY: Whenever I hear from parents about their difficulty in getting kids to eat vegetables I think about dishes like this. What kid is not going to respond to the sweet and crunchy mix of apples, raisins, and pecans? They form the absolutely pitch-perfect accompaniment to acorn squash, a naturally sweet vegetable that is literally a fiber heavyweight, delivering a sizeable 9 grams of fiber per cup, not to mention 896 mg of potassium (twice that of a banana) and almost 2 mg of iron. Fun fact: In addition to keeping the proverbial doctor away, apples are a great source of a little-known mineral called *boron*, which is increasingly being seen by scientists as essential for bone health. In animal studies, low boron intake is associated with abnormal bone growth and development. In humans, patients affected with arthritic joints show lower levels of boron in their bones than those without arthritis.

In a medium-size bowl, mix together the Sucanat, cinnamon, nutmeg, cardamom, and salt. Add the apple, raisins, and pecans and toss to coat thoroughly. Stuff each half of the squash with one-fourth of the mixture and drizzle 1 teaspoon of butter over the top of each. Pour the cider into the slow cooker.

If you have a large cooker (6 or 7 quarts [5.7 or 6.6 L]), place the squash halves side by side, cut sides up, in the cooker, cover, and cook. If you have to stack them, wrap each half tightly in foil before stacking (to keep the contents inside) and cook with water, not cider. Cook on high for 4 hours, or on low for 8 hours, or until the squash is very tender.

YIELD: 4 servings

PER SERVING: Calories 277.6; Calories From Fat 84.3; Total Fat 9.9 g; Cholesterol 0 mg; Sodium 155.5 mg; Potassium 1,010.6 mg; Total Carbohydrates 51 g; Fiber 6 g; Sugar 18.2 g; Protein 3.2 g

SUMMERY, COLORFUL HERBED CARROTS AND GREEN BEANS

INGREDIENTS

1 pound (454 g) baby carrots

2 tablespoons (30 ml) olive oil

1 pound (454 g) fresh green beans, trimmed

½ teaspoon salt

1 tablespoon (15 ml) freshly squeezed lime juice

1 tablespoon (1 g) minced fresh cilantro

1 tablespoon (4 g) minced fresh dill

1 tablespoon (6 g) minced fresh mint

FROM DR. JONNY: One of the only good pieces of advice I ever heard from a dietitian was this: shop for color. It's so simple yet so completely true, and it bypasses the need for any complicated nutritional science. Bottom line: foods that have the most color usually have the most antioxidants and other health-supporting plant compounds. (For instance, the compounds that make blueberries blue or raspberries red actually protect these plants from free radical damage, and they do the same thing for your cells!) All of which brings me to this colorful recipe. The orange color of carrots tells you they are brimming with important nutrients called carotenoids (like beta-carotene), which are only found in red and yellow fruits and vegetables. And green beans, while not exactly the biggest nutritional heavyweight in the vegetable kingdom, nonetheless contain a nice helping of folate, potassium, and vitamin A, not to mention about 20 percent of the Daily Value for manganese, a trace mineral that's important for metabolism, growth, reproduction, and peak brain function. And man, those colors are gorgeous!

Place the carrots in a slow cooker. Drizzle the oil over all and toss lightly to coat. Cover and cook on high for 1½ hours or on low for 3 hours. Add the green beans, sprinkle the salt over all, and toss to coat. Cook for an additional 30 to 60 minutes, until the vegetables reach the desired tenderness. Toss gently with the lime juice and herbs before serving.

YIELD: 8 servings

PER SERVING: Calories 69; Calories From Fat 31.2; Total Fat 3.5 g; Cholesterol 0 mg; Sodium 194.3 mg; Potassium 272.2 mg; Total Carbohydrates 9.2 g; Fiber 3.7 g; Sugar 3.5 g; Protein 1.5 g

ORANGE IRON-RICH BEETS WITH WALNUTS

INGREDIENTS

½ cup (120 ml) freshly squeezed orange juice

2 tablespoons (30 ml) sherry vinegar

2 pounds (908 g) whole beets, unpeeled, stemmed

¼ cup (30 g) roasted chopped walnuts (optional)

FROM DR. JONNY: Have you often wondered why beets are red? I didn't think so—not on your top ten must-know list. But since this is a beet recipe, I'll tell you anyway! The red color actually comes from a plant compound in beets called *betacyanin*, which researchers believe could protect against the development of cancerous cells and might even play a role in reducing the inflammation that is a big part of heart disease (as well as every other degenerative disease we know of). Beets also contain fiber, potassium, and a decent amount of folate. The walnuts provide heart-healthy monounsaturated fat along with fiber and minerals and provide a nice textural balance to the beets. The sherry and orange lend a light, complementary flavor note and blend beautifully with the sweet beets. Fun fact: A study from the *Journal of Applied Physiology* found that athletes drinking organic beet juice for six consecutive days were able to cycle for 92 seconds longer than athletes given a placebo to drink. This translates into approximately a 2 percent reduction in the time needed to cover a set distance!

In a small bowl, whisk together the orange juice and sherry. Place the whole beets in the slow cooker and pour the juice mixture over all. Cover and cook on low for about 3 hours, or to the desired tenderness. Stir well and remove the beets to cool. When cool enough to handle, slip the skins off with your fingers (or use a paper towel to protect your hands from the staining juices). Quarter the beets and top with the walnuts, if using.

YIELD: 8 servings

PER SERVING: Calories 80.2; Calories From Fat 21.7; Total Fat 2.6 g; Cholesterol 0 mg; Sodium 88.7 mg; Potassium 419.4 mg; Total Carbohydrates 13.2 g; Fiber 3.5 g; Sugar 9.1 g; Protein 2.5 g

IRON-POWER GARLIC SPINACH WITH ROASTED REDS

INGREDIENTS

2 teaspoons olive oil

1 sweet onion, chopped

4 cloves garlic, minced

½ teaspoon ground cumin

½ teaspoon each salt and black pepper

2 roasted red peppers, chopped

1 can (14 ounces, or 392 g) fire-roasted diced
  tomatoes, drained

4 or 5 dashes hot pepper sauce, to taste

3 packages (10 ounces, or 280 g) frozen
  chopped spinach (do not thaw)

For Optional Garnish

¼ cup (60 g) plain low-fat Greek yogurt

1 tablespoon (15 ml) freshly squeezed
  lemon juice

1 clove garlic, minced

¼ teaspoon salt

FROM DR. JONNY: The ingredients list in this recipe is kind of like an "all-star" team of superfoods. There's not a lightweight in the bunch. Spinach is one of the great vegetables of all time, providing vitamin A, manganese, folic acid, magnesium, iron, vitamin C, and a powerful anti-inflammatory called *quercetin* (which I take as a supplement on a daily basis). What's more, spinach is a great source of calcium, and one of the best sources of the important heart-protective, bone-supporting nutrient, vitamin K. Garlic, one of the oldest medicinal foods on the planet, is a powerful antioxidant that is also antimicrobial and antiviral. Plus, compounds in garlic have been shown in many lab studies to be chemoprotective (anticancer). And I haven't even touched on the reds: roasted red peppers have a high vitamin C content and tomatoes contain the cancer-fighting antioxidant lycopene. High-protein Greek yogurt rounds out the superstar team of fabulous foods in this scrumptious recipe.

Heat the oil in a large skillet over medium heat. Add the onion and cook for 5 to 6 minutes, or until starting to soften. Add the garlic and cook for 30 seconds, stirring constantly. Remove from the heat and stir in the cumin, salt, pepper, peppers, tomatoes, and hot pepper sauce.

Place the frozen spinach on the bottom of the slow cooker and pour the onion mixture evenly over the top. Cover and cook on low for 4 to 5 hours, or until heated through.

To make the garnish: Combine the yogurt, lemon juice, garlic, and salt in a small bowl and whisk thoroughly. Store in the fridge to let the flavors combine. To serve, stir the spinach gently to mix, adjust the seasonings to taste, and top with the garnish, if using.

YIELD: 6 servings

PER SERVING: Calories 122.9; Calories From Fat 22.3; Total Fat 2.6 g; Cholesterol 0.6 mg; Sodium 409.7 mg; Potassium 938.7 mg; Total Carbohydrates 19.9 g; Fiber 7.4 g; Sugar 7.7 g; Protein 7 g

WHOLE-GRAIN ASIAN SHIITAKE BARLEY

FROM DR. JONNY: Barley is a low-glycemic grain that is an excellent source of dietary fiber, particularly soluble fiber. The particular type of soluble fiber in barley is called *beta-glucan*, which has been shown in research to promote healthy blood sugar by slowing the absorption of sugar (glucose) into the bloodstream. In a study reported in the *Journal of the American College of Nutrition* (of which I am a proud member), subjects who ate cookies and crackers made with barley flour enriched with beta-glucan fiber experienced significant reductions in glucose and insulin response compared to their responses after eating the same foods made with whole wheat flour. This is a decidedly low-cal recipe that sports a nice combination of chewy grains and crunchy water chestnuts. Note: According to www.barleyfoods.org, barley on average contains about 5 to 8 percent gluten, something to be aware of if you're gluten-sensitive.

INGREDIENTS

1 cup (184 g) barley groats
6 dried shiitake mushrooms (about ½ ounce, or 14 g), coarsely chopped
1 yellow onion, finely chopped
1 can (8 ounces, or 225 g) sliced water chestnuts, drained
2 ribs celery, sliced
3 cups (705 ml) vegetable broth
2 cloves garlic, minced
½ teaspoon white pepper
1½ tablespoons (23 ml) low-sodium tamari
1 tablespoon (15 ml) mirin (or cooking sherry)
½ cup (50 g) sliced scallion

Combine the barley, chopped dried mushrooms, yellow onion, water chestnuts, and celery in a slow cooker. Add the vegetable broth, garlic, and white pepper and stir to combine. Cover and cook on high for 2 to 3 hours, or on low for 4 to 5 hours, until most of the liquid has been absorbed and the barley is tender. Add the tamari and mirin for the last half hour of cooking time. Stir in the scallions just before serving.

YIELD: 4 servings
PER SERVING: Calories 243.4; Calories From Fat 27.3; Total Fat 3.1 g; Cholesterol 1.9 mg; Sodium 1,541.3 mg; Potassium 583.3 mg; Total Carbohydrates 47.3 g; Fiber 7.3 g; Sugar 6.3 g; Protein 8.3 g

FROM CHEF JEANNETTE

Barley groats (also called hulled barley) are the most nutritious, whole-grain form of barley. Pearl barley is a little more processed, with the bran layers removed. It is easier to find, and only requires about three-fourths of the cooking time of the whole groats, so if you make the substitution, start checking for doneness at about 1½ hours on high or 3 hours on low. To speed barley groat cooking time, soak it for 3 to 6 hours in fresh water, drain, and cook, reducing the liquid slightly and cooking time by about 1 hour.

For a richer flavor, roast the dry barley grains in 1½ tablespoons (23 ml) ghee in a large skillet over medium heat for 8 to 10 minutes, or until starting to brown.

LOW-CARB SPICE-RUBBED SPAGHETTI SQUASH

INGREDIENTS

1 teaspoon paprika

1 teaspoon garlic powder

1 teaspoon onion powder

$\frac{1}{2}$ teaspoon dried oregano

$\frac{1}{2}$ teaspoon dried thyme

$\frac{1}{2}$ teaspoon cayenne pepper

$\frac{1}{2}$ teaspoon freshly ground black pepper

$\frac{1}{2}$ teaspoon salt

1 medium spaghetti squash

$\frac{1}{2}$ cup (120 ml) vegetable broth or water

1 tablespoon (15 ml) olive oil (or unsalted butter, diced)

FROM DR. JONNY: Back when I was first starting out as a nutritionist and personal trainer at Equinox Fitness Clubs in the early '90s, clients would frequently tell me they couldn't stand vegetables. I'd tell them to melt some butter over them (remember, I'm not afraid of healthy fat, and that includes butter!), season them within an inch of their life, and enjoy! My thinking: if the price of an extra hundred or so calories (from the butter) is going to get you to eat a whole plate of broccoli, I'd call that a bargain! It's kind of the same deal here. Spaghetti squash isn't a great nutritional heavyweight, but it is incredibly low in calories and provides 2.2 grams of fiber (plus about half the potassium in a banana) for a single 42-calorie 1-cup (225 g) serving. Problem is, it's a tiny bit bland. Chef Jeannette comes to the rescue with this pungent spice rub that really kicks the taste quotient up a few notches! This filling, low-carb winter squash is both delicious and incredibly easy to make.

In a small bowl, mix the spices together and set aside.

Using a heavy chef's knife or a cleaver, slice the squash in half lengthwise. Using a heavy spoon, scrape out all the seeds and connective threads and discard.

Pour the broth into the slow cooker. Lay the squash halves on a counter surface, cut sides up, and drizzle half of the oil into each squash half. Gently rub the oil with your fingers to evenly coat all the cut flesh. (If you are using butter, distribute the chopped pieces evenly into the "bowls" of each half.) Sprinkle each half evenly with the rub mixture (you may have some rub left over). Arrange the squash in the slow cooker so the cut sides are up. Cover and cook on high for $3\frac{1}{2}$ to 4 hours, or on low for 7 to 8 hours, or until the squash is fork-tender. Spoon the flesh out of the skins (discarding the skins) and/or pull the individual strands apart, if desired, to serve.

YIELD: 4 to 6 servings (or more if your squash is large)

PER SERVING: Calories 52.5; Calories From Fat 23.8; Total Fat 2.7 g; Cholesterol 0.2 mg; Sodium 453.2 mg; Potassium 129.8 mg; Total Carbohydrates 7.2 g; Fiber 1.6 g; Sugar 2.4 g; Protein 1 g

FIBER-FANTASTIC MEXI BEANS

FROM DR. JONNY: I probably don't have to tell you about the downside of beans. Enter kombu, a kind of edible kelp that's widely eaten in Japan and Asia. Kombu happens to do a fine job of decreasing the flatulence factor! These beans have a clean, fresh flavor with subtle hints of Mexican spice—completely different from the canned version. Fun fact: Hippocrates, the father of modern medicine, once said: "Passing gas is necessary to well-being."

INGREDIENTS

1 piece dried kombu (about 1 by 2 inches [2.5 by 5 cm]) (optional)

1 ½ tablespoons (23 ml) olive oil

1 large yellow onion

1 jalapeño pepper, seeded and finely chopped (optional)

4 cloves garlic, minced

2 teaspoons ground cumin

1 teaspoon dried oregano

½ teaspoon chili powder

½ teaspoon hot paprika

1 pound (454 g) dried black beans, rinsed and picked through

6 cups (1.4 L) no-sodium vegetable broth (or water)

2 tablespoons (30 ml) apple cider vinegar

Salt and cracked black pepper, to taste

¼ cup (4 g) chopped fresh cilantro or chives (optional)

Lime slices (optional)

Soak the kombu, if using, in a small bowl of water for 5 to 10 minutes, or until tender. Chop finely and set aside.

In a large Dutch oven or soup pot, heat the oil over medium heat. Add the onion and cook for about 6 minutes, or until tender. Add the jalapeño, if using, garlic, cumin, oregano, chili powder, and paprika and cook for about 30 seconds, stirring constantly. Add the black beans and broth, stir to combine, and increase the heat to bring the mixture to a boil. When the mixture reaches a full boil, remove from the heat and carefully transfer the contents to a slow cooker, stir in the prepared kombu, if using, cover, and cook on high for 3 to 5 hours, or until the beans are tender to the squeeze.

Stir in the vinegar, season to taste with salt and pepper, and cook for about 15 minutes longer. Garnish with the cilantro and lime slices, if using.

YIELD: about 8 cups (2 kg) (½ cup [125 g] per serving)
PER SERVING: Calories 120.7; Calories From Fat 15; Total Fat 1.6 g; Cholesterol 0 mg; Sodium 61.1 mg; Potassium 455.7 mg; Total Carbohydrates 19.3 g; Fiber 7.4 g; Sugar 1 g; Protein 6.3 g

FROM CHEF JEANNETTE

These beans freeze beautifully. Chill leftovers completely in the fridge overnight, transfer to an airtight, freezer-safe container, and store in the freezer. I like to portion them out in quart-size, freezer zip-closure bags, suck the air out to seal, freeze flat, and then stack them like records once frozen to save space in the freezer. For best taste, thaw them overnight in the fridge (instead of in the microwave) and reheat.

Salt slows the cooking process of beans, so don't add any until very near the end of cooking time. If using broth, make sure it's sodium-free.

Another key to improving the digestibility of beans is to cook them to full tenderness. Undercooked beans are definitely a "musical fruit." The quickest version is to bring them to a boil and then slow cook them for several hours, as described in this recipe. Another method is to cover the rinsed beans with at least 1 inch (2.5 cm) of water and allow them to soak overnight (soaking in the fridge will prevent any bacteria growth). Drain the beans and cover with fresh hot water in the recipe amounts indicated. Cook in the slow cooker on high for 4 hours.

WINE-BRAISED ANTIOXIDANT-RICH ARTICHOKES

INGREDIENTS

For Artichokes

4 whole, fresh artichokes
1 cup (235 ml) dry red wine
1 cup (235 ml) vegetable broth (or water)
1 teaspoon dried oregano
¼ teaspoon black peppercorns
¼ cup (25 g) chopped celery

For Dip

¼ cup (60 g) plain low-fat Greek yogurt
¼ cup (60 g) natural, organic mayonnaise
2 teaspoons freshly squeezed lemon juice
2 teaspoons Dijon mustard
2 tablespoons (6 g) minced fresh chives
1 shallot, minced
¼ teaspoon each salt and white pepper

FROM CHEF JEANNETTE

To choose a fresh artichoke, look for a firm, heavy, medium green one with compact center leaves. To eat a steamed artichoke, pull the leaves off, dip lightly, and drag the base ends through your teeth, scraping off the tender pulp and discarding the tougher parts of the leaves. When all the leaves are gone, scoop out the thistly fibers (choke) and enjoy the tender "heart" (base) and stem.

FROM DR. JONNY: Artichokes are known to be a "liver-friendly" food, and artichoke extract is often included in comprehensive liver formulas. Why? Because the plant is a wonderful source of *silymarin*, the active ingredient in the most important herb for liver health, milk thistle. The leaves also contain a number of active chemical compounds that have been found to be beneficial across a range of health issues. And let's not even talk about artichoke's antioxidant power! . . . Okay, let's. One of the largest studies of antioxidants in food, conducted by the U.S. Department of Agriculture and published in the *Journal of Agriculture and Food Chemistry*, ranked artichokes seventh among the top 100 foods! Artichokes are a nutrient superstar because they provide more than 15 percent of your total Recommended Daily Allowance (RDA) for four or more different vitamins and minerals. One medium artichoke contains 72 mg of magnesium, a whopping 425 mg of heart-healthy potassium, and a substantial 6.5 grams of fiber. And that's all for a miserly 60 calories! A good nutritional deal, no matter how you slice it!

To make the artichokes: Rinse the artichokes and trim off any thorny leaf ends. Slice off the stems at the base and remove any small leaves on the base.

Combine the wine, broth, oregano, peppercorns, and celery in the slow cooker. Place the artichokes, bases down, into the cooker. Cover and cook for 4½ to 5 hours on low, or until the lower leaves pull away easily and the base is fork-tender.

To make the dip: While the artichokes are cooking, in a small bowl, whisk together the yogurt, mayonnaise, lemon juice, mustard, chives, shallot, salt, and pepper until well incorporated. Adjust the seasonings to taste and set aside in the refrigerator for the flavors to develop while the artichokes cook. Serve each artichoke with one-fourth of the dip.

YIELD: 4 servings
PER SERVING: Calories 274; Calories From Fat 113.6; Total Fat 12.6 g; Cholesterol 6.5 mg; Sodium 799.7 mg; Potassium 717.1 mg; Total Carbohydrates 25.4 g; Fiber 8.2 g; Sugar 1.7 g; Protein 7.2 g

NUTS FOR WILD RICE

FROM DR. JONNY: This interesting combination of wild rice and brown rice just seems to beg for an answer to the question: "What's the difference between them, anyway?" So, because you asked (I'm kidding), here's the answer: wild rice is somewhat lower in calories and higher in protein. It's also quite a bit lower in carbs. The two distinct tastes of these whole grains blend beautifully. As for the nutritional benefits of whole grains, it's pretty clear that they're wildly better than the processed kind. A three-year prospective study of more than 200 postmenopausal women with cardiovascular disease, published in the *American Heart Journal*, showed that those eating at least six servings of whole grains each week experienced a significantly reduced progression of atherosclerosis, the buildup of plaque that narrows the vessels through which blood flows. Cheese, eggs, and evaporated skim milk add protein to help offset the carbs from the rice, making this a low-glycemic side dish that could easily do double duty for a vegetarian main course!

INGREDIENTS

Olive oil cooking spray

1 can (12 ounces, or 353 ml) evaporated skim milk

3 eggs

1/2 teaspoon each salt and freshly ground pepper

2 cups (330 g) cooked brown rice (brown basmati or rose brown work well)

1 cup (165 g) cooked wild rice

4 large shallots, chopped

1/3 cup (33 g) finely chopped celery

1/2 cup (55 g) toasted slivered almonds (unsalted)

1/2 cup (68 g) toasted pine nuts (unsalted)

1/3 cup (40 g) chopped toasted walnuts (unsalted)

1 cup (115 g) shredded sharp Cheddar cheese

1/2 cup (75 g) crumbled feta cheese

1/4 cup (15 g) chopped fresh parsley (optional)

Lightly spray (or butter) the insert in the slow cooker and set aside (not necessary if your slow cooker has a nonstick surface).

In a large bowl, combine the milk, eggs, salt, and pepper and whisk to incorporate. Add the rices, shallots, celery, nuts, and cheeses and mix gently to combine.

Spoon the mixture evenly into the prepared slow cooker, cover, and cook on high for 3 to 4 hours, or on low for 5 to 7 hours, until set (a fork inserted into the center should come out clean). Sprinkle with the parsley before serving, if using.

YIELD: 8 servings

PER SERVING: Calories 369.8; Calories From Fat 194.4; Total Fat 22.7 g; Cholesterol 104.4 mg; Sodium 428.7 mg; Potassium 417.3 mg; Total Carbohydrates 27.2 g; Fiber 3.2 g; Sugar 7.4 g; Protein 17 g

Appetizers and Snacks

You might not think of the slow cooker when you think about whipping up snacks or appetizers, but you should. It's one of the easiest ways to prepare healthy snacks on the planet. Slow cook them in batches so you always have something nutritious and delicious on hand!

APPETIZERS

High-Fiber, Puréed White Bean Dip with Rosemary Oil

Tangy Grass-Fed Meatballs

Low-Carb Cheesy Spinach-Artichoke Dip

Flavorful Free-Range Chicken Wings

Antioxidant-Rich Bubbling Black Bean Dip

Rich Reuben Dip with Flu-Fighting Sauerkraut

Mediterranean Stuffed Grape Leaves

Clean and Tasty Pizza Fondue

Low-Carb Sesame Turkey Meatballs

Protein-Rich Pastured Chicken Liver Pâté

Hot and Hearty Red, White, and Blue Crab Dip

SNACKS

Cheesy Gluten-Free Spoonbread

Whole-Grain Crunchy Party Mix

Sweet, Lower-Sugar Rosemary Mixed Nuts

Baba Ghanoush: Aromatic Antioxidants

Dark Chocolate Trail Mix for a Crowd

Eye-Poppin' Lean and Clean Pecans

Sugar-Balancing Cinnamon Almonds

Lightly Sweetened Autumnal Fruit Butter

Nutty Lentil All-Veg Pâté

INGREDIENTS

2 tablespoons (30 ml) rosemary olive oil

1 medium sweet onion, finely diced

4 cloves garlic, minced

2 cans (15 ounces, or 420 g each) Great
    Northern beans

1 can (14.5 ounces, or 406 g) roasted diced
    tomatoes, drained, juice reserved

³⁄₄ teaspoon salt

½ teaspoon cracked black pepper

½ teaspoon Sucanat

½ cup (30 g) chopped fresh flat-leaf parsley

FROM CHEF JEANNETTE

To make your own rosemary oil infusion, combine 2 cups (470 ml) extra-virgin olive oil and 4 to 6 stems (4 inches, or 10 cm each) tender, fresh rosemary in a 1-, 1 ½-, or 2-quart (1, 1.4, or 1.9 L) slow cooker. (You can also add 4 to 6 crushed cloves of garlic.) Cover and cook on low for 2 to 3 hours, to the desired strength (cool a teaspoon of oil carefully before tasting). Remove the insert from the cooker and allow the oil to cool to room temperature. Strain the oil through a double layer of cheesecloth into a sterile glass jar and discard the solids. (To sterilize beforehand, run the jar and lid through the hottest cycle of your dishwasher, or submerge in a pot of boiling water for at least 2 minutes and allow to air-dry.) Seal the jar and store in the refrigerator for up to 1 month.

Serving Suggestions: This dip is fantastic served with crisp vegetable sticks. It is so low in calories and high in fiber and protein that it can also be eaten like hummus: over a bed of greens, in a wrap with lots of chopped lettuce, or even stuffed into half a hollowed-out tomato.

PURÉED WHITE BEAN DIP WITH ROSEMARY OIL

FROM DR. JONNY: As someone who has spent a lot of years helping people lose weight and eat healthier, I can tell you that one of the biggest challenges people face is giving up foods and snacks that they love. Chef Jeannette and I have always been conscious of that, so we try to figure out ways to create familiar and delicious foods and snacks but with "stealth" health benefits—sometimes replacing some of the worst ingredients usually found in these foods, sometimes doing a complete overhaul, and sometimes making subtle changes that boost the nutritional value. Case in point: dips. Everyone loves them, but the commercial versions are filled with chemicals, sweeteners, sodium, and inferior ingredients. Not this version. Just look at the ingredients. Beans are fiber heavyweights and loaded with antioxidants. Garlic is a great medicinal food that diminishes the risk of certain cancers and lowers blood pressure to boot. Tomatoes are loaded with lycopene and vitamin C. And onions provide sulfur compounds that are good for the skin and quercetin, which is good for everything (including substantially reducing inflammation). Not an artificial ingredient, chemical, or preservative in sight. This dip has great staying power and makes a fabulous snack. Note: If you're not buying premade oil, it will need to be infused with the herbs ahead of time.

Heat the oil over medium heat in a large skillet. Add the onion and cook for about 7 minutes, or until very soft but not yet brown. Add the garlic and sauté for 1 minute. Transfer the contents into a 2-quart (1.9 L) slow cooker.

Add the beans and a couple of tablespoons (30 ml) of the reserved tomato juice to a food processor. Process until mostly smooth, scraping down the sides as necessary. Transfer the bean purée to the slow cooker and add the drained tomatoes, salt, pepper, and Sucanat. Stir gently until well combined, adding in a little more of the tomato juice if the mixture is too dry. Cover and cook on high for 1 to 2 hours, or low for 2 to 3 hours, until hot and creamy. Stir in the parsley and serve warm.

YIELD: 12 servings

PER SERVING: Calories 133.1; Calories From Fat 22.6; Total Fat 2.6 g; Cholesterol 0 mg; Sodium 152 mg; Potassium 477 mg; Total Carbohydrates 21.8 g; Fiber 5.2 g; Sugar 3.6 g; Protein 5.9 g

TANGY GRASS-FED MEATBALLS

FROM DR. JONNY: There is nothing like the slow cooker for locking in flavor and moisture, and these slow-cooked, savory meatballs are a perfect example. Moist and incredibly delicious, they have a cider-y, horseradish bite you'll adore. And if you missed our frequent memos on grass-fed meat, let me give you the executive summary: higher in omega-3s and lower in (inflammatory) omega-6s, they have a far better balance of omega fats than their unfortunate brethren on factory farms (also known as CFOs for "controlled feedlot operations"—as different from the family-run farms I visited as a kid as the name implies). Grass-fed meat also contains a wonderful cancer-fighting fat called CLA (conjugated linoleic acid), which is notably absent in factory-farmed meat. Also notably absent: antibiotics, steroids, and growth hormone. Notably present: fabulous flavor.

INGREDIENTS

1 ½ pounds (680 g) leanest ground beef (or use 1 pound [454 g] beef and ½ pound [225 g] leanest ground turkey)

¾ cup (180 ml) low-fat milk

1 egg, lightly beaten

⅔ cup (55 g) whole rolled oats

3 cloves garlic, minced

½ small yellow onion, minced

¼ cup (12 g) finely chopped chives (optional)

1 teaspoon salt

½ teaspoon cracked black pepper

¾ cup (180 g) low-sugar ketchup

⅓ cup (80 ml) water

2 tablespoons (30 ml) apple cider vinegar

1 tablespoon (15 g) horseradish (optional)

1 tablespoon (20 g) honey

In a medium-size bowl, gently mix together the beef, milk, egg, oats, garlic, onion, chives, if using, salt, and pepper. Without overhandling, form into 1-inch (2.5 cm) meatballs and arrange them in the slow cooker.

In a small bowl, whisk together the ketchup, water, vinegar, horseradish, if using, and honey until well combined. Pour the sauce evenly over the meatballs and cook on low for 6 to 8 hours, or until the beef is cooked all the way through (no pink remaining).

YIELD: 8 to 10 servings

PER SERVING: Calories 145.8; Calories From Fat 37.5; Total Fat 4.4 g; Cholesterol 64.1 mg; Sodium 504 mg; Potassium 292.6 mg; Total Carbohydrates 41.9 g; Fiber 0.7 g; Sugar 3.3 g; Protein 16.7 g

LOW-CARB CHEESY SPINACH-ARTICHOKE DIP

INGREDIENTS

1 tablespoon (15 ml) olive oil

1 small sweet onion, finely diced

2 cloves garlic, minced

1 jar (7.5-ounce, 210 g) marinated, grilled artichoke hearts, drained and chopped (or use regular marinated)

1 can (14 ounces, or 420 g) artichoke hearts in water, drained and chopped

1 package (10 ounces, or 280 g) frozen chopped spinach, thawed, drained, and squeezed well to remove all excess moisture

¼ cup (60 g) natural mayonnaise

2 cups (225 g) shredded Cheddar cheese

½ cup (40 g) shredded Parmesan cheese

FROM CHEF JEANNETTE

Serving Suggestions: This dip is delicious served with baked corn chips, on whole-grain crackers, or for a low-carb option, with crisp vegetable sticks such as celery, carrot, bell pepper, or cucumber rounds.

FROM DR. JONNY: I'll bet you never thought of an artichoke as a vegetable superstar, but that's exactly what it is. A 2004 study published in the *Journal of Agricultural and Food Chemistry* used updated technology to rank the antioxidant content of more than 100 foods, and artichokes came in seventh! Which isn't that surprising; after all, one medium-size artichoke contains 72 mg of magnesium, 425 mg of potassium, and a substantial 6.5 grams of fiber (all for a measly 60 calories!). And I'm sure I don't have to tell you about spinach, one of the healthiest vegetables on earth, with its generous helping of heart-healthy, bone-supporting vitamin K, vitamin C, iron, and plant chemicals called *flavonoids*, which function both as antioxidants and as anticancer agents. How can you lose? This dip is low in carbs and has minimal impact on your blood sugar. Suggestion: Don't spoil this great recipe with some dumb processed "cheese food" product. Go for the gusto with a nice, healthy, and real cheese!

Heat the oil in a large skillet over medium-high heat. Add the onion and cook until softened but not browned, 4 to 5 minutes. Add the garlic and cook for 30 seconds, stirring constantly. Spoon the onion and garlic into a slow cooker. Add the artichokes, spinach, mayonnaise, and cheeses and stir gently to combine. Cook on high for 1 to 2 hours, or on low for 2 to 3 hours, until well melted and bubbly. Stir well with a heavy spoon to combine before serving.

YIELD: 10 servings

PER SERVING: Calories 215.4; Calories From Fat 133.1; Total Fat 15 g; Cholesterol 30.1 mg; Sodium 321.1 mg; Potassium 369.8 mg; Total Carbohydrates 11.4 g; Fiber 5.1 g; Sugar 2.2 g; Protein 10.9 g

FLAVORFUL FREE-RANGE CHICKEN WINGS

INGREDIENTS

⅔ cup (160 ml) low-sodium tamari

2 cups (470 ml) no-sodium chicken broth (or use half freshly squeezed orange juice)

½ cup (120 ml) dry white wine

¼ cup (60 ml) sesame oil

2 tablespoons (12 g) minced fresh ginger

4 cloves garlic, minced

1 tablespoon (20 g) honey, Sucanat, or xylitol

4 pounds (1.8 kg) chicken wings

1 tablespoon (16 g) toasted sesame seeds (optional)

FROM CHEF JEANNETTE

It's a time-saver to cook the wings whole, but if you'd prefer the classic "wing and drummette" sections, simply cut each whole wing at the two joints to separate them into three pieces and discard the wing tips.

FROM DR. JONNY: When I was a kid we took family vacations in a small resort in upstate New York called Deerpark Farm, which was actually exactly as described—a real working farm that was also a small resort with cabins, a children's program, tennis, and a pool. I remember the farm part really well. Chickens ran around pecking at whatever chickens peck at, the owners dutifully collected eggs every day, the cows ranged around on pasture, and the dogs chased cars. Those chickens were truly free-range. We know now that when animals are left to graze (or peck) at their natural food supply they produce meat (and eggs and milk) that is significantly different from their factory-farmed brethren. When chickens roam around (as opposed to being confined in battery cages all their lives) they peck at all sorts of things, like worms, insects, and whatever else is in their path. The result is that their meat has far more omega-3 fats, and is not contaminated with all the chemicals and hormones given to animals raised in close confinement. So I never recommend any meat (chicken, beef, or anything else) that wasn't raised on its natural diet. Use free-range chicken in this recipe, preferably from small local farms, and use the slow cooker to marinate it, giving it plenty of time to develop its full flavor. You'll get a fabulous, flavorful, high-protein dish with none of the chemicals and steroids found in factory-farmed chickens.

Combine the tamari, broth, wine, oil, ginger, garlic, and honey in a glass 9 x 13-inch (23 x 33 cm) baking dish or large shallow bowl. Whisk well to combine. Add the chicken wings and toss gently to coat. Seal and marinate in the refrigerator overnight, turning occasionally to recoat.

Transfer the contents to 6- or 7-quart (5.7 or 6.6 L) slow cooker, cover, and cook on low for 3 to 4 hours, until the chicken is cooked through but still tender. Drain, discard the marinade, sprinkle the sesame seeds over the wings, and serve.

YIELD: about 20 servings

PER SERVING: Calories 249.3; Calories From Fat 157.7; Total Fat 17.6 g; Cholesterol 69.9 mg; Sodium 447.6 mg; Potassium 173.9 mg; Total Carbohydrates 2.3 g; Fiber 0.1 g; Sugar 1 g; Protein 18.3 g

ANTIOXIDANT-RICH BUBBLING BLACK BEAN DIP

INGREDIENTS

¹⁄₃ cup (45 g) pickled jalapeño peppers

2 cans (15 ounces, or 420 g each) black beans, rinsed and drained

Juice and zest from ¹⁄₂ lime

1 teaspoon ground cumin

1 teaspoon chili powder

³⁄₄ teaspoon salt

1 cup (260 g) prepared salsa

¹⁄₂ cup (8 g) chopped fresh cilantro (or chopped scallion)

¹⁄₄ cup (34 g) toasted pepitas, for garnish

FROM CHEF JEANNETTE

Serving Suggestions: Serve with baked corn chips, on whole-grain crackers, or for a low-carb option, with crisp vegetable sticks such as celery, carrot, bell pepper, or cucumber.

FROM DR. JONNY: Just about everyone knows the main nutritional selling point of beans is fiber. (Approximately 15 whopping grams per cup!) But what's less known is that beans, including black beans, are antioxidant powerhouses. The ORAC test measures the total antioxidant power of a given food by looking at how all the compounds in that food work together—much like evaluating the performance of a basketball team rather than just the individual players. On the ORAC scale, black beans score extremely high, higher than such powerhouses as blueberries, apples, and even plums. This black bean dip is sizzling with the flavors of jalapeño peppers, with their nice dose of capsaicin, the stuff that makes them hot but also helps lower pain and inflammation! This high-fiber, high-protein dip is so rich in flavor you could say, as my mother frequently did about any snack she liked, "I could make a meal of this!"

Place the jalapeños in the food processor and pulse a few times to chop. Add the beans, lime juice and zest, cumin, chili powder, and salt, and process until smooth, scraping down the sides as necessary. Transfer the mixture to a 2-quart (1.9 L) slow cooker and stir in the salsa until well combined. Cover and cook on high for 1 to 2 hours, or low for 2 to 3 hours, until hot and creamy. Stir in the cilantro and garnish with the pepitas.

YIELD: 12 servings

PER SERVING: Calories 81.6; Calories From Fat 3.5; Total Fat 0.4 g; Cholesterol 0 mg; Sodium 494.7 mg; Potassium 274.9 mg; Total Carbohydrates 15.1 g; Fiber 5.4 g; Sugar 0.7 g; Protein 5.2 g

RICH REUBEN DIP WITH FLU-FIGHTING SAUERKRAUT

INGREDIENTS

8 ounces (225 g) corned beef, shredded

1 jar (32 ounces, or 896 g) high-quality sauerkraut, drained

8 ounces (225 g) Neufchâtel cheese, chopped

8 ounces (225 g) shredded Swiss cheese

8 ounces (225 g) low-fat sour cream

1 pound (454 g) baby carrots

Whole-grain rye cocktail bread

FROM DR. JONNY: Okay, you're wondering how sauerkraut helps fight flu? (I know, I know. It sounds like a bad riddle.) The thing of it is, sauerkraut is a naturally fermented food, putting it in the elite company of other legendary health foods like yogurt, miso, tempeh, real olives (not the chemically ripened ones in the jar!), and the Korean food kimchi. When foods are naturally fermented, they produce a wonderful, healthy group of bacteria that we know as *probiotics*. Probiotics are powerful stimulators of the immune system, not to mention the fact that they help protect the environment of your gut and assist with the digestion and assimilation of nutrients. And sauerkraut is filled with these probiotics. In fact, it's one of the few foods that contains a specific bacterium called *Lactobacillus plantarum*, which is known to boost the immune system by increasing antibodies that fight infectious diseases. Hence the clever "flu-fighting" moniker in the recipe title. (Well, I thought it was clever.) This rich flavorful dip is a creamy indulgence.

Combine the corned beef, sauerkraut, cheeses, and sour cream in the slow cooker. Cover and cook on low for 2 hours, or until the cheeses are melted. Stir very well before serving with the carrots and rye bread.

YIELD: 16 servings

PER SERVING: Calories 159.9; Calories From Fat 99.9; Total Fat 11.3 g; Cholesterol 37.4 mg; Sodium 659.4 mg; Potassium 252.3 mg; Total Carbohydrates 6.6 g; Fiber 2.5 g; Sugar 2.6 g; Protein 8.5 g

MEDITERRANEAN STUFFED GRAPE LEAVES

INGREDIENTS

Olive oil cooking spray

1 pound (454 g) leanest ground lamb

1 small red onion, finely chopped

2 cloves garlic, minced

1 cup (165 g) cooked brown rice (golden rose brown rice or brown basmati works well)

1/3 cup (50 g) raisins

1 teaspoon salt

1/2 teaspoon freshly ground pepper

1/2 cup (48 g) chopped fresh mint

1/3 cup (80 ml) freshly squeezed lemon juice, divided

About 48 grape leaves, drained and rinsed

2 teaspoons olive oil

1 1/2 cups (353 ml) low-sodium vegetable broth or water

FROM CHEF JEANNETTE

If using fresh leaves, first submerge in boiling water for about 30 seconds, drain, and rinse in cold water to soften.

FROM DR. JONNY: Besides being ridiculously low in calories (fewer than 3 calories per leaf!), grape leaves are nutritionally dense, containing 44 mg of calcium, 33 mg of potassium, and an unbelievable amount of beta-carotene and vitamin A (1,943 mg and 3,303 IUs, respectively), not to mention a hefty 210 mcg dose of those eye-friendly carotenoids lutein and zeaxanthin—all for one 11-calorie, 4-leaf serving. No wonder they talk about how healthy the Mediterranean diet is! Lamb is always a great choice when it comes to protein foods, and the onions and garlic add their usual benefits, which include sulfur compounds for beautiful skin and cancer-fighting allicin (formed when the garlic is crushed in cooking). What's more, garlic is high in antioxidants as well as being anti-inflammatory, antibiotic, and antiviral. Did I mention that this dish tastes as great as it looks? The gentle heat of the slow cooker is absolutely perfect for cooking tender, delicate grape leaves. This dish would be right at home at a beach resort on the Greek Isles.

Spray the insert of a slow cooker thinly with olive oil and set aside.

In a large skillet over medium-high heat, combine the lamb, onion, and garlic and cook for 5 to 6 minutes, stirring frequently, until the meat is cooked through (no pink remaining). Remove from the heat, drain off the excess fat, and fold in the rice, raisins, salt, pepper, mint, and 2 tablespoons (30 ml) of the lemon juice. Set aside.

Lay out one grape leaf, shiny side down, and place a heaping tablespoon (15 g) of lamb filling near the bottom of the leaf (stem side). Fold in the sides of the leaf over the filling and roll from the wide bottom side upward. Place the roll, seam side down, against the side of the slow cooker insert. Continue to fill each leaf and pack them close together to prevent unrolling, stacking them in layers. Whisk the remaining 3 1/2 tablespoons (50 ml) lemon juice and the olive oil into the broth and pour evenly over the stuffed leaves. Cover and cook on low for about 4 hours, or until the stuffed leaves are tender.

YIELD: 12 servings

PER SERVING: Calories 163.5; Calories From Fat 91.6; Total Fat 10.1 g; Cholesterol 27.6 mg; Sodium 236.1 mg; Potassium 168.5 mg; Total Carbohydrates 10.8 g; Fiber 2.1 g; Sugar 3.7 g; Protein 7.7 g

CLEAN AND TASTY PIZZA FONDUE

INGREDIENTS

8 ounces (225 g) leanest ground turkey

1 small yellow onion, finely chopped

4 cloves garlic, minced

1 can (28 ounces, or 784 g) crushed tomatoes

1 can (6 ounces, or 168 g) tomato paste

½ cup (120 ml) hot water

1 tablespoon (1.3 g) dried parsley

1 teaspoon Sucanat or xylitol

1 teaspoon salt

1 teaspoon dried basil

1 teaspoon dried oregano

½ teaspoon red pepper flakes (optional)

¼ cup (20 g) shredded Parmesan cheese

8 ounces (225 g) mozzarella cheese, cut into
    ½-inch (1.3 cm) cubes

2 cups (480 g) baby carrots

½ loaf whole-grain or sourdough bread, cut
    into 1-inch (2.5 cm) cubes (or use 1 small
    whole-grain pizza crust, toasted and cut
    into strips)

FROM CHEF JEANNETTE

Time-Saver Tip: To save time, use 2 cans
(15 ounces, or 420 g each) high-quality pizza
sauce in place of the homemade (crushed
tomatoes through oregano). If you do that,
you may also want to add 2 crumbled links
(4 ounces, or 112 g each) Italian chicken
sausage to the turkey for more flavor.

FROM DR. JONNY: When I was a student at Juilliard in New York
(more decades ago than I wish to admit, thank you very much), I had
one dish that I could make to impress the women I invited to my bachelor pad on Central Park West. The dish was fondue. It was just coming
into style at the time and considered oh-so-cosmopolitan and vaguely
European, and I thought I was the bomb serving it in my little fondue
maker from Crate & Barrel. But regular fondue is all cheese, and not
even necessarily very good cheese. And let's not even talk about how
many calories it has. This modern, urbane "fondue" is very flavorful yet
way lighter on the cheese, and spiked with protein from lean ground
turkey and antioxidants from the tasty tomato sauce. Chef Jeannette
cleverly decided to use mozzarella cheese as one of the "dippers" (versus
the main ingredient!) to control the amount you consume. Brilliant. A
word to the wise: Swap out the bread for dipping and use more crudités!
You'll never miss the processed carbs and your body will thank you for
the added nutrients.

In a large skillet over medium heat, combine the turkey, onion, and garlic
and cook for about 8 minutes, or until the meat is cooked though and no
pink remains. Transfer the contents to a slow cooker and add the crushed
tomatoes, tomato paste, water, parsley, Sucanat, salt, basil, oregano, red
pepper flakes, and Parmesan. Stir well to mix, cover, and cook on low for
3 to 4 hours, until hot and melted. Stir and serve with the mozzarella,
carrots, and bread for dipping.

YIELD: 16 servings
PER SERVING: Calories 150; Calories From Fat 38; Total Fat 4.3 g; Cholesterol
21.7 mg; Sodium 518.5 mg; Potassium 365.8 mg; Total Carbohydrates 19.2 g;
Fiber 2.9 g; Sugar 3.3 g; Protein 10 g

LOW-CARB SESAME TURKEY MEATBALLS

INGREDIENTS

1 ½ pounds (680 g) leanest ground turkey

1 egg, beaten

⅓ cup (5 g) finely chopped cilantro

2 tablespoons (16 g) toasted sesame seeds

1 tablespoon (6 g) minced fresh ginger

3 cloves garlic, minced

¼ teaspoon cayenne pepper

2 cups (470 ml) low-sodium chicken broth

½ cup (120 ml) low-sodium tamari

½ cup (120 ml) mirin

½ cup (125 g) white miso paste

1 ½ tablespoons (12 g) kudzu dissolved in 2 tablespoons (30 ml) chicken broth or water (optional)

FROM DR. JONNY: Ever since I wrote my book *Living Low Carb: Controlled Carbohydrate Eating for Long-Term Weight Loss*, I've been identified as a "low-carb" kind of guy. That's not altogether wrong— I've long maintained that sugar is way more damaging to our health and our waistline than fat ever was, and I think we eat entirely too many processed carbs in general. So with that said, I'm delighted to introduce this perfect low-carb recipe, which will neither play havoc with your blood sugar nor raise your fat-storing hormones. The recipe also features kudzu, one of the most interesting ingredients to come down the pike in a while. It's a plant that's native to China and Japan, and is loaded with plant chemicals called *isoflavones*, which are both anti-inflammatory and antimicrobial. The sesame seeds and miso give this low-calorie turkey meatball recipe a deep Japanese flair. Fun fact: Kudzu grows so fast, especially in the Southern United States, that it's been nicknamed "the vine that ate the South." Harvard Medical School researchers are currently studying kudzu as a possible way to treat alcohol cravings.

In a large bowl, combine the turkey, egg, cilantro, sesame seeds, ginger, garlic, and cayenne pepper. Mix gently and form 1½-inch (3.8 cm) meatballs—do not overhandle the meat. Arrange the meatballs in the slow cooker insert.

In another bowl, whisk together the chicken broth, tamari, mirin, and miso and pour over the meatballs. Cover and cook on high for 3 to 3½ hours, until the meatballs are cooked through and no pink remains. Remove and serve the meatballs as is or, to accompany with sauce, transfer the liquid to a medium-size pan on the stove over medium-high heat. Bring to a boil, add the dissolved kudzu, and stir for 1 to 2 minutes, until thickened. Serve with the meatballs.

YIELD: 8 servings

PER SERVING: Calories 235.3; Calories From Fat 90.1; Total Fat 10.2 g; Cholesterol 93.6 mg; Sodium 1,579.3 mg; Potassium 323.3 mg; Total Carbohydrates 14.5 g; Fiber 1.3 g; Sugar 5.2 g; Protein 21.4 g

PROTEIN-RICH PASTURED CHICKEN LIVER PÂTÉ

INGREDIENTS

5 ½ tablespoons (75 g) unsalted butter (preferably organic), divided, plus more for the dish

1 red onion, finely chopped

1 pound (454 g) raw chicken livers (from organic chickens raised on pasture), cleaned (deveined)

2 cloves garlic, minced

¾ teaspoon salt

½ teaspoon cracked black pepper

2 tablespoons (30 ml) dry sherry (such as fino, or use brandy)

2 teaspoons finely minced fresh rosemary (or ¾ teaspoon dried and finely chopped)

1 teaspoon fresh thyme (or ½ teaspoon dried)

Zest from 1 lemon

FROM DR. JONNY: I'm not sure where the expression "What am I, chopped liver?" came from, but it does a disservice to this much-maligned food. Chicken liver is a rich source of protein, very low in sodium, and a decent source of vitamins like thiamin, zinc, copper, vitamins A and C, riboflavin, niacin, and quite a few others. The one reason it gets a bad rap is that it's relatively high in cholesterol, but readers who have followed my work know that I don't think this is the problem it's cracked up to be. (The liver makes most of the body's cholesterol, and the amount we eat has negligible effect on our blood levels.) My one and only caution about chicken liver is this: because the liver is "detox central" in the body, it's likely to be a repository for a lot of chemicals, medicines, and artificial ingredients. I strongly recommend you only get organ meats from organically raised chickens, preferably free-range. And because this mineral-rich pâté is not exactly a "low-cal" dish, remember to consume sparingly!

Butter a small, shallow casserole dish or terrine and set aside. (It must have a lid and fit into your slow cooker.)

Melt 3 tablespoons (45 g) of the butter in a large skillet over medium heat, add the onion, and cook for about 5 minutes. Add the livers and cook for about 4 minutes, stirring occasionally. Stir in the garlic, salt, and pepper and cook for another minute. Mash slightly and stir in the sherry, rosemary, thyme, and remaining 2 ½ tablespoons (30 g) butter and cook another couple of minutes. Remove from the heat, transfer the mixture to a food processor, and purée to the desired consistency. Stir in the lemon zest and transfer to the prepared casserole dish, cover, and place in a 6- or 7-quart (5.7 or 6.6 L) slow cooker. Slowly add water to come halfway up the sides of the casserole dish, cover the slow cooker, and cook on low for 6 to 7 hours, until very tender and cooked through. Unplug the slow cooker and remove the covers to cool enough to remove the casserole dish from the hot water.

YIELD: 12 servings

PER SERVING: Calories 99.1; Calories From Fat 63.2; Total Fat 7.1 g; Cholesterol 144.4 mg; Sodium 173.6 mg; Potassium 96.4 mg; Total Carbohydrates 1.4 g; Fiber 0.3 g; Sugar 0 g; Protein 6.6 g

HOT AND HEARTY RED, WHITE, AND BLUE CRAB DIP

INGREDIENTS
1 pound (454 g) lump blue crabmeat
2 roasted red pepper halves, finely chopped
$\frac{1}{3}$ cup (75 g) natural mayonnaise
$\frac{1}{3}$ cup (38 g) shredded pepper Jack cheese
$\frac{1}{3}$ cup (27 g) shredded Parmesan cheese
1 teaspoon hot pepper sauce
$\frac{1}{2}$ teaspoon salt
$\frac{1}{2}$ cup (8 g) chopped fresh cilantro

FROM CHEF JEANNETTE

Serving Suggestions: This dip is delicious served on whole-grain crackers, or for a low-carb option, with crisp vegetable sticks such as celery, carrot, bell pepper, or cucumber.

FROM DR. JONNY: Blue crab is almost pure protein—and very low in calories to boot. (One cup [118 g] packs more than 24 grams of protein into a measly 112 calories.) And blue crab is a surprisingly good source of selenium, which in my opinion is one of the most important trace minerals we don't get enough of. (Low levels of selenium have been linked to higher levels of prostate cancer.) Our easy dip is a delicious blend of seafood with a bit of cheese and mayo, but way less than you'll find in traditional crab dips, which, sad to say, are *mostly* cheese and mayo with a little bit of imitation crabmeat thrown in for good measure. Those delicious roasted red peppers add more than 190 mg of vitamin C. The pepper Jack cheese and hot sauce give the whole shebang a nice taste kick.

Combine the crabmeat, red peppers, mayonnaise, cheeses, hot pepper sauce, and salt in a 2-quart (1.9 L) slow cooker and mix gently to combine. Cover and cook on high for 1 to 2 hours, or on low for 2 to 3 hours, until hot and melted. Add the cilantro and stir well with a heavy spoon before serving.

YIELD: 8 to 10 servings
PER SERVING: Calories 135.6; Calories From Fat 81.8; Total Fat 9 g; Cholesterol 50.9 mg; Sodium 384.8 mg; Potassium 194.2 mg; Total Carbohydrates 1.4 g; Fiber 0.5 g; Sugar 0 g; Protein 11.6 g

INGREDIENTS

Olive oil cooking spray

2 eggs

¾ cup (105 g) high-quality stone-ground cornmeal

1¼ cups (163 g) fresh corn kernels (or frozen, thawed)

⅔ cup (75 g) low-fat cottage cheese

2 tablespoons (30 ml) unrefined corn oil (or olive oil)

1 tablespoon (15 g) Sucanat or xylitol

2 teaspoons baking powder

Several dashes of hot pepper sauce, to taste (optional)

½ teaspoon salt

½ cup (58 g) shredded sharp Cheddar cheese

CHEESY GLUTEN-FREE SPOONBREAD

FROM DR. JONNY: If this is the first time you've encountered the term *gluten-free*, a word of explanation is in order. Gluten is a protein, and it's found in grains like wheat, rye, and barley. And it's a big problem for many people. When it becomes a huge problem, it's diagnosed as celiac disease, a condition in which the intestinal villi (tiny little projections that come out from the walls of the small intestine) are seriously damaged when they come into contact with gluten. One in 133 people have full-blown celiac disease, but many more are affected with a much lesser version of this syndrome, which is usually called *gluten sensitivity* or *gluten intolerance*. Symptoms of gluten intolerance can range all over the map, but when people who are sensitive to gluten stop eating it, their symptoms, which can include bloating, brain fog, aches, and pains, clear up almost immediately. Hence the huge explosion of gluten-free products on the market. Here we've created one of our own. This is a moist, wheat-free (and therefore gluten-free) bread that you can actually eat with a spoon. No kidding. It's warm, soothing, and satisfying and just begs to be enjoyed either on its own or as a side dish. The cottage cheese adds a nice protein boost! Hint: Just to be safe, avoid the GMO cornmeal and go for organic.

Spray the insert of a 2-quart (1.9 L) slow cooker with olive oil and set aside.

Add the eggs to a large mixing bowl and whisk until lightly beaten. Add the cornmeal, corn, cottage cheese, corn oil, Sucanat, baking powder, hot pepper sauce, if using, and salt and mix to combine. Spoon the batter into the prepared slow cooker, cover, and cook on low for 2 to 2½ hours, until the center is set. Sprinkle an even layer of cheese over the top, cover, and cook for 5 to 10 minutes longer, until the cheese melts.

YIELD: 8 servings

PER SERVING: Calories 159; Calories From Fat 71.7; Total Fat 8.1 g; Cholesterol 61.8 mg; Sodium 407.7 mg; Potassium 134.4 mg; Total Carbohydrates 14.9 g; Fiber 1.6 g; Sugar 2.6 g; Protein 7.7 g

WHOLE-GRAIN CRUNCHY PARTY MIX

INGREDIENTS

2 cups (62 g) natural whole wheat Chex-style cereal

2 cups (62 g) natural whole oat Chex-style cereal

2 cups (56 g) whole-grain "O's"-style cereal

1 pound (454 g) roasted mixed nuts, unsalted

1 cup (30 g) whole-grain mini pretzel twists or sticks

¼ cup (55 g) unsalted butter, melted

2 teaspoons Worcestershire sauce (use organic to avoid high-fructose corn syrup)

1 teaspoon granulated garlic

1 teaspoon curry powder

¾ teaspoon garlic salt

½ teaspoon onion powder

½ teaspoon cayenne pepper

FROM DR. JONNY: So what's a recipe for party mix doing in a nice healthy cookbook like this? Actually it's a slow cooker favorite, but unfortunately it's usually made from conventional cereals. If that sugar hit weren't enough, most commercial mixes use refined white flour (can everyone say "boo") and high-fructose corn syrup. So making this better wasn't as much of a challenge as you might think—after all, the commercial stuff couldn't get much worse! Now we did use cereals—after all, what's a party mix without the Chex? But we boosted the quality considerably by using natural, whole-grain cereal without artificial ingredients. We added nuts for their fiber, minerals, and monounsaturated fat (great for the heart), and we eliminated a whole lot of calories by halving the usual amount of butter (with virtually no sacrifice in taste or texture). (We strongly recommend organic butter!) Our much-better-for-you version still maintains all the spicy, satisfying crunch of the classic version!

Combine the cereals, nuts, and pretzels in a 6-quart (5.7 L) slow cooker and mix gently to combine.

In a small bowl, whisk together the butter, Worcestershire, granulated garlic, curry, garlic salt, onion powder, and cayenne pepper. Drizzle over the mix and fold very gently to coat without breaking the cereal. Cover and cook on low for 3 hours, frequently stirring gently. Remove the lid for the last hour of cooking time to aid with the drying. Or cook uncovered on high for 2 hours, stirring frequently.

YIELD: about 2 quarts (775 g) or 16 servings
PER SERVING: Calories 257; Calories From Fat 155.6; Total Fat 18.4 g; Cholesterol 7.6 mg; Sodium 190.5 mg; Potassium 271.5 mg; Total Carbohydrates 17.8 g; Fiber 4.6 g; Sugar 2.8 g; Protein 7.7 g

SWEET, LOWER-SUGAR ROSEMARY MIXED NUTS

INGREDIENTS

2 teaspoons unsalted butter

2 teaspoons Sucanat

2 or 3 dashes hot sauce

3 tablespoons (5 g) minced fresh rosemary

½ teaspoon salt

3 cups (435 g) roasted mixed nuts, unsalted

FROM DR. JONNY: As many of you know, I'm a native New Yorker, and we walk everywhere. And since this is the custom in that city, there's a plethora of street vendors selling every kind of snack you can imagine, as New Yorkers seem constitutionally unable to walk down the street without a cell phone in one hand and a junk food snack in the other. But I digress. One of the most popular fixtures on New York street corners is the candied nuts man. And in the old days, I was a steady customer. I justified this ridiculously fattening treat by saying it had nuts in it—but the truth is, candied nuts are basically swimming in heavy syrup with enough sugar to prompt a diabetic coma. (I'm exaggerating, but still.) No sugar or junky cheap frying oil here—just some Sucanat and healthy butter. The low heat and long cooking time of the slow cooker allow for the gentle absorption of the light sweetener and the pungent richness of the rosemary. Best of all, these nuts are as fragrant and flavorful as I remember the New York street vendor nuts to be, despite being treated with a light hand and much better nutrition. Note: This recipe works with any nut or combo of nuts. Try with cashews, my personal fave.

In a small saucepan over medium heat, combine the butter, Sucanat, hot sauce, rosemary, and salt and cook, stirring frequently, until the butter is melted and the ingredients are well incorporated. Add the nuts to a 2- to 4-quart (1.9 to 3.8 L) slow cooker and drizzle the butter mixture over all. Stir gently to thoroughly coat and cook on low, uncovered, for 1 to 2 hours, stirring occasionally. Serve warm or at room temperature. Store in an airtight container in the fridge.

YIELD: 3 cups (435 g)

FOR ENTIRE RECIPE: Calories 2,576.2; Calories From Fat 1,899.6; Total Fat 226.7 g; Cholesterol 20.4 mg; Sodium 1,173.4 mg; Potassium 3,125.3 mg; Total Carbohydrates 88.9 g; Fiber 49.6 g; Sugar 28.3 g; Protein 91.7 g

BABA GHANOUSH: AROMATIC ANTIOXIDANTS

FROM DR. JONNY: I like the color of eggplant so much I bought a car that's the same color! (Okay, not exactly, but it was such a good opening sentence I couldn't resist!) The thing of it is, the rich color that makes eggplant purple is a member of a family of plant chemicals called anthocyanins, the pigments that make blueberries blue, raspberries red, and, yes, eggplants purple. One compound in particular that has been isolated from eggplant pigments is called *nasunin*, which, like other members of the anthocyanin family, is a powerful antioxidant, eating up free radicals that cause serious damage to your cells and DNA. Eggplant is filling, is incredibly low in calories (35 per cup!), and has 2.5 grams of fiber in a 1 cup (100 g) serving. This is a low-calorie, mild-tasting dip with some nice protein and fiber. Try it warm with steamed veggies or cold with crudités.

INGREDIENTS

2 eggplants (about 2 pounds, or 908 g), peeled
   and cut into 1-inch (2.5 cm) cubes

¾ teaspoon salt

⅓ cup (80 g) raw tahini

⅓ cup (80 ml) freshly squeezed lemon juice

4 large cloves garlic, minced

½ teaspoon freshly ground pepper

⅓ cup (77 g) plain, low-fat Greek yogurt

FROM CHEF JEANNETTE

Time-Saver Tip: Do not peel or drain the raw eggplants. Halve them lengthwise and cook in the slow cooker as directed until very soft. Remove the cooked eggplant and place in a colander or fine-mesh sieve in the sink to drain for at least 30 minutes. Once cool, press out any remaining liquid with a wooden spoon, scoop the flesh out of the skins, and discard the skins. Follow the rest of the recipe instructions as written, but add ½ teaspoon salt, or to taste.

Toss the eggplant cubes with the salt and let them drain in a colander or fine-mesh sieve in the sink for 1 hour. Transfer the drained eggplant to a slow cooker and cook on high for 3 to 4 hours, or on low for 6 to 7 hours, or until very soft. Transfer the eggplant to a fine-mesh sieve and press with a large wooden spoon to drain out excess liquid. Place the drained eggplant in the bowl of a mixer and add the tahini, lemon juice, garlic, and pepper and beat on low until very well mixed. Stir in the yogurt, adjust the seasonings to taste, and serve.

YIELD: 12 servings

PER SERVING: Calories 63.7; Calories From Fat 28.9; Total Fat 3.5 g; Cholesterol 0.4 mg; Sodium 156.5 mg; Potassium 231.4 mg; Total Carbohydrates 7.5 g; Fiber 3.3 g; Sugar 2 g; Protein 2.4 g

DARK CHOCOLATE TRAIL MIX FOR A CROWD

INGREDIENTS

1 ½ pounds (680 g) highest quality dark
  chocolate bark (preferably organic)

12 ounces (336 g) highest quality dark chocolate
  (such as Callebaut or Dagoba organic)

1 ½ pounds (680 g) roasted mixed nuts

6 ounces (168 g) juice-sweetened tart cherries

4 ounces (112 g) whole-grain mini twist pretzels
  or whole-grain Chex-style cereal (optional)

FROM DR. JONNY: I'm probably dating myself, but I actually remember when trail mix first came out. I remember hiking the Delaware Water Gap with one of my brother's friends, an experienced hiker, and he used to bring these plastic baggies filled with nuts, raisins, and M&M's. Not long afterward I started seeing prepared bags of similar concoctions sold in what were then quaintly called "health food" stores. Now trail mix is a common item in every grocery store and comes with every possible mix of nuts, raisins, dried fruit, chocolate, and pretzels that you can imagine. I've even seen it in prepackaged "100-calorie snack" packs perfect for lunchboxes. And by the way, that's a good thing. Trail mix is one of those really good-for-you things that you can easily get kids to eat—just don't tell them it's "health food." Which our version definitely is. We use cocoa-rich dark chocolate because of the health-promoting flavanols in cocoa, which have been shown to support heart health and blood pressure. We also use tart cherries, a fruit that has gained a ton of attention from studies showing that they help control body weight (in animals) and help reduce inflammation (in people). Use any nuts you like—all of them contain minerals and fiber and a dollop of protein for good measure. Remember, though, that this is, after all, a "candy," so it's higher in sugar and calories than many other treats. Moderation is the key to enjoying this wonderfully healthy mix of delectables. Note: This recipe makes a really big batch, so get ready to share with friends!

Layer the chocolates on the bottom of the slow cooker. Pour the nuts on top and cover. Cook on low for 1½ to 2½ hours, until the chocolate is fully melted (start checking at 90 minutes). Stir gently to thoroughly mix.

Remove the insert from the cooker, uncover, and let cool for 30 minutes. Fold in the cherries. Gently fold in the pretzels, if using, and turn carefully with a spoon to coat all without breaking the pretzels.

Lay out two 2-foot (61 cm) lengths of waxed paper and drop the mixture by tablespoonfuls onto the paper. Allow to cool completely. The pieces will harden as they cool. Store in the refrigerator.

YIELD: about 4 pounds (1.8 kg) (about 30 servings)
PER SERVING: Calories 313.3; Calories From Fat 194.7; Total Fat 24.7 g; Cholesterol 0.8 mg; Sodium 40.8 mg; Potassium 157.2 mg; Total Carbohydrates 26.3 g; Fiber 6.4 g; Sugar 0.4 g; Protein 7.6 g

EYE-POPPIN' LEAN AND CLEAN PECANS

INGREDIENTS

3 cups (435 g) whole roasted pecans (or whole
     roasted almonds), unsalted

1 teaspoon olive oil

2 or 3 dashes of Worcestershire sauce (use
     organic to avoid high-fructose corn syrup)

1 ½ teaspoons chili powder

½ teaspoon chipotle pepper, or more to taste

¾ teaspoon garlic powder

½ teaspoon cayenne pepper

¼ teaspoon salt

FROM DR. JONNY: Nuts, as you probably know, are one of the great original health foods. Five—count 'em, five—major studies (including the Physicians Health Study, the Iowa Women's Health Study, and the Nurses Health Study) have examined the relationship between nut consumption and the risk of cardiovascular disease and all have found an inverse relationship (more nuts equals a lower risk). This recipe mixes pecans (or almonds) with some edgy, hot spices that give them real bite and character, and cooking them in the slow cooker allows the spicy flavors to penetrate—no extra oils needed! In fact, with 1 scant teaspoon of heart-healthy olive oil, you can power up 3 full cups (435 g) of nuts with a tongue-tickling kickiness. Enjoy!

Add the nuts to a 2- to 4-quart (1.9 to 3.8 L) slow cooker. Drizzle with the olive oil and Worcestershire. Evenly sprinkle the spices over all and mix well with a wooden spoon to thoroughly coat. Cook on low for 1 hour. Remove the lid, stir, and cook uncovered for about 30 minutes longer. Serve warm or at room temperature. Store in an airtight container in the fridge.

YIELD: 3 cups (435 g)

FOR ENTIRE RECIPE: Calories 3,001; Calories From Fat 2,620.5; Total Fat 312.7 g; Cholesterol 0 mg; Sodium 625.9 mg; Potassium 1,871 mg; Total Carbohydrates 60.4 g; Fiber 40.7 g; Sugar 17.7 g; Protein 40.3 g

INGREDIENTS

2 tablespoons (14 g) ground Saigon cinnamon

1/4 teaspoon ground allspice

1 teaspoon powdered arrowroot (or use cornstarch)

1 egg white

1 tablespoon (20 g) 100 percent maple syrup

3/4 teaspoon vanilla stevia (our favorite brand is NuNaturals)

1/4 teaspoon salt

1 pound (454 g) raw almonds

FROM CHEF JEANNETTE

For a sugar-free version, omit the syrup and replace it with 3/4 teaspoon additional NuNaturals vanilla stevia.

Variation: Substitute raw cashews for the almonds or use a mix of both. You can also substitute raw cacao powder for the cinnamon for chocolaty almonds.

SUGAR-BALANCING CINNAMON ALMONDS

FROM DR. JONNY: First, let's talk about the myth that nuts are inherently "fattening." They're not. High in calories? Yes. But consider this: two major epidemiologic studies from Harvard showed that those who eat the most nuts tend to have the lowest—not the highest—body mass indexes (BMIs). This doesn't mean you can scarf down 10 ounces (280 g) a day in addition to your regular diet—but if you replace a given amount of calories (especially junk calories from processed carbs) with an equal number of calories from almonds, you'll be doing yourself a favor on two counts. One, general health. (Nuts are rich sources of minerals, fiber, and even a little protein). Two, weight management. Now of course, once you get into snacks like this one, which are, let's face it, candied almonds, you're talking the potential for excess calories, but it doesn't really have to be that way. We used only a small amount of sweetener (pure maple syrup and vanilla stevia, which has virtually no impact on your blood sugar and few calories). We also used cinnamon, which, in addition to providing scrumptious flavor, has been known to help moderate blood sugar. The result is lightly sweet and cinnamon-y—so tempting you'll have to work hard to resist the temptation to overindulge!

Combine the cinnamon, allspice, and arrowroot in a gallon-size (3.8 L) zip-closure bag and set aside.

In a large bowl, whisk together the egg white, maple syrup, vanilla stevia, and salt until light and frothy. Add the almonds and toss well to coat. Pour the almonds into the bag with the cinnamon mixture. Seal the bag and shake it to coat the almonds thoroughly and evenly. Pour them gently into a slow cooker, cover, and cook on low for 1 hour, then stir to break them up and turn them and cook, uncovered, for 1 to 2 more hours, stirring occasionally, until very dry. Remove and spread on waxed paper for 15 to 20 minutes until completely cool. Store in an airtight container in the refrigerator.

YIELD: 16 servings

PER SERVING: Calories 170.4; Calories From Fat 117.4; Total Fat 14 g; Cholesterol 0 mg; Sodium 40.3 mg; Potassium 210.4 mg; Total Carbohydrates 8 g; Fiber 4 g; Sugar 1.9 g; Protein 6.3 g

LIGHTLY SWEETENED AUTUMNAL FRUIT BUTTER

INGREDIENTS

3 large McIntosh apples, unpeeled, cored, and
   sliced
4 large Bartlett pears, unpeeled, cored, and
   sliced
¼ cup (36 g) raisins
1 cup (235 ml) pear nectar (for sweeter butter)
   or apple cider
2 tablespoons (40 g) blackstrap molasses
⅓ cup (80 g) Sucanat
1 tablespoon (8 g) grated fresh ginger
½ teaspoon ground cinnamon
½ teaspoon ground nutmeg

FROM DR. JONNY: Back in the day when I was still naive about nutrition and thought it was fine to eat anything as long as it had no fat, I discovered fruit jellies. And I thought they were the mother lode—no fat, made only with fruit (and, of course, a ton of sugar, but I wasn't concerned with that then), and a great taste. Well, that was then. Now we know that fruit butters are still a great choice as a spread, but not because they have no fat—rather, because the best ones are almost entirely made of fruit with just a smattering of other minor ingredients. So you're essentially buttering your toast, or French toast, or anything else you want to butter, with "essence of apple" (or whatever fruit butter you're using). This version is the perfect example of how to make a fruit butter. It's only lightly sweetened using cider, molasses, and a tiny bit of Sucanat (no sugar or high-fructose corn syrup, common ingredients in commercial fruit jams). And this one is even healthier because we leave the skins on, and the skins are where so many nutrients (and fiber) are often concentrated. Note: This recipe has a long cooking time, but who cares? The prep is quick!

Combine the apples, pears, and raisins in the bottom of a 4-quart (3.7 L) slow cooker.

In a medium-size bowl, whisk together the nectar, molasses, Sucanat, ginger, cinnamon, and nutmeg until well combined. Pour it over the fruit, cover, and cook on low for 8 to 10 hours. Remove the cover, stir gently, and cook uncovered for 6 to 8 hours more, or until very thick and most of the juices have evaporated. Purée until smooth with an immersion blender (or cool and purée in a regular blender or food processor). Store in tightly sealed glass containers in the refrigerator; this will keep for up to a month.

YIELD: about 3 quarts (2.8 L)
FOR ENTIRE RECIPE: Calories 1,450.4; Calories From Fat 25.4; Total Fat 3 g; Cholesterol 0 mg; Sodium 53.3 mg; Potassium 3,095.6 mg; Total Carbohydrates 382.8 g; Fiber 45.8 g; Sugar 274.8 g; Protein 7 g

NUTTY LENTIL ALL-VEG PÂTÉ

FROM DR. JONNY: Lentils, carrots, goat cheese, walnuts. How can anyone not love that? This mild vegetarian "pâté" stands on its own nutritional merits, providing more nutrition than you have a right to ask from anything that has the word *pâté* in the title. Lentils are one of the best foods in the world, providing almost 18 grams of protein and almost 16 grams of fiber per cup, not to mention a host of valuable vitamins and minerals; carrots deliver vitamin A and the powerful anti-oxidant beta-carotene; walnuts provide minerals and fiber and are a rich source of plant-based omega-3 fat; and goat cheese provides another few grams of protein plus extraordinary taste and texture. This is a super-healthy high-fiber snack, or you can serve it as an appetizer and watch the compliments fly by.

INGREDIENTS

1 tablespoon (15 ml) olive oil
1 large yellow onion, chopped
1 cup (110 g) shredded carrot
1 ½ cups (288 g) green lentils
4 cups (940 ml) no-sodium vegetable broth
1 bay leaf
½ teaspoon black pepper
¾ teaspoon salt
⅔ cup (80 g) toasted walnuts, finely chopped
½ cup (115 g) chèvre (or feta)
Juice of 1 lemon, or to taste
¼ cup (12 g) chopped chives, for garnish
   (optional)

In a large skillet, heat the oil over medium heat. Add the onion and cook for about 5 minutes, until soft. Transfer the contents to a slow cooker. Add the carrot, lentils, broth, bay leaf, and pepper and stir gently to combine. Cover and cook on high for about 3 hours, or low for 5 to 6 hours, until the lentils are very tender. Remove the bay leaf and stir well or purée with an immersion wand to the desired consistency. Stir in the salt, walnuts, chèvre, and a little of the lemon juice at a time until the pâté achieves the desired tang. Serve warm, garnished with the chives, if using.

YIELD: 10 servings
PER SERVING: Calories 202.7; Calories From Fat 74.2; Total Fat 8.4 g; Cholesterol 6.7 mg; Sodium 322.3 mg; Potassium 379.5 mg; Total Carbohydrates 21.5 g; Fiber 9.9 g; Sugar 2.3 g; Protein 10 g

FROM CHEF JEANNETTE

Serving Suggestions: This pâté is terrific rolled into tender lettuce leaves, scooped with red bell pepper spears, or served on whole-grain crackers.

Drinks, Desserts, and Breakfasts

These drinks, desserts, and breakfasts are fun and delicious. They add a sweetness to holidays, special events, or any day when you need a lift! Our slow cooker drink recipes are always 100 percent healthy, so no need to feel guilty!

DRINKS

Irish Moss Tonic

Clean Classic Wassail

Hot Vitamin C–Pop Cranberry Cider

Resveratrol-Raising Fresh Grape Delight

Habanero-Spiked "Red Hot" Cider

Lower-Cal Vanilla Bean Chai

DESSERTS

Steamy, Creamy, High-Calcium Chai Pudding

Juice-Sweetened Tropical Fruit Compote

Gingered Honey Pears with Cinnamon Sticks

Low-Cal Cocoa Tapioca

Glorious Glazed Bananas

Low-Sugar Lemon Honey Custard

Fibered-Up Strawberry Sourdough Bread Pudding

Antioxidant-Rich Sweet Potato Carrot Pudding

Low-Sugar Choco-nutty Rice Pudding

Spiced Candied Apples and Yams with Raw Chocolate Drizzle

Antioxidant-Burst Raspberry Peach Cobbler

Lower-Sugar Raisin-Orange Pumpkin Pie Pudding

Fresh Pineapple with Coconut Lime Rum Sauce

Strawberry-Lime Antioxidant Granita

BREAKFASTS

Fruit 'n Nutty Overnight Breakfast Groats

Eggy Spiced Whole-Grain Breakfast Bread Pudding

IRISH MOSS TONIC

FROM DR. JONNY: Every year, Chef Jeannette runs a healthy eating retreat in the tropics. (This year she took a group to St. John for a week of great food and healthy living seminars—nice work if you can get it!) And every year she comes back with new discoveries. The year we were writing this book, it was Irish carrageen moss. Irish carrageen moss isn't moss—it's an edible seaweed. It's extremely popular in raw food cuisine because of its ability to thicken sauces and because it is a terrific gelling agent. Raw chefs also like it for mousses and pies because it makes a wonderful, creamy (and nutritious) base. The moss is about 10 percent protein and rich in minerals, especially iodine and sulfur (the latter being really good for your skin—just think "sulfur baths"). This creamy, satisfying drink is a great way to get the health properties of this interesting ingredient.

INGREDIENTS
1 packed cup (55 g) whole leaf Irish carrageen
    moss, wild-crafted is best (see Resources)
½ cup (120 ml) freshly squeezed lime juice
    (about 4 large limes)
2 cups (470 ml) water
¾ cup (180 g) erythritol or Sucanat
2 cinnamon sticks
4 cups (940 ml) unsweetened vanilla
    almond milk
½ teaspoon vanilla stevia (we like NuNaturals)

Rinse and drain the Irish moss well several times to remove as much of the sea salt as possible. Combine the moss and lime juice in a small glass container, cover, and allow to soak overnight in the fridge. Transfer the contents to a slow cooker, add the water, sweetener, and cinnamon sticks, stir, cover, and cook on low for 1 to 2 hours, or until the sweetener is dissolved, the mixture is hot and thick, and the seaweed is pale and gelid. Remove the insert, uncover and allow to cool.

Add the cooled mixture to a blender and blend well until totally smooth. (You can store in the fridge at this point and blend with the additional contents later, or blend them in now and then chill in the fridge.) Add the almond milk and vanilla stevia and blend until smooth and creamy. Chill in the refrigerator to the desired temperature. Store in the refrigerator for up to 2 days.

YIELD: about 6 cups (1.4 L)
FOR ENTIRE RECIPE: Calories 941.8; Calories From Fat 102.4; Total Fat 11.7 g; Cholesterol 0 mg; Sodium 23.8 mg; Potassium 146.3 mg; Total Carbohydrates 218.7 g; Fiber 15.2 g; Sugar 145.9 g; Protein 10.2 g

CLEAN CLASSIC WASSAIL

FROM DR. JONNY: *Wassail* refers to an ancient tradition called "wassailing," which was done in the cider-producing countries in England. The purpose of the traditional wassailing ritual was to "awaken" the cider trees and scare away evil spirits to better guarantee a good harvest of autumn fruit. Meanwhile, wassail the beverage is a hot, spicy punch or mulled cider, traditionally made with sugar, ginger, cinnamon, and nutmeg. (Mouthwatering, right?). Our version uses the slow cooker to great effect, allowing the apples to cook slowly (duh!) in a bit of ale and sherry. And any drink made from apples can't be bad—loaded with vitamins, nutrients, and a great source of the anti-inflammatory flavonoid quercetin, the apple blends beautifully with the spices, creating a drink that's warming and delicious. Drink enough of this and you can carol all snowy-night long! Fun fact: *Wassail* actually comes from the salute "waes hail," a contraction of the Middle English phrase *waes heil*, meaning "good health" or "be healthy."

INGREDIENTS

3 McIntosh or Winesap apples, peeled, cored, and coarsely chopped

⅓ cup (80 g) Sucanat (or ⅓ cup [80 g] sugar and 1 teaspoon blackstrap molasses)

1 quart (946 ml) nut brown ale, divided

1½ cups (353 ml) dry sherry, divided

¾ teaspoon ground cinnamon

½ teaspoon ground nutmeg

¼ teaspoon ground cloves

¼ teaspoon ground allspice

¼ cup (32 g) grated fresh ginger

6 thin slices fresh lemon (around the equator)

Place the prepared apples in the slow cooker and sprinkle evenly with the Sucanat. Gently pour ⅔ cup (160 ml) of the ale and ¼ cup (60 ml) of the sherry over the apples. Cover and cook on high for 1 to 2 hours, or until the apples are soft.

Purée the cooked apples and juices with an immersion wand or in a blender to the consistency of applesauce.

Return the apples to the slow cooker and turn it down to low. Add the remaining 3⅓ cups (786 ml) ale, the remaining 1¼ cups (293 ml) sherry, cinnamon, nutmeg, cloves, and allspice. Using your hand, squeeze the juice out of the grated ginger into the ale mixture. Mix gently to combine well. Float the lemon slices on top. Cover and cook on low for 15 to 30 minutes, until the mixture is hot (do not let it boil).

YIELD: 10 to 12 servings

PER SERVING: Calories 116.9; Calories From Fat 1.5; Total Fat 0.1 g; Cholesterol 0 mg; Sodium 2.5 mg; Potassium 73.4 mg; Total Carbohydrates 13 g; Fiber 1 g; Sugar 9 g; Protein 0.2 g

HOT VITAMIN C–POP CRANBERRY CIDER

FROM DR. JONNY: One of the topics magazine editors keep asking me to write about is incredibly healthy foods that most people don't eat regularly. The thinking is we all know about salmon and blueberries, but what don't we know about? One food that keeps popping up on those lists is cranberries. They have one of the highest antioxidant ratings (called the ORAC score) and are loaded with phenols (plant chemicals that are known to be highly protective against a wide range of health problems), and research shows that several bioactive compounds in cranberries are toxic to a variety of cancer tumor cells. And of course, there's the well-established ability of cranberries and cranberry juice to prevent urinary tract infections. This cider is a unique and tasty way to incorporate fresh cranberries into your diet. This tangy juice is rich in vitamin C, lightly sweet, and mellowed by the warming spices. It's great either hot or cold!

INGREDIENTS

1 gallon (3.8 L) 100 percent pure fresh cider with no additives

12 ounces (336 g) fresh cranberries (or frozen, thawed)

4 cinnamon sticks

2 tablespoons (13.2 g) ground cloves

4 to 6 thin slices fresh lemon (around the equator)

Combine the cider, cranberries, cinnamon, and cloves in the slow cooker. Float the lemon slices on top and cook on high for 3 to 4 hours, or on low for 4 to 5 hours.

Strain and serve hot or cold.

YIELD: 1 gallon (3.8 L)

FOR ENTIRE RECIPE: Calories 2,125.6; Calories From Fat 73.3; Total Fat 8.9 g; Cholesterol 0 mg; Sodium 168.7 mg; Potassium 5,007.6 mg; Total Carbohydrates 535 g; Fiber 45.5 g; Sugar 7 g; Protein 5.8 g

FROM CHEF JEANNETTE

For the best flavor and richest nutrients, look for unpasteurized cider that has been treated with UV light to prevent bacterial growth.

Time-Saver Tip: Combine the cider, cranberries, cinnamon, and cloves in a large soup pot and bring to a boil over medium-high heat. Carefully transfer the contents to the slow cooker, add the lemon slices, and cook on high for 1 hour.

RESVERATROL-RAISING FRESH GRAPE DELIGHT

INGREDIENTS

4 pounds (1.8 kg) fresh Concord grapes

7 cups (1.6 L) water, divided

$\frac{1}{2}$ to $\frac{2}{3}$ cup (120 to 160 g) honey, to taste

Juice and zest of $\frac{1}{2}$ lemon

FROM DR. JONNY: The search for the fountain of youth has been going on for thousands of years, with legends and reports of such a fountain dating back to the writings of the Greek Herodotus in the fifth century BCE. More recently, scientists discovered that we can extend life span (at least in animals) by restricting calories. This has worked in every species tested, from yeast cells to fruit flies to, more recently, monkeys. Researchers found that calorie restriction appears to activate certain longevity genes known as the SIRT genes. Unfortunately, restricting calories isn't a hugely popular strategy among humans! Fortunately, these same scientists have also discovered a substance in food that can "turn on" the longevity genes almost as well as a Spartan, calorie-restricted diet. The substance is a plant chemical called *resveratrol*, and it's the ingredient in red wine that makes red wine such a healthy drink (in moderation, of course). Resveratrol is found in the skins of darkly colored grapes (there's none to speak of in white wine). So you don't actually have to drink wine to get resveratrol; you can get it from grapes. And you should! It's great for you. In addition to showing tremendous potential as an anti-aging compound, resveratrol from grapes (or wine) is a powerful antioxidant, helping to protect your cells and DNA from damage. This clean distillation of the pure juice is a sweet treat sure to delight the taste buds. Word to the wise: this drink is also terrific cold!

Place the grapes and 2 cups (470 ml) of the water in a large soup pot and bring to a boil over high heat, stirring frequently. Boil for 1 minute, stirring constantly, then remove from the heat. Strain the contents of the pot through a double-mesh sieve into a slow cooker, pressing hard on the fruit to extract all juices. Discard the pulp, skin, and seeds. Stir in the remaining 5 cups (1.2 L) water, honey, and lemon juice and zest, cover, and cook on low for 3 hours. Serve hot or chilled.

YIELD: 9 cups (2.1 L)

FOR ENTIRE RECIPE: Calories 1,774.6; Calories From Fat 24.3; Total Fat 2.9 g; Cholesterol 0 mg; Sodium 93.1 mg; Potassium 3,606.9 mg; Total Carbohydrates 470.6 g; Fiber 16.8 g; Sugar 420.8 g; Protein 13.7 g

HABANERO-SPIKED "RED HOT" CIDER

FROM DR. JONNY: When I was a kid we'd go on family vacations to Deerpark Farm in upstate New York. Every week we'd drive into town, where they had a big general store that featured buckets of every kind of candy you can imagine, most of which wound up uneaten in leftover Halloween bags. But one of those candies came to mind when I tried this spicy drink—those little "red hots" that burned your tongue but felt so good in your mouth. Spicy, cinnamon-y, with just enough of an overtone of peppery fire to make your eyes water. This cider is loaded with capsaicin, courtesy of the habanero chile peppers. Among other things, capsaicin helps turn off pain signals in the body, and is a potential treatment for arthritis and neuropathy. Good stuff!

INGREDIENTS

1 gallon (3.8 L) 100 percent pure fresh cider with no additives

1 or 2 habanero or jalapeño peppers, seeded and sliced

6 cinnamon sticks

FROM CHEF JEANNETTE

For the best flavor and richest nutrients, look for unpasteurized cider that has been treated with UV light to prevent bacterial growth.

Take care when slicing chile peppers: it's best to use rubber gloves to protect your skin from the hot oils, and never, ever rub your eyes!

Place the cider in the slow cooker and add the prepared chiles and cinnamon. Heat on high for 1 to 2 hours, or on low for 2 to 3 hours, or until the desired spiciness is reached. After the first hour, test for heat at half-hour intervals. Strain out and discard all solids and serve the cider warm or cold.

YIELD: 1 gallon (3.8 L)

FOR ENTIRE RECIPE: Calories 2,082.3; Calories From Fat 55.6; Total Fat 7 g; Cholesterol 0 mg; Sodium 140.7 mg; Potassium 4,752 mg; Total Carbohydrates 529.3 g; Fiber 48.5 g; Sugar 0.5 g; Protein 5.6 g

INGREDIENTS

8 orange pekoe tea bags

¼ cup (60 g) xylitol or erythritol

½ cup (64 g) grated fresh ginger

6 cinnamon sticks

2 tablespoons (8 g) lightly crushed whole
   cardamom pods

2 teaspoons whole cloves

½ teaspoon whole black peppercorns

2 star anise (optional)

1 whole vanilla bean

8 cups (1.9 L) water

1 teaspoon vanilla stevia (we like NuNaturals)

2 cups (470 ml) unsweetened vanilla
   almond milk

FROM CHEF JEANNETTE

If you aren't concerned about sugars,
substitute high-quality honey. If you'd prefer
to use a zero-calorie natural sweetener,
omit the sugar alcohols and sweeten each
individual mug to taste with a couple
additional of drops of vanilla stevia.

If you don't wish to use a vanilla bean, omit
it and add 1 teaspoon vanilla extract to the
tea when you add the milk.

LOWER-CAL VANILLA BEAN CHAI

FROM DR. JONNY: Okay, all you chai lovers (yup, I'm talking to you, Sally Starbucks), here are a couple of things you need to know about your favorite drink. One, even though green tea gets the lion's share of the press on health benefits, black tea is no also-ran. One review article in the medical journal *Stroke* reported that individuals consuming 3 or more cups (705 ml) of black tea a day had a 21 percent lower risk of stroke than those consuming less than 1 cup (235 ml) a day. And black tea is loaded with health-giving polyphenols and antioxidants. The second thing you need to know is that there's quite a controversy about the effect of milk on the antioxidant power of tea (black or any other kind). Most data indicate that adding milk neutralizes many of the health-giving properties of compounds found in tea (like those antioxidants and polyphenols). However, research from Germany published in the *European Heart Journal* found that it's the proteins in milk, called *casein*, that cancel out the positive effects. So in this wonderful chai recipe, we used unsweetened almond milk, which should have no negative impact on all those good things in the tea, because there's no casein in almond milk. And if that weren't enough, our version uses a healthy sweetener (xylitol or erythritol), which has virtually no impact on your blood sugar. Personally, I think it tastes as good as the expensive cup you get at you-know-where.

Combine the tea bags, xylitol, ginger, cinnamon sticks, cardamom pods, cloves, peppercorns, and star anise, if using, in a 4-quart (3.8 L) slow cooker.

Carefully slice the vanilla bean lengthwise to open it. Using the point of your knife, scrape out all the seeds and add them to the tea and spices. Gently pour the water over all. Cover and cook on high for 2 to 3 hours, or to the desired strength. Strain the mixture through a double-mesh sieve and discard the spices. Return the liquid to the slow cooker and stir in the vanilla stevia and almond milk. Cook for 10 minutes, or until heated through.

YIELD: 8 servings

PER SERVING: Calories 87.7; Calories From Fat 12.4; Total Fat 1.6 g; Cholesterol 0 mg; Sodium 13.3 mg; Potassium 90.7 mg; Total Carbohydrates 23.4 g; Fiber 6.9 g; Sugar 0.2 g; Protein 1.6 g

STEAMY, CREAMY, HIGH-CALCIUM CHAI PUDDING

INGREDIENTS

2 cans (12 ounces, or 353 ml) evaporated
    skim milk

1/3 cup (80 g) small pearl tapioca

1/2 cup (120 g) Sucanat (or substitute xylitol or
    erythritol for part or all of the Sucanat for
    less sugar)

3/4 teaspoon ground cinnamon

3/4 teaspoon ground cardamom

3/4 teaspoon ground ginger

1/2 teaspoon ground mace

1/4 teaspoon ground cloves

1/4 teaspoon black pepper

Pinch of salt

1 egg, beaten

FROM DR. JONNY: If you've read through enough of these intros you know I have a major, almost addictive, weakness for several desserts—cheesecake, ice cream, and pudding being at the top of the list. And none of those are exactly low-calorie items. But replacing cream or even whole-fat milk with evaporated skim does a lot to lighten the caloric load, and best of all, it boosts the nutrition substantially. (Did you know, for example, that 1 cup [235 ml] of evaporated skim milk has 742 mg of calcium, nearly 50 percent more than a similar amount of regular skim milk?) Evaporated skim is also loaded with potassium (850 mg versus the 422 in a medium-size banana) and phosphorus (499 mg), an important constituent of human bones. It's also high in protein (19 grams per cup of evaporated milk, plus, of course, the egg), making this a high-protein dessert as well as an utterly delectable one.

Pour the milk into a slow cooker and whisk in the tapioca, Sucanat, cinnamon, cardamom, ginger, mace, cloves, pepper, and salt. Cover and cook on low for 90 minutes. Remove the cover and whisk in the egg until well incorporated. Cover and cook on low for 30 minutes more. Whisk well before serving.

YIELD: 9 servings

PER SERVING: Calories 136.4; Calories From Fat 7; Total Fat 0.8 g; Cholesterol 26.9 mg; Sodium 138.3 mg; Potassium 295.8 mg; Total Carbohydrates 25.8 g; Fiber 0.3 g; Sugar 20.6 g; Protein 7.2 g

JUICE-SWEETENED TROPICAL FRUIT COMPOTE

INGREDIENTS

2 cups (330 g) chopped fresh pineapple, ³⁄₄ cup (180 ml) juice reserved

2 ripe mangoes, peeled, pitted, and chopped

4 ripe kiwis, peeled and chopped

2 cups (340 g) chopped ripe honeydew melon

2 ripe bananas, peeled and sliced

1 tablespoon (15 ml) freshly squeezed lime juice

2 teaspoons lime zest

¹⁄₄ cup (20 g) shaved coconut

1 ¹⁄₂ tablespoons (16 g) quick-cooking tapioca

FROM DR. JONNY: Compotes originated in France in the 1600s. They were made by immersing fruit in water with sugar and spices and simmering over gentle heat. But compotes are perfectly suited for slow cookers, which simmer and mix the flavors perfectly. This unique version of the classic compote features tropical fruits, all of which are high in water and nutrient dense—meaning that, for not too many calories, you get a whole lot of nutrition (the opposite, of, say, cheesecake or ice cream, which are high in calories and not so high in nutrients). There's a load of vitamin C here (from the kiwi, melons, pineapple, and mangoes), beta-carotene from the mangoes, and the digestive enzyme bromelain from the pineapple. The added kick from the coconut-lime combo puts this dish over the taste top. I dare you not to love it!

Combine all the ingredients in a slow cooker and stir gently to combine. Cook on high for 2 to 3 hours, or on low for 4 to 5 hours, until the fruit is very tender. Stir well before serving.

YIELD: 8 to 10 servings

PER SERVING: Calories 113.8; Calories From Fat 8.9; Total Fat 1.1 g; Cholesterol 0 mg; Sodium 15 mg; Potassium 387.4 mg; Total Carbohydrates 27.6 g; Fiber 3.4 g; Sugar 19.1 g; Protein 1.3 g

FROM CHEF JEANNETTE

Serving Suggestions: This compote is excellent chilled and stirred into Greek yogurt for a light dessert, or served warm over pancakes or waffles for a filling snack or dessert.

GINGERED HONEY PEARS WITH CINNAMON STICKS

INGREDIENTS

6 Anjou pears, peeled

1 1/2 cups (353 ml) pear nectar

1 cup (235 ml) water

1/2 cup (160 g) honey

1/2 cup (120 ml) ginger brandy or Poire William

6 thick slices fresh ginger, about the size of quarters

3 cinnamon sticks

2 tablespoons (16 g) minced candied ginger (optional)

FROM DR. JONNY: Years ago when I lived in New York City I was close friends—and a fellow practitioner with—Oz Garcia, the legendary self-taught guru of anti-aging nutrition and the "nutritionist to the stars" for more A-list names than you can imagine. He used to always make these shakes for his clients using pear juice as the base. When I asked him why, he said that in twenty years of practice he has found that pear juice never causes bad or allergic reactions or problems with digestion, is tolerated by just about everyone, and tastes great. Really ripe delicious Anjou pears are just heaven to bite into, and Chef Jeannette has taken the sublime and made it, well, *more* sublime by seasoning with ginger, honey, and cinnamon. (The names of those three spices together sounds almost as good as they taste! And it could be the name of a singing group. But I digress.) The sweetness comes from the fruit and the mineral-rich raw honey, but the base is pure fruit—one of the healthiest desserts you can choose.

Arrange the pears in a single layer in a slow cooker.

Combine the nectar, water, honey, brandy, ginger root, and cinnamon sticks in a medium-size saucepan over medium-high heat and bring to a boil, stirring frequently. Let the mixture boil for 30 seconds, and then pour evenly over the pears. Cover and cook on high for 2 to 3 hours, or on low for 4 to 5 hours, until the pears are soft, removing the lid and basting the pears for the last half hour of cooking time. Remove the cinnamon sticks and ginger coins and serve warm with a little sauce poured over the top and garnished with the candied ginger crumbles, if using.

YIELD: 6 servings

PER SERVING: Calories 326.1; Calories From Fat 3.7; Total Fat 0.5 g; Cholesterol 0 mg; Sodium 8.7 mg; Potassium 244.2 mg; Total Carbohydrates 76.1 g; Fiber 9.7 g; Sugar 51.6 g; Protein 1.2 g

LOW-CAL COCOA TAPIOCA

FROM DR. JONNY: I'm absolutely daffy for tapioca in any form. And this recipe is the easiest way I know to whip up a rich, creamy tapioca dessert with virtually no fuss. So let's talk for a moment about chocolate and cocoa. Real cocoa (more on that in a moment) is a rich treasure trove of plant chemicals called *flavanols*, which have been found to have a huge number of health benefits. Just a few months before this book was being written, a study in *Circulation*, the prestigious journal of the American Heart Association, found that women who ate a small amount of chocolate every week had lower risks of heart disease. This comes on the heels of a ton of research showing that cocoa flavanols lower blood pressure and improve blood flow, making blood platelets less sticky. The key to getting these benefits is to use high-cocoa chocolate; there's no flavanols in white or milk chocolate, so you should always choose a dark chocolate that has no less than 60 percent cocoa. The evaporated skim milk in this recipe is low-cal, and using xylitol as a sweetener keeps the calorie count down and blunts the impact on your blood sugar. Just for good measure we threw in a couple of eggs both for creaminess and for extra protein. You'll love this chocolaty tapioca as much as I do. I promise.

INGREDIENTS

2 cans (12 ounces, or 353 ml each) evaporated skim milk

2 eggs

¼ cup (28 g) dark cocoa powder (such as Cacao Barry Extra Brute)

¼ cup (60 g) xylitol or erythritol

3 tablespoons (45 g) Sucanat (or substitute more xylitol or erythritol for a no-added sugar option)

1 teaspoon vanilla stevia (we like NuNaturals)

½ teaspoon ground cinnamon

¼ teaspoon salt

⅓ cup (58 g) small pearl tapioca

In a medium-size bowl, whisk together the evaporated milk and eggs until smooth and well incorporated. Whisk in the cocoa powder, xylitol, Sucanat, stevia, cinnamon, salt, and tapioca. Transfer the contents to a slow cooker. Cook on low for 2 hours, whisking well at 1 hour. Whisk well at the end of cooking time to break up the bottom layer and incorporate the lumps before serving.

YIELD: 6 servings

PER SERVING: Calories 210.9; Calories From Fat 20.4; Total Fat 2.3 g; Cholesterol 75.6 mg; Sodium 267.1 mg; Potassium 447.9 mg; Total Carbohydrates 38.4 g; Fiber 0.9 g; Sugar 20.9 g; Protein 12.5 g

GLORIOUS GLAZED BANANAS

INGREDIENTS

1 tablespoon (14 g) unsalted butter or coconut
oil, softened

4 large bananas (ripe but not soft), peeled and
halved lengthwise

2 tablespoons (30 g) Sucanat or xylitol

2 tablespoons (30 ml) freshly squeezed lime
juice

2 tablespoons (30 ml) coconut rum

½ teaspoon vanilla stevia (we like NuNaturals)

FROM DR. JONNY: Whenever I get together with friends for dinner, either in a restaurant or at home, they always look at me with guilt when it comes time for dessert. I think they think I'm the food police and am going to pronounce them criminals the moment they dig into that Death by Chocolate Cake. But the thing of it is, I love sweets and desserts (and yes, even sugar—there, I've said it!) as much as the next person, probably a lot more if you want to know the truth. So when I can find a dessert that has built-in damage control for my blood sugar and waistline, I'm thrilled. Here, Chef Jeannette has taken the simple (and healthy) banana, and made its natural sweetness the centerpiece of this dessert. One tablespoon of butter or coconut oil adds only about 100 or so calories, all good fat (yes, you heard that right), and the only additional sweetener comes from noncaloric (or virtually noncaloric) xylitol or Sucanat plus stevia. The rum adds a flavor that perfectly complements the vanilla overtones of the stevia and the freshly squeezed lime juice. You're gonna love this, I promise. And it's easy enough that even I can prepare it in a New York minute.

Smear the butter evenly over the bottom of the slow cooker insert. Lay the bananas, cut sides down, in one layer on the bottom (you may have to cut them in half widthwise to get them to fit).

In a small bowl, whisk together the Sucanat, lime juice, rum, and vanilla stevia, and drizzle evenly over the bananas. Cover and cook for on low about 2 hours, or until the bananas are hot and tender.

YIELD: 8 servings

PER SERVING: Calories 92.1; Calories From Fat 14.6; Total Fat 1.7 g; Cholesterol 3.8 mg; Sodium 2 mg; Potassium 248.4 mg; Total Carbohydrates 19.6 g; Fiber 1.8 g; Sugar 11.4 g; Protein 0.8 g

INGREDIENTS

3 cups (705 ml) low-fat cow's milk (preferably organic)

5 eggs

½ cup (120 g) honey

2 teaspoons vanilla extract

2 teaspoons lemon zest

Pinch of salt

FROM CHEF JEANNETTE

There is a trick for retrieving dishes from the hot insert or hot water baths in slow cookers: make temporary handles out of aluminum foil. Working with 18- to 24-inch (46 to 61 cm) lengths of foil, fold the sheets vertically until they are 2 to 3 inches (5 to 7.5 cm) wide and several layers thick. You'll need at least 4 strips. Arrange them in the bottom of the cool, dry slow cooker insert like the spokes of a wheel (good for round dishes) or parallel—2 running lengthwise and 2 running widthwise—evenly spaced (good for rectangular or square dishes), and set the filled dish on top. Bring the ends of the foil strips together in the center and fold them together tightly to make a handle that will lift and support the dish. Add your water and cook, and then you can remove the dish at the end of cooking time without waiting for it to cool.

LOW-SUGAR LEMON HONEY CUSTARD

FROM DR. JONNY: This recipe says "clean and fresh" all over it. Simple, basic ingredients combine to make a luscious, rich custard that I have to tell you I love as a dessert if only because it is one of the few I can think of that is high in protein and low in sugar and still tastes great. Real whole foods like eggs contribute nutrients like choline for the brain and lutein and zeaxanthin for the eyes; the protein comes from the eggs and the milk. We go light on the sweetener, keeping glycemic impact low. Highly recommended: raw, cold-pressed honey for its richer array of enzymes and nutrients. And if you can get raw milk, I strongly recommend it. At the very least, use organic milk, and don't try to save on calories by going nonfat. Recent research shows that there is a compound in milk fat called TPA (trans-palmitoleic acid) that boosts heart health and helps regulate blood sugar!

Place a 6-cup (1.4 L) shallow glass baking dish into the center of a 6-quart (5.7 L) slow cooker. Using a spouted container, slowly add water to the cooker until the level reaches halfway up the empty baking dish. Set aside.

In a medium-size saucepan, heat the milk over medium heat until steaming hot, but not boiling.

While the milk is heating, in a large bowl, whisk together the eggs, honey, vanilla, lemon zest, and salt. When the milk is ready, slowly add ¼ cup (60 ml) of the milk to the egg mixture, whisking it in to coddle the eggs. Slowly pour the remaining milk into the eggs, whisking constantly. Gently pour the custard mix into the prepared baking dish in the slow cooker. Cover and cook on high for 2 to 4 hours, until almost set (the center will not be fully set). Remove the cover, turn off the heat, and let cool until you are able to handle the baking dish enough to remove. Serve soft and hot or chill for a couple of hours to fully set.

YIELD: 4 to 6 servings

PER SERVING: Calories 210.8; Calories From Fat 59.1; Total Fat 6.6 g; Cholesterol 186 mg; Sodium 158.1 mg; Potassium 256.7 mg; Total Carbohydrates 29.6 g; Fiber 0.1 g; Sugar 29.9 g; Protein 9.4 g

FIBERED-UP STRAWBERRY SOURDOUGH BREAD PUDDING

INGREDIENTS

Neutral cooking oil spray

4 cups cubed slightly stale sourdough bread (³/₄- to 1-inch [2 to 2.5 cm] cubes)

¹/₃ cup (37 g) toasted sliced almonds

1 can (12 ounces, or 353 ml) evaporated skim milk

4 eggs

²/₃ cup (160 g) Sucanat

1 teaspoon vanilla stevia (we like NuNaturals)

1 teaspoon ground cinnamon

¹/₂ teaspoon ground coriander

1 ¹/₂ tablespoons (11 g) toasted wheat germ

2 cups (340 g) sliced fresh strawberries

Cinnamon Yogurt, Optional

¹/₄ cup (60 g) plain, low-fat Greek yogurt

³/₄ teaspoon ground cinnamon (optional)

2 teaspoons honey

FROM DR. JONNY: You might be surprised to hear me talk about bread because it's one of the starchy carbs I tend to avoid, at least most of the time. But the truth is that all bread is not created equal. Researchers at the University of Guelph in Canada studied four types of bread, trying to determine the differences in health effects. They fed subjects either white bread, whole wheat bread, whole wheat bread with barley, or sourdough bread, and then measured indicators of how efficiently their bodies metabolized the carbohydrates, checking, for example, blood sugar and insulin levels. The results were dramatic: those who ate the sourdough showed the most positive responses (i.e., blood sugar control) and—best of all—those positive responses continued after eating a second meal later in the day that didn't include bread! Our sourdough bread pudding is filling and sweet but with way less sugar (and fewer calories) than standard-issue bread puddings. We cut the calories (but not the flavor) by using evaporated skim milk and added four eggs to beef up the protein content. The wheat germ adds extra fiber and vitamin E. Chef Jeannette recommends finishing this off with a dollop of cinnamon yogurt, and I agree wholeheartedly!

Spray a slow cooker insert with oil. Place the bread cubes in the slow cooker and sprinkle with the almonds.

In a medium-size bowl, whisk together the evaporated milk, eggs, Sucanat, stevia, cinnamon, and coriander until well blended and pour evenly over the bread mixture. Toss gently to coat. Sprinkle the wheat germ over all, cover, and cook on low for 4 to 5 hours, until the pudding is mostly set. Allow to cool to desired thickness (it will continue to set as it cools).

To make the cinnamon yogurt: If using, in a small bowl, whisk together the yogurt, cinnamon, and honey until very well mixed. Serve the bread pudding topped with the strawberries and a dollop of the cinnamon yogurt, if using.

YIELD: 10 servings

PER SERVING: Calories 295.6; Calories From Fat 49.9; Total Fat 5.7 g; Cholesterol 86.5 mg; Sodium 387.6 mg; Potassium 327.4 mg; Total Carbohydrates 50.1 g; Fiber 3 g; Sugar 21.9 g; Protein 12.8 g

ANTIOXIDANT-RICH SWEET POTATO CARROT PUDDING

INGREDIENTS

1 cup (235 ml) high-quality heavy cream

1 egg

3 tablespoons (45 g) Sucanat or xylitol,
    or to taste

1 teaspoon vanilla extract

1 1/2 teaspoons ground cinnamon

1/2 teaspoon ground cardamom

1/4 teaspoon ground cloves

1/2 teaspoon salt

2 cups (220 g) grated sweet potato

2 cups (220 g) grated carrot

1 small baking apple, such as McIntosh, peeled,
    cored, and grated

FROM DR. JONNY: So here's a little nutrition trivia for you: When vegetables or fruits are orange or yellow it means they are filled with beta-carotene and other members of the carotenoid family. They're also rich in vitamin A. One cup (130 g) of carrots contains more than 21,000 IUs of vitamin A, 10,000 mcg of beta-carotene, and 4,000 mcg of its relative, alpha-carotene, and that's not counting the fiber, calcium, and potassium. And sweet potatoes are hardly nutritional lightweights. One medium sweet potato has almost 4 grams of fiber, a whopping 542 mg of potassium, 13,000 mcg of beta-carotene, and almost 22,000 IUs of vitamin A. Now before you panic about the heavy cream, remember that cream is a perfectly good food as long as you use it in moderation—this recipe has 2 tablespoons (30 ml) per serving. Cream has no carbs, and if you choose organic (if you can get raw, even better!) you've got nothing to worry about. We used very little added sweetener for this pudding because the carrots and sweet potatoes provide plenty on their own. Plus, the fiber in the veggies, the protein in the milk, and the cinnamon spice all work beautifully together to lower the glycemic impact of this unique, rich, spicy, veggie-based dessert.

In a mixer, beat together the cream, egg, Sucanat, vanilla, cinnamon, cardamom, cloves, and salt.

Combine the grated sweet potato, carrot, and apple in a slow cooker. Pour the cream mixture over all and cook on high for 2 to 3 hours, or on low for 4 to 6 hours, until the vegetables are tender. Using an immersion blender (or a regular blender or food processor), purée the mixture until mostly smooth.

YIELD: 8 servings

PER SERVING: Calories 279; Calories From Fat 138.4; Total Fat 15.7 g; Cholesterol 89.6 mg; Sodium 267.3 mg; Potassium 403.8 mg; Total Carbohydrates 33.7 g; Fiber 3.3 g; Sugar 23.1 g; Protein 3.2 g

LOW-SUGAR CHOCO-NUTTY RICE PUDDING

INGREDIENTS

2 cans (12 ounces, or 353 ml each) evaporated skim milk

½ cup (120 g) xylitol or Sucanat

⅓ cup (106 g) honey or rice syrup

¼ cup (28 g) high-quality cocoa powder (or use ⅓ cup [37 g] raw cacao powder)

¾ cup (143 g) long-grain brown or brown basmati rice

½ cup (55 g) sliced almonds

1 teaspoon vanilla extract

1 teaspoon ground cinnamon

¼ teaspoon ground cardamom or cloves (optional)

FROM DR. JONNY: If you've read any of our other cookbooks you know my "hit list" of all-time favorite desserts, health benefits be dammed: chocolate pudding, chocolate graham crackers, tapioca pudding, ice cream, cheesecake, and . . . (drum roll, please) . . . rice pudding! But, and there's a "but," rice pudding is usually made with white rice and whole-fat homogenized milk, not to mention a ton of added sugar. We've cleaned up the recipe, making it "health food worthy" by substituting whole-grain brown rice and evaporated skim milk. We also used very little sweetener, and if you choose xylitol you'll cut down on the sugar load even more. Cocoa is a rich source of plant chemicals called *flavanols*, which can lower blood pressure and protect the heart. Sweet, satisfying, and filling, this treat really hits the spot. Fun tip: Try this as a breakfast, either alone or as an accompaniment to a couple of eggs. Wow.

Combine all the ingredients in a slow cooker and mix gently. Cook on low for about 5 hours, or until the rice is tender and the pudding reaches the desired thickness. Stir well before serving.

YIELD: 8 servings

PER SERVING: Calories 286.5; Calories From Fat 47.7; Total Fat 5.7 g; Cholesterol 3.8 mg; Sodium 111.4 mg; Potassium 433.3 mg; Total Carbohydrates 53 g; Fiber 3.3 g; Sugar 35 g; Protein 10.8 g

SPICED CANDIED APPLES AND YAMS WITH RAW CHOCOLATE DRIZZLE

INGREDIENTS

³/₄ cup (180 ml) pure apple cider

¹/₃ cup (106 g) honey

2 cinnamon sticks

4 whole cloves

4 allspice berries

1 yam, peeled and cut into ¹/₂-inch (1.3 cm) dice (or sweet potato)

3 Granny Smith apples, unpeeled, cored, and halved

For Chocolate Drizzle

2 tablespoons (14 g) dark cocoa powder (such as Callebaut Extra Brute)

2 tablespoons (14 g) raw cacao powder (or use more cocoa powder)

2 tablespoons (40 g) brown rice syrup

2 tablespoons (30 ml) unsweetened vanilla almond milk

1 teaspoon melted coconut oil

¹/₂ teaspoon vanilla stevia (we like NuNaturals)

Pinch of salt

FROM DR. JONNY: Here's another example of Chef Jeannette's amazing talent for creating unusual combinations of ingredients in a way that makes you think, "Why didn't someone think of this before?" The tang of the apples in this dish creates a perfect harmony with the soft sweetness of the yams, made even more perfect by the visual harmony of the rich red and orange. An unexpected flavor delight is added by the dark chocolate, which is loaded with plant compounds called *flavanols*, which have been found to lower blood pressure as well as the risk of heart disease. This sweet-as-pie dessert has a minimum of added sugar—not needed because of the inherent sweetness of the cooked yams and apples. Fun fact, courtesy of Alan Gaby, M.D., nutritional medicine specialist: Cinnamon is an ancient herbal medicine mentioned in Chinese texts as long ago as 4,000 years. Did I mention that this dessert is ridiculously delish?

Combine the cider and honey in the slow cooker and whisk to combine. Add the cinnamon sticks, cloves, allspice, and yam and toss to coat. Stir the mixture gently, add the apples, cut side up, and baste the apples with the liquid. Cover and cook on high for 2 hours, or until the apples and yams are tender, basting one or two times at the end of cooking time.

When the fruit is tender, make the chocolate drizzle: In a small bowl, whisk together the cocoa and cacao powders, rice syrup, almond milk, coconut oil, stevia, and salt until very smooth.

To serve, remove the apples and place one half on each plate. Spoon an equal amounts of yams into the halves, and drizzle lightly with the chocolate sauce.

YIELD: 6 servings

PER SERVING: Calories 188.7; Calories From Fat 14.9; Total Fat 1.6 g; Cholesterol 0 mg; Sodium 65.6 mg; Potassium 162.8 mg; Total Carbohydrates 41 g; Fiber 6.9 g; Sugar 24.9 g; Protein 1.3 g

ANTIOXIDANT-BURST RASPBERRY PEACH COBBLER

INGREDIENTS

Neutral cooking oil spray

1 pint (250 g) fresh raspberries or 1 bag
(10 ounces, or 280 g) frozen, thawed and
drained

2 ½ pounds (1.1 kg) fresh, ripe peaches,
unpeeled, pitted, and sliced, or 2 bags
(16 ounces, or 454 g each) frozen, thawed
and drained

¼ cup (71 g) frozen orange juice concentrate,
thawed

1 ½ tablespoons (12 g) kudzu or quick-cooking
tapioca

2 teaspoons orange zest

¼ cup (60 g) plus 2 tablespoons (30 g) Sucanat
or xylitol, divided

2 teaspoons ground cinnamon, divided

½ teaspoon ground cloves

1 teaspoon vanilla stevia (we like NuNaturals)

⅓ cup (27 g) rolled oats

⅓ cup (37 g) toasted sliced almonds

¼ cup (30 g) oat flour or whole wheat pastry
flour

4 tablespoons (56 g) unsalted butter, chopped
(or coconut oil, softened)

Pinch of salt

FROM DR. JONNY: What's not to like about peaches and raspberries? Seriously. Two good-looking fruits that are relatively low in sugar, are high in fiber (a whopping 8 grams per cup for raspberries), and extremely delicious. And surprisingly perfect for the slow cooker, which brings out the fruits' natural sweetness. Classic cobblers are made from sugar, butter, flour, and milk—as you might guess, I'm not a fan. Our version is a lot lower in sugar and overall carbs, and a lot higher in fiber (from the oats and almonds). The stevia plus the xylitol or Sucanat give this cobbler all the extra sweetness you could possibly want. Fun fact: Researchers at Harvard Medical School are exploring the possibilities of using an extract from the kudzu plant as a means to treat alcoholic cravings.

Spray the inside of the slow cooker insert lightly with cooking oil. Combine the raspberries and peaches in the prepared insert.

In a small cup, combine the melted juice concentrate and kudzu, mixing well to blend, and pour it over the fruit.

Sprinkle in the zest, ¼ cup (60 g) of the Sucanat, 1 teaspoon of the cinnamon, cloves, and vanilla stevia, and stir gently to evenly coat.

In a small bowl, combine the oats, almonds, flour, remaining 2 tablespoons (30 g) Sucanat, butter, remaining 1 teaspoon cinnamon, and salt and work them together until the mixture forms large crumbs. Sprinkle evenly over the fruit, cover, and cook on high for 2 hours.

YIELD: 6 servings
PER SERVING: Calories 320.2; Calories From Fat 112.3; Total Fat 13.2 g; Cholesterol 20.4 mg; Sodium 52.1 mg; Potassium 584.9 mg; Total Carbohydrates 77.9 g; Fiber 7.8 g; Sugar 34.7 g; Protein 5.6 g

LOWER-SUGAR RAISIN-ORANGE PUMPKIN PIE PUDDING

INGREDIENTS

Neutral cooking oil spray

5 eggs

1 can (28 ounces, or 784 g) high-quality
    pumpkin purée

1 can (12 ounces, or 353 g) evaporated skim milk

½ cup (160 g) 100 percent maple syrup, or
    more, to taste

2 teaspoons orange zest

1 teaspoon orange extract (or vanilla)

1 teaspoon ground cinnamon

½ teaspoon ground cloves

½ cup (75 g) raisins

FROM DR. JONNY: Here's a little mnemonic device to use next time someone asks you at a cocktail party, "What's so great about pumpkin?" (I'm assuming that you actually *attend* cocktail parties where people ask such questions, admittedly a stretch, but work with me here!) The mnemonic device? "P" stands for pumpkin and potassium. While most of us tend to think of bananas when it comes to potassium, pumpkin leaves them in the dust, providing about 33 percent more potassium per cup than a medium-size banana. And why should you care? Because several large studies suggest that increased potassium intake is associated with decreased risk of stroke as well as a generally healthier heart and lower blood pressure. Pumpkin's also ridiculously low in calories, very low in sugar, and high in fiber. This light pudding also makes a great breakfast. Seriously. Note: Canned pumpkin is one of the few exceptions to the "don't buy vegetables in the can" rule. But if you can find it, get organic; Chef Jeannette finds it has the richest flavor.

Lightly spray the insert of a slow cooker with cooking oil and set aside. Place the eggs in a mixer and beat until smooth. Add the pumpkin, evaporated milk, syrup, zest, extract, cinnamon, and cloves and beat until well combined. Stir in the raisins, add the mixture to the slow cooker, and cook on high for 4 to 4½ hours, or until set.

YIELD: 6 servings

PER SERVING: Calories 274.9; Calories From Fat 43.7; Total Fat 4.8 g; Cholesterol 178.8 mg; Sodium 480.6 mg; Potassium 725 mg; Total Carbohydrates 48.6 g; Fiber 5 g; Sugar 36.4 g; Protein 12.1 g

FRESH PINEAPPLE WITH COCONUT LIME RUM SAUCE

INGREDIENTS

2 tablespoons (30 ml) coconut rum

1 fresh pineapple, peeled and quartered lengthwise, 1 tablespoon (15 ml) juice reserved

Juice and zest of 1 lime

½ to 1 teaspoon vanilla stevia (we like
NuNaturals), to taste, or use 1 to
2 teaspoons Sucanat or xylitol

4 teaspoons (7 g) coconut flakes

FROM DR. JONNY: Who doesn't love pineapple? This rich, juicy fruit conjures up thoughts of tropical paradises and mixed drinks with parasols on the beach. Along with all the lovely beach-y associations, pineapple is a nutritious gem. Its main claim to fame is an amazing substance called *bromelain*, a rich source of enzymes with many health benefits, including aiding digestion, speeding wound healing, and reducing inflammation. It's also a natural blood thinner, preventing excessive blood platelet stickiness. And on top of that, pineapple has almost 100 percent of the Daily Value for manganese, an essential trace mineral needed for healthy skin, bone, and cartilage formation. Hot pineapple is a unique taste treat, and slow cooking really brings out the natural sweetness of the fruit.

FROM CHEF JEANNETTE

Fresh pineapple doesn't ripen after picking, so choose a ripe one: the leaves should be green and look fresh, the "eyes" on the skin plump. It should be firm and give off a strong, sweet smell of pineapple. To prepare it, twist the crown from the pineapple, slice it in half the long way, and then quarter it. You can then cut out the core and cut off the rind.

In a small bowl, whisk together the rum, pineapple juice, lime juice and zest, and vanilla stevia. Lay the pineapple pieces in the slow cooker and pour the sauce over all. Cover and cook on low for 3 to 4 hours, or until very tender. Garnish with the coconut to serve.

YIELD: 8 servings
PER SERVING: Calories 69.7; Calories From Fat 3.3; Total Fat 0.4 g; Cholesterol 0 mg; Sodium 4.8 mg; Potassium 135 mg; Total Carbohydrates 16.9 g; Fiber 1.9 g; Sugar 11.6 g; Protein 0.7 g

STRAWBERRY-LIME ANTIOXIDANT GRANITA

INGREDIENTS

1 ½ pounds (680 g) fresh strawberries, stemmed and halved

1 cup (235 ml) water

3 tablespoons (45 g) erythritol or Sucanat

3 tablespoons (45 ml) freshly squeezed lime juice

½ to 1 teaspoon vanilla stevia, to taste

1 teaspoon lime zest

FROM DR. JONNY: Granita is a tasty and easy summertime treat that doesn't require any special equipment, goes together like a dream, and has basically two ingredients. The problem is that one of those ingredients is sugar—meaning that granitas have the potential for doing serious damage to your blood glucose and most probably your waistline. No problemo. We substituted erythritol (or if you like, Sucanat), thereby eliminating the problem. Erythritol is a sweet-as-sugar sugar alcohol that has virtually no calories (okay, 0.02 calories per gram) and does zilch to your blood sugar. (It's also been approved by the World Health Organization.) Along with the erythritol we use a bit of stevia, another completely healthy sweetener. (We like NuNaturals vanilla stevia because it's a high-quality product and unlike most stevias on the market has virtually no aftertaste.) The other main ingredient in this two-star affair is strawberries, like all berries a health bonanza. Strawberries contain chemicals found to protect cells against cervical and breast cancer. In addition, they contain tons of protective plant compounds like phenols and anthocyanins, well known for their antioxidant capacity. This is one dessert you'll never have to feel guilty about eating. Refreshing, light, and bright on a hot summer day!

In a 3-quart (2.8 L) slow cooker, combine the strawberries, water, and erythritol, and stir well. Cover and cook on high for 2 to 3 hours, until the strawberries have mostly broken down.

Cool slightly and transfer the contents to a blender or food processor and process until very smooth. Strain the mixture through a fine-mesh sieve into a 9 x 11-inch (23 x 28 cm) baking pan, pressing well to extract all the juices, then discard the pulp and seeds. Stir in the lime juice, vanilla stevia, and zest.

Cover with a rubber top (if using Pyrex) or plastic wrap and place in the freezer. Freeze for 3 to 4 hours, stirring at least once an hour to break up the ice chunks. If freezing overnight, break into pieces and process briefly in the food processor just before serving.

YIELD: 6 servings

PER SERVING: Calories 60.9; Calories From Fat 2.9; Total Fat 0.4 g; Cholesterol 0 mg; Sodium 2.5 mg; Potassium 183.4 mg; Total Carbohydrates 15.4 g; Fiber 2.3 g; Sugar 11.7 g; Protein 0.8 g

FRUIT 'N NUTTY OVERNIGHT BREAKFAST GROATS

INGREDIENTS

¾ cup (60 g) whole oat groats

¼ cup (20 g) whole wheat or rye berries

4 cups (940 ml) water

½ cup (75 g) whole raw almonds

½ cup (75 g) raw sunflower seeds

¼ cup (36 g) sesame seeds (raw or toasted)

1 cinnamon stick (optional)

¼ teaspoon ground cardamom (optional)

¼ teaspoon ground nutmeg (optional)

¾ cup (110 g) fresh or dried berries of your choice (try fresh blueberries or dried goji berries)

FROM CHEF JEANNETTE

If you can't find whole oat groats, use steel-cut oats (steel-cut are just chopped groats), which are readily available at most supermarkets, but you may need to decrease the cooking time—start checking at 6 hours.

Serving Suggestions: For sweeter oatmeal, stir in half a mashed banana or ½ to ¾ cup (123 or 185 g) unsweetened applesauce before serving. To sweeten with no added sugars, add ¼ cup (60 g) xylitol (or to taste) or 1½ teaspoons NuNaturals vanilla stevia. Oat groats also work as a savory dish: simply omit the sweet spices when cooking and season to taste with a small amount of tamari sauce before serving. They're also great with chopped chives or scallion stirred in, even for breakfast! To add a little more calcium and some friendly intestinal flora, stir 2 to 3 tablespoons (30 to 45 g) plain yogurt into individual portions of either the sweet or the savory version.

FROM DR. JONNY: There's not much we nutritionists agree on these days, or so it seems, but I can't think of anyone from any end of the nutritional spectrum who wouldn't agree that this is an absolutely terrific addition to the breakfast menu. Yes, it's a bit high carb (and might not be suited to absolutely *everyone*), but consider this: the groats are one of the slowest-burning carbs on the planet, with a very low glycemic load and a very high amount of fiber. Between the groats and the nuts, and the low-glycemic berries, you're in no danger of going on the blood sugar roller coaster with this in your tummy. And it's not just the positive effect this combo will have on your immediate energy that makes this recipe a winner. Berries are loaded with antioxidants, which help fight one of what I call "the Four Horsemen of Aging": oxidative damage, or, as we like to say, "rusting from within." The sesame seeds add a whopping 75 percent of the Daily Value for copper and almost half the Daily Value for manganese. And check out the combination of spices! If you like them as much as I do, these groats will quickly become one of your breakfast faves.

Combine the oats, wheat berries, water, almonds, sunflower and sesame seeds, and, if using, the cinnamon stick, cardamom, and nutmeg in a 2-quart (1.9 L) slow cooker. Cook on low for 9 hours or overnight. Stir in the berries, let warm for 5 minutes, and serve.

YIELD: 4 to 6 servings

PER SERVING: Calories 288.4; Calories From Fat 122; Total Fat 14.3 g; Cholesterol 0 mg; Sodium 15 mg; Potassium 134.6 mg; Total Carbohydrates 33.1 g; Fiber 7.9 g; Sugar 5.7 g; Protein 9.9g

EGGY SPICED WHOLE-GRAIN BREAKFAST BREAD PUDDING

INGREDIENTS

1 teaspoon unsalted butter or coconut oil, softened

9 slices high-fiber sprouted or whole-grain bread

2 teaspoons ground cinnamon, divided

1 can (12 ounces, or 353 ml) evaporated skim milk

5 eggs

2 tablespoons (14 g) toasted wheat germ

2 tablespoons (40 g) 100 percent maple syrup

¾ teaspoon vanilla stevia (we like NuNaturals)

¼ teaspoon ground cardamom

¼ teaspoon ground allspice

¼ teaspoon ground cloves

FROM DR. JONNY: Bread pudding might not seem like a dish that a carb-conscious guy like me would recommend, especially not for breakfast, but this is a bread pudding with a difference. First, we use whole-grain bread, preferably sprouted grains such as Ezekiel brand bread, but you can use any multigrain bread that has at least 2, preferably 3 or more grams of fiber per slice. (The added wheat germ bumps up the fiber a bit as well.) Second, we use a generous helping of five eggs to convert this into a high-protein breakfast. Third, we use evaporated skim milk, which provides the creaminess of cream without the calories and adds even more protein to the mix. Cinnamon is well known to reduce the glycemic (sugar) impact of food, and the only sweetener we use is a touch of syrup. This is a healthy and delicious overhaul of a formerly high-carb, low-nutrient dish, and your family will love it! Plus, it actually tastes like bread pudding, one of my all-time favorite deserts. Bonus: it's incredibly easy to make!

Lightly coat the slow cooker insert with the butter. Arrange the bread in layers, using 1 teaspoon of the cinnamon to sprinkle a bit on each layer. Set aside.

In a medium-size bowl, combine the evaporated milk, eggs, wheat germ, syrup, vanilla stevia, remaining 1 teaspoon cinnamon, cardamom, allspice, and cloves and whisk together until smooth. Pour the mixture evenly over the bread, cover, and cook on low for 6 to 8 hours, until set. Remove the cover for the last 45 minutes of cooking time to evaporate excess liquid.

YIELD: 8 servings

PER SERVING: Calories 203.3; Calories From Fat 48.6; Total Fat 5.4 g; Cholesterol 135.4 mg; Sodium 251 mg; Potassium 314.8 mg; Total Carbohydrates 26.2 g; Fiber 3.3 g; Sugar 11 g; Protein 12.8 g

Resources

FISH, POULTRY, AND MEAT

Broken Arrow Ranch
www.brokenarrowranch.com/index.htm
Venison and other wild game meats

Diamond Organics
www.diamondorganics.com
Organic/free-range/grass-fed animal and plant foods, including buffalo, turkey, and dairy, plus a raw selection

Natural Lamb Co-Op
www.naturallambcoop.com
Pasture-raised lamb

Novy Ranches
www.novyranches.com
Grass-fed beef

U.S. Wellness Meats
www.grasslandbeef.com
Grass-fed meats and dairy products

Vital Choice
www.vitalchoice.com
Wild-caught fish

OTHER FOODS

Barlean's
www.barleans.com
Flax products, coconut oil, and other omega-3 products

Living and Raw Foods
www.rawfoods.com
Raw foods, including goji berries, cacao powder, and agave nectar

NuNaturals
https://nunaturals.com
Alternative sweeteners

The Raw Food World
www.therawfoodworld.com
Irish moss

RECOMMENDED READING

The Environmental Working Group
www.ewg.org

Fast Food Nation by Eric Schlosser

Food Rules by Michael Pollan

In Defense of Food by Michael Pollan

Nourishing Traditions by Sally Fallon

The Omnivore's Dilemma by Michael Pollan

Acknowledgments

FROM JONNY AND JEANNETTE:

We would like to extend our deep gratitude to the unequaled team at Fair Winds, especially our favorite editor, Cara Connors, our organizational queen Tiffany Hill, and our guide Will Kiester. Thanks also to Bill Bettencourt for the gorgeous photos. Special thanks, as always, to our extraordinary agent, Coleen O'Shea.

In addition, Jeannette would like to extend a warm thank-you to her testers, tasters, and clients for their indispensable feedback and ideas for the recipes, especially Frank and Karen Knapp, Jodi Bass, Judie Porter (thanks, Mom!), and Tracee Yablon Brenner, and her beloveds, Jay, Jesse, and Julian. Thanks also to Mary Weaver, owner of Newport Cooks gourmet cooking school in Rhode Island, for sharing a favorite recipe.

About the Authors

JONNY BOWDEN, PH.D., C.N.S., a board-certified nutritionist with a master's degree in psychology, is a nationally known expert on nutrition, weight loss, and health. He is the nutrition editor for *Pilates Style*, a contributing editor for *Clean Eating*, and a columnist for both *America Online* and *Better Nutrition*. His work has been featured in dozens of national publications (print and online) including *The New York Times*, *The Wall Street Journal*, *Forbes*, *Time*, *Oxygen*, *Marie Claire*, *W*, *Remedy*, *Diabetes Focus*, *US Weekly*, *Cosmopolitan*, *Family Circle*, *Self*, *Fitness*, *Allure*, *Essence*, *Men's Health*, *Weight Watchers*, *Prevention*, *Woman's World*, *InStyle*, *Fitness*, *Natural Health*, and *Shape*. He is the author of *The Most Effective Ways to Live Longer*, *The 150 Most Effective Ways to Boost Your Energy*, and *The 100 Healthiest Foods to Eat During Pregnancy* (coauthored with Allison Tannis, R.D.). A popular, dynamic, and much sought-after speaker, he's appeared on CNN, Fox News, MSNBC, ABC, NBC, and CBS, and speaks frequently around the country.

Dr. Jonny is also the author of the award-winning *Living Low Carb: Controlled Carbohydrate Eating for Long-Term Weight Loss*, *The Most Effective Natural Cures on Earth*, *The Healthiest Meals on Earth*, *The Most Effective Ways to Live Longer Cookbook*, *The 150 Healthiest 15-Minute Recipes on Earth*, *The 150 Healthiest Comfort Foods on Earth*, and his acclaimed signature best seller, *The 150 Healthiest Foods on Earth*.

You can find Dr. Jonny's DVDs, *The Truth about Weight Loss* and *The 7 Pillars of Longevity*, his popular motivational CDs, free newsletter, free audio programs, and many of the supplements and foods recommended in this book on his website, www.jonnybowden.com. You can also follow him on twitter.com/jonnybowden.

He lives in Southern California with his beloved animal companions Emily (a pit bull) and Lucy (an Argentine Dogo).

JEANNETTE BESSINGER, the Clean Food Coach (www.thecleanfoodcoach.com), recognized by *Better Homes and Gardens* magazine as among the nation's leading experts in food and nutrition, is on a mission to empower overweight women in the primes of their lives with the knowledge, tools, and support they need to reclaim their health, rediscover their waistlines, and resore their self-confidence. By emphasizing clean, natural, real-food choices, Jeannette guides appreciative women to achieve permanent weight loss, celebrate the end of chronic health problems, and really believe—at a gut level—that the second half of life can be the best half.

Jeannette is a board-certified health counselor, whole foods chef, and award-winning lifestyle and nutrition educator. She is the author and co-author of seven books featuring healthy eating, including *The 150 Healthiest 15-Minute Recipes on Earth, Simple Food for Busy Families,* and *Great Expectations: Best Food for Your Baby and Toddler.*

Designer and lead facilitator of a long-running and successful hospital-based lifestyle change program, she is a consultant to national public and private groups and coalitions working to improve the health of people stuck in the sand traps of the Standard American Diet (S.A.D.).

Jeannette's nutrition and clean food perspectives have been showcased in more than fifty media outlets, including *Consumer Reports, Clean Eating, Better Nutrition, Redbook Magazine, Parenting, Martha Stewart Living,* NPR, and NBC News Health Check, influencing women around the world.

She lives in Portsmouth, Rhode Island, with her patient husband, two amazing teenagers, three dogs, and pesky cat.

Index

Best-selling Books by Acclaimed Nutritionist
JONNY BOWDEN, PH.D., C.N.S.

The 150 Healthiest Foods on Earth

The Surprising, Unbiased Truth about What You Should Eat and Why

"*The 150 Healthiest Foods on Earth* is simply delightful! The information is accurate; the presentation is a visual feast. All in all, reading this book is a very satisfying experience."

—Christiane Northrup, M.D., author of
Mother-Daughter Wisdom, *The Wisdom of Menopause*, and
Women's Bodies, Women's Wisdom

The Most Effective Natural Cures on Earth

The Surprising, Unbiased Truth about What Treatments Work and Why

"I reference this beautifully written and illustrated review of the best cures on the planet so often that it lives on my desk rather than the bookshelf."

—Mehmet C. Oz, M.D., coauthor of
You: The Owner's Manual

The Most Effective Ways to Boost Your Energy

The Surprising, Unbiased Truth about Using Nutrition, Exercise, Supplements, Stress Relief, and Personal Empowerment to Stay Energized All Day

"Get everyone you love to read my friend Dr. Jonny's brilliance!"

—Mark Victor Hansen, coauthor of
Chicken Soup for the Soul

The Healthiest Meals on Earth

The Surprising, Unbiased Truth about What Meals to Eat and Why

"What a simply irresistible book with mouthwatering recipes from all around the world! I plan to use this book as a resource guide and as a gift for all the people I truly care about."

—Ann Louise Gittleman, Ph.D., C.N.S., *New York Times* best-selling author of *The Fat Flush Plan*, *Zapped*, and *Before the Change*

The 150 Healthiest 15-Minute Recipes on Earth

The Surprising, Unbiased Truth about How to Make the Most Deliciously Nutritious Meals at Home in Just Minutes a Day

"A gem of a book and a collector's piece for all of Dr. Jonny's fans!"

—Ann Louise Gittleman, Ph.D., C.N.S., *New York Times* best-selling author of *The Fat Flush Plan*, *Zapped*, and *Before the Change*

The 100 Healthiest Foods to Eat During Pregnancy

The Surprising, Unbiased Truth about Foods You Should Be Eating During Pregnancy but Probably Aren't

"Another great book from Jonny Bowden! In his signature expert style, Jonny, along with Allison Tannis, recommends the healthiest foods and spices for pregnant women … all pregnant women should read this book."

—Dean Raffleock, D.C., C.C.N., author of *A Natural Guide to Pregnancy and Postpartum Health*

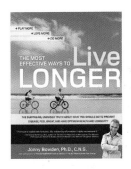

The Most Effective Ways to Live Longer

The Surprising, Unbiased Truth about What You Should Do to Prevent Disease, Feel Great, and Have Optimum Health and Longevity

"A must-read for anyone who wants to live longer! Jonny Bowden takes the lessons we've learned from the world's longest-lived people and offers a research-backed formula for the rest of us to get the most good years out of our lives."

—Dan Buettner, author of *The Blue Zones: Lessons on Living Longer from the People Who've Lived the Longest*

The Most Effective Ways to Live Longer Cookbook

The Surprising, Unbiased Truth about Great-Tasting Food That Prevents Disease and Gives You Optimal Health and Longevity

"Lusciously healthy and mouthwatering recipes—all beautifully organized into five key body systems. Another nutritional masterpiece from Dr. Jonny Bowden!"

—Deirdre Rawlings, Ph.D., author of *Foods That Help Win the Battle Against Fibromyalgia*

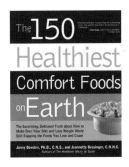

The 150 Healthiest Comfort Foods on Earth

The Surprising, Unbiased Truth about How You Can Make Over Your Diet and Lose Weight While Still Enjoying the Foods You Love and Crave

"This book tantalizes my taste buds and is everything I love—real comfort food that is as nutritious as it is delicious!"

——Holly Clegg, author of the trim&TERRIFIC® cookbook series

Unleash Your Thin...

The Missing Link to a Slim, Sexy, and Healthy Body

Most diets actually work…IF you follow them. Where most diets FAIL, however, is that they don't tell you HOW to keep the weight off for good in the REAL WORLD by dealing with the temptations, cravings, stressful situations, 24x7 availability of cheap, unhealthy food, and other obstacles that are constantly getting in your way, sabotaging your weight loss efforts. Everyone can lose weight, but the challenge is keeping it off for good…until now.

In this program you will learn how to unleash your natural ability to be thin while dissolving fat from your waist, hips, and belly. You'll also discover how to trigger your behavior control switch to help you rewire your brain to break old habits that make you sick, fat, tired, and depressed and create NEW habits that will automatically help you be fit, trim, happy, and health for life…and all WITHOUT feeling deprived.

Unleash Your Thin is written by Jonny Bowden, Ph.D., C.N.S., known as The Rogue Nutritionist, a world-renown authority on nutrition and weight loss. He's a board certified nutritionist and best-selling author with a master's degree in psychology and counseling.

In this groundbreaking program, you'll learn:
- ✓ The secret to turning ON your fat burning hormone and turning OFF your fat storage hormone…
- ✓ How to eliminate the intense urges, wild cravings, and irresistible temptations that constantly sabotage your weight loss efforts…
- ✓ Simple tips to protect yourself from our toxic food environment, which has been engineered to keep you sick and fat no matter what you try…
- ✓ Why nearly everything you've ever heard about nutrition and weight is completely wrong…
- ✓ How to rewire your brain and your body to automatically unleash the thin person that's hidden inside you once and for all…

Download a FREE Sneak Preview of *Unleash Your Thin* at:
http://UnleashYourThin.com/jonny
Available for a limited time only so act now!